INVESTING IN CONVERTIBLE SECURITIES

YOUR COMPLETE GUIDE TO THE RISKS AND REWARDS

JOHN P. CALAMOS

Dearborn
Financial Publishing, Inc.

Executive Editor: Kathleen A. Welton
Project Editor: Roseann P. Costello
Copy Editor: Pat Stahl
Interior Design: Edwin Harris
Cover Design: Stuart Paterson

© 1988 by John P. Calamos

Published by Dearborn Financial Publishing, Inc.

10   9   8   7   6   5   4   3   2

LIBRARY OF CONGRESS
Library of Congress Cataloging-in-Publication Data

Calamos, John P.
    Investing in convertible securities / John P. Calamos.
      p.   cm.
    Includes index.
    ISBN 0-88462-736-5
    1. Convertible preferred stocks. 2. Convertible bonds.
I. Title.
HG4661.C32 1988
332.63'2044—dc19   88-10104
                      CIP

Contents

Implications of Convertible Preferred Program. Hedging
Convertible Preferreds. Covered Call Writing with Convertible
Preferreds. Tax Holding Period Requirements. Hedging
Convertible Preferred Portfolios. Hedging with Index Put
Options. Summary.

Acknowledgments

This book has evolved from practical day-to-day experience as a portfolio manager of convertible securities and from the academic theories that help explain the complexity of our capital markets. It would not have been possible without the dedication, patience and direct and indirect help from others. The goal is to continually seek better tools that allow for the proper evaluation of investment opportunities and thereby manage money effectively. The book details and explains these tools as they apply to convertibles, many of which have not previously been published.

To the extent that we have accomplished that, I want to acknowledge Nick P. Calamos, Director of Research at Calamos Asset Management, for the fundamental contributions he has made to the development of convertible price theory and its applications as outlined in this book. His probing curiosity in the employment of academic theories to our decision-making process, along with the critical thought necessary to fully develop an idea into a useful investment management tool have provided an invaluable contribution without which this book could not have accomplished its purpose.

I also am indebted to my wife, Jackie, for her patience and support, as well as for her direct contribution in editing and preparation of the manuscript.

In addition, I am indebted to Michael D. Brailov, Senior Trader at Calamos Asset Management. His support and keen commentary were extremely helpful throughout the preparation of the book. The many charts and exhibits to better communicate complicated concepts were accomplished by John P. Calamos, Jr. Also my colleagues at Calamos Asset Management, Joyce A. Cagnina, Robert M. Slotky and Nancy J. Annicella, have shared my interest in convertible money management throughout the years and have provided valuable support and encouragement. Laura Munson, my secretary, is greatly appreciated for her assistance in meeting deadlines and typing the manuscript.

The book could not have been completed without the support of the staff at Calamos Asset Management. The main benefit of running your own firm is to help create an environment that is interesting, challenging and productive. It is gratifying to be associated with people who not only share your enthusiasm for an idea, for a goal, but who also are instrumental in achieving that goal.

Preface

The purpose of this book is to provide a guide to investing in convertible securities. It does not presume to predict the direction of long-term interest rates, bond or stock prices. It does seek to develop the most appropriate and effective ways in which investors can control risk and return through the use of convertible securities. So versatile are convertible securities—employed either alone or in connection with other financial instruments—that in many cases the investor may be able to gain above-average returns while reducing risk. The most attractive strategy for one investor at a particular time may involve simply purchasing convertibles; for another it may be the writing of call options against convertibles or the use of put options with convertibles. The use of warrants or various convertible hedging techniques might be another consideration. Alternative convertible strategies differ at times, depending on their opportunity for reward and their associated risks.

The material that follows is designed to provide a reference guide to various convertible strategies, each with its own risk/reward characteristics. The applications in this guide are not meant to be all-inclusive or directed exclusively toward any one category of investor; some of the strategies are appropriate for conservative investors, while others would be better suited to speculators or hedgers.

The techniques and strategies discussed herein have evolved over the years and are dynamic in nature. They will continue to change, as do the capital markets in which they compete. An ancillary goal of this reference guide is to develop a decision-making mechanism by which the reader assembles a frame of reference to evaluate convertible opportunities. This book is not simply about the development of mathematical formulas to describe complex relationships—although these calculations are important and must be done properly. My goal is to provide the reader with *insight* into how the decision-making process of a convertible specialist can be used with flexibility and success.

Lastly, the reader must recognize how difficult it is to compete in our complex capital markets. Therefore, I have included past examples to bridge the gap between theory and reality. This is done to illustrate the contribution of theoretical analysis and to show its limits in the real world. Formula-type investment strategies often seem foolproof, except when applied with dollars. If it were not so, I'm sure there would be many more wealthy mathematicians than there are.

The capital marketplace can be compared to Socrates' parable of the cave. Each market player makes decisions based on how he or she views the world. Each, locked into position in the cave, views only the shadows on the cave wall in front of him, never being able to turn and see the fire outside the cave and the real figures that make the distorted images on the cave's wall. Each player has to determine reality but sees only distorted shadows. The number of variables that influence the capital markets is so immense that, even with computers, statistics, macroeconomics and microeconomics and capital pricing theory, we can quantify only a fraction of them. Like the parable of the cave, investors do not know all factors that influence the market, but we know some things. In the end, our insight—derived from education and experience—becomes a crucial factor in the decision-making process. The more knowledge we can obtain by quantifying as many variables as possible, the better equipped we will be to decipher the distorted figures on the wall of Wall Street.

Thus, the successful convertible strategist, or any serious investor, does not just apply neat mathematical formulas, but instead meshes accurate theoretical analyses with critical thought. I hope that this book will contribute to the reader's understanding of the convertible segment of the capital markets, because the greater the understanding derived through experience and thought, the greater the probability of success.

PART
I

INTRODUCTION

1
Background and Review

Convertible securities have been overlooked for many years by investors. They have not been in widespread use because, unlike the stock and bond markets, convertibles are not widely discussed in the financial press. Also, their complexity causes many investors to ignore their investment merits. And until recently the convertible market's relatively small size lacked the depth needed to develop complete investment strategies.

This market atmosphere changed dramatically in the 1980s, and the use of convertible securities by investors has grown significantly since then. The dramatic increase in convertible bond offerings by corporations has fueled the new issue market and sparked interest among the larger institutional investors. This interest is spilling over to pension funds and individual investors. In response to such interest, many mutual funds have been formed that invest primarily in convertible securities. Several investment managers and bank trust departments have set up separate departments in order to manage convertible portfolios.

Another important reason for the recent interest in convertible securities is the volatility of the financial markets in the early seventies. The end of the great bull market of the 1960s ushered in a market environment that caused many investors to rethink traditional investment strategies. No longer were investors able to simply buy and hold common stocks for growth of capital. No longer were pension funds and conservative investors content to hold long-term corporate and government bonds while their principals varied wildly with the extreme changes in interest rates.

The opening of the Chicago Board Option Exchange (CBOE) in 1973 and the passage of the Employees Retirement Income Security Act (ERISA) in 1974 both fostered the growth of nontraditional investment strategies. The CBOE showed investors different ways to reduce market volatility by utilizing stock options, index options and other investment vehicles. Learning to properly use these new vehicles undoubtedly costs some investors dearly. Similarly, ERISA challenged the traditional prudent man rule and legal lists of the past by recognizing modern techniques of portfolio management.

As investors' knowledge increased, they were no longer convinced that the traditional mix of stocks and bonds was the optimum strategy, nor were they willing to ride the performance roller coaster. Investing today requires a continual search for ways to control risk and protect assets while still achieving above-average returns on investment. Therefore, it is not surprising that convertible securities are gaining advocates in many parts of the financial community as a specific investment strategy to be used throughout the market cycle.

The purpose of this book is to show the serious investor how to use convertibles in pursuing investment strategies that can achieve above-average returns at low risk. Although the book is written on a basic level, the evaluation of convertible securities is complex and requires that the serious investor take time to translate convertible theory into profitable strategies. It is also useful to place convertibles into historic and academic perspective, so a brief history of convertibles is presented along with a review of modern portfolio theory.

CONVERTIBLES AND MODERN PORTFOLIO THEORY

Convertible investing, like common stock investing, is both simple and complex. After all, there are just two ways a stock can move: up or down. Because of this fact, many people see themselves as experts in the stock market. With the prodding of stockbroker salesmen, many investors feel as qualified as a professional by merely reading the financial press. Nonetheless, investing today requires more than a casual reading of the financial press or market letters; it requires serious study and a basic knowledge of the science of investing.

"Science is a way of approaching the natural world through a process of questioning, hypothesizing and experimentation. Contrary to popular belief, it does not consist primarily of gathering facts or determining truth in any absolute sense. On the contrary, one of the principal tasks of each new generation of scientists is to modify, and in some cases overthrow, the truth handed down to them."[1]

The science of investing is like the natural sciences in that both include a body of knowledge that has evolved over time. Investors who do not have this knowledge are at a serious disadvantage in the marketplace. The tools are not infallible, but they are necessary for understanding the complexities of the financial markets.

A starting point in understanding investing today is to understand security analysis and modern portfolio theory (MPT). Of course, some investors who have never formally studied security analysis or heard of MPT have done well in their investments. Investing, like most other sciences, is also based on common sense. Security analysis, as developed by Graham and Dodd, and MPT have refined those common sense beliefs into tools for the professional investor. Some tools become outdated as new tools are developed. Others become so clouded in mathematical derivations that they are far removed from the original common sense principles, or the realities of the marketplace, and so prove to be worthless tools for the investor.

Security analysis or value investing deals with the in-depth investigation of a given security. It is concerned with a business and its finances over the long run and usually is not concerned with short-term price moves. If a security is attractive, the purchase is made today, recognizing that the market may not fairly value the security for many years. Graham and Dodd worked in 1934, outlining for the professional analyst the principles of value investing. Warren Buffet is their well-known current disciple and epitomizes this type of investing.

MPT as we know it today was an outgrowth of the pioneering work of Harry Markowitz. His paper on portfolio theory, published in 1952, laid the groundwork for MPT. The theory came into prominence because it was able to explain why the "gunslingers" of the 1960s were so successful, albeit for a short time. MPT theorized that their returns were based on assuming high risk. They were merely gamblers, and

---

[1]Thomas S. Kuhn, *The Structure of Scientific Revolutions*. (Chicago: University of Chicago Press, 1962).

FIGURE 1.1   Risk/Reward Relationship

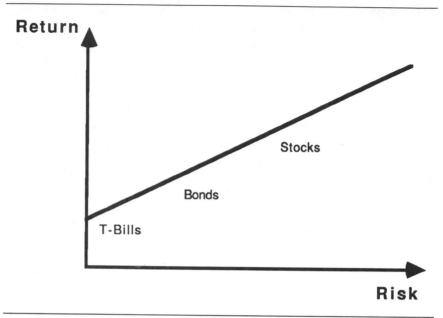

gamblers occasionally win. This high-risk/high-return strategy disinte-grated in the bear market and recession of the early seventies, and MPT was there to explain the reason for the debacle. MPT explains in-vestment performance in terms of risk versus return: Investors commit funds today in the hope of obtaining an expected future reward. The risk/return spectrum shown in figure 1.1 indicates the no-risk invest-ment of U.S. Treasury bills as compared to the higher-risk investment of common stocks. For every unit of risk assumed, the higher the re-turn an investor can expect. Risk and return can be quantified by using this linear relationship.

As figure 1.1 indicates, the no-risk investment of Treasury bills be-comes the zero-risk point, while blue-chip stocks become the average risk. By choosing any investment other than U.S. Treasury bills the in-vestor expects a higher return. This linear relationship between risk and reward remains intact over the long term.

Risk/reward over the long run has been calculated to indicate the historical risk/reward relationship. This is clearly indicated in the 55-year study of stocks, bonds, bills and inflation. Figure 1.2 shows this

FIGURE 1.2   Long-Term Risk/Return Relationship

Total Annual Returns 1926–1981

	Geometric Mean	Arithmetic Mean
Common Stocks	9.1%	11.4%
Corporate Bonds	3.6	3.7
Treasury Bonds	3.0	3.1
Treasury Bills	3.0	3.1
Inflation	3.0	3.1

SOURCE: R.G. Ibbotson and R.A. Sinquefield, *Stocks, Bonds, Bills and Inflation: The Past and the Future*. The Financial Analysts Research Foundation, 1982.

information. The aberrations from this relationship tend to smooth out over time.

In addition, MPT distinguishes between business risk, or *unsystematic risk*, and market risk, called *systematic risk*. Unsystematic risk is based on factors specific to the company. For example, during a roaring bull market, companies can falter through mismanagement or other factors that can cause their stock price to decline. A portion of the total stock prices' change or variance, estimated to be about 38 percent,[2] is due to these factors and ten percent due to industry factors. Most investors have a common sense understanding that diversification is important in portfolio management. In MPT terms, diversification can offset unsystematic risk to a large extent.

The remaining 52 percent of the total stock price variance represents systematic risk and is due to the ebb and flow of market sentiment. In bear markets, like the stock market of 1974 and the stock market crash of 1987, even very financially sound companies fell dra-

---

[2]Benjamin F. King, "Market and Industry Factors in Stock Price Behavior," *The Journal of Business* 39 no. 1, Pt. 2 (January 1966): 139–190.

matically in value. In bull markets, market sentiment is high, causing investors to bid prices of securities to higher levels. Systematic risk is influenced by both internal factors of the economy as well as political factors, all of which are difficult to predict. As difficult as the risk factors are to measure, MPT does attempt to quantify them. Unlike unsystematic risk, which is easily controlled through diversification, systematic risk is difficult to control; and as our capital markets expand, it is becoming more and more difficult all the time. Controlling market risk is one of the single most difficult problems investment professionals face on a day-to-day basis. The stock market crash of 1987 is a dramatic example of the importance of controlling general market risk. Convertibles are important because, if properly used, they can provide a means to control both systematic and unsystematic risk.

However, investing today is not typically done for 55-year periods. Some investors consider one year to be long-term investing. For shorter periods of time, there is little solace derived from the fact that eventually the capital market line relationship will eventually come into balance. As the famous economist Keynes aptly put it, we're all dead in the long run. Over the short run, the relationship exists between *expected* risk and *expected* return. It is this relationship with which we are most concerned. The most important ingredient is the risk expectation, which is based on the most recent risk experience. The variability of stock prices on a periodic basis becomes the key measure of risk expectation. If recent volatility exceeds normal volatility, risk expectations should rise. The marketplace should then price the asset classes to reflect the expectation of superior reward—which should lead to a better chance of actually *achieving* superior reward. If convertibles as an asset class are providing superior risk adjusted returns, then the marketplace would eventually adjust for the aberration.

Therefore, understanding convertibles as an asset class as well as a derivative security helps in determining how they should be evaluated. It is also useful to review the historical development of convertibles.

HISTORICAL REVIEW OF CONVERTIBLE SECURITIES

With the explosive growth of the convertible market in the 1980s and its introduction to many investors for the first time, one may conclude that convertibles are new. In fact, convertibles have been used by investors dating back to the 1800s. Generally, two types of securities provide the capital of a corporation: stocks and bonds. It's relatively simple to organize a corporation and provide for the issuance of common stocks and corporate bonds. It's quite another matter to sell these securities to the investing public. Convertible securities came into being as a way to make securities more attractive to the investing public.

Financing the building of the railroads in the 1800s was not always an easy task. The convertible clause was added to first mortgage bonds to entice investors. The Chicago, Milwaukee & St. Paul Railway, for example, used many convertible issues for financing between 1860 and 1880. In 1896, that company had 12 separate convertible issues outstanding, most bearing a seven percent coupon. As the country and its railroads grew, it became easier to market new bonds. The convertible clause virtually disappeared as a feature in new issues for a period of 20 years.

At the turn of the century, the convertible clause reappeared with the Baltimore & Ohio Railroad's issuance of $15 million of four percent ten-year debentures convertible into common stock at par. In that same year (1901), the Union Pacific Railroad issued $100 million four percent mortgage bonds convertible into common stock at par. Many others followed, including the Pennsylvania Railroad and the Erie. Besides the railroads, convertibles during this era were issued by the Brooklyn Rapid Transit, Distillers Securities Corporation, Lackawanna Steel Company, International Steam Pump Co., Consolidated Gas Company of New York, Brooklyn Union Gas Co., International Paper and Western Union Telegraph. Westinghouse Electric & Manufacturing Co. brought convertible issues to the market in 1906, and General Electric offered its stockholders the right to subscribe to a convertible bond issue in 1907.[3]

The American Telephone & Telegraph Co. first authorized $150 million of four percent convertible bonds in 1906. Over the years, AT&T has sold at least nine separate issues of convertible bonds, most of them through subscription rights to stockholders. During this period, companies like AT&T issued convertible bonds because they brought in a wider class of shareholders than would have been available with a stock offering. Due to business practices at the time, many financial institutions that had funds available were not allowed to buy

---

[3]Thomas Gibson, *Special Market Letter 1908* (New York: Gibson, 1908).

common stock.[4] Bonds, however, were approved, so buying convertible bonds was a way around the "no common stock" rules.

This historical review, besides providing an interesting footnote to the convertible market, explains why convertibles have become popular recently. They have been used over the years to entice investors to buy the companies' securities. This added kicker is not needed in less volatile periods, so the issuance of convertibles diminishes. A number of factors have caused record growth in the convertible market in recent years. One is the volatility of the bond market to the point where bonds are as volatile as stocks. This uncertainty in the financial markets and the volatility it has fostered have forced companies to add the convertible option as an additional feature to their preferred stock or bond issuances, thereby making them more attractive to buyers.

The dramatic growth of the capital markets is also a factor. With many new companies coming to the market, the convertible issue provides an incentive to buy these unseasoned securities. The technological developments of our age provide a fertile field for new ideas and for companies that need capital to develop those ideas. MCI Communications and others financed much of their dramatic growth by issuing convertible bonds. A record number of new issues in the emerging growth sector was brought to the market in 1986. This portion of the market has expanded so much that a whole new sector has been created, called by some the "junk bond" or "high yield" market.

The expansion to a global market has fostered the growth of new convertibles offered by blue-chip companies. Many seasoned or high capitalization companies seeking worldwide distribution of their securities offer convertible bonds to foreign investors in the Eurobond market, not unlike AT&T's use of convertibles some 60 years ago. This practice will probably grow with the continued internationalization of the securities markets.

Now that we have looked at the history of convertibles, what about their potential as an investment in the coming years? Convertibles have been providing higher risk-adjusted returns over the past 15 years. In today's market environment, they continue to provide a means by which investors can achieve above-average returns at low risk.

---

[4]Benjamin Graham, *The Intelligent Investor: A Book of Practical Counsel* (New York: Harper, 1954), p. 121.

To illustrate how convertibles can yield such returns, we must first review the basics of convertible securities. Part I discusses these basics and defines the types of convertible securities. It also details commonly used terms and techniques in the convertible evaluation process.

Part II discusses the development of a theoretical fair price value for a convertible security. It explains how fair value is determined and, once determined, how it can be applied.

Part III outlines different strategies in the use of convertibles. These encompass the full spectrum of the market, including convertible hedging techniques.

2

What Are Convertibles?

Convertibles are corporate securities (usually preferred stock or bonds) that may be exchanged for a specified number of another form (usually common shares) at a prestated price as defined by the corporation upon issuance.

Investors in the capital markets traditionally invest in either debt instruments or common stocks. Most feel that fixed-income vehicles offer security and income, while common stocks offer capital appreciation. Convertible securities combine the elements of both and, therefore, contain investment characteristics of both debt and equity securities. In general, convertible securities include both convertible preferred stocks and convertible bonds. Convertibles are best understood by studying convertible bonds.

Convertible bonds are a specific type of corporate bond issued by corporations. The issuing company guarantees to pay the specified coupon interest, usually semiannually, and the par value, usually $1,000 per bond, upon maturity. Although convertible bonds may be junior to other long-term debt instruments, they have the same attributes of straight corporate bonds plus an additional feature: At the holder's option, the bond can be exchanged for the underlying common stock of the company at any time. This important feature completely changes the investment characteristics of the bond.

Convertible bonds are hybrid issues, part bond and part stock. The evaluation process should take both parts into consideration. The convertible bond income characteristics include the coupon rate, maturity date, call features and financial quality. The equity side includes the analyst's opinion as to the future prospects of the company, the risk measures of the common stock and how much equity participation the convertible bond represents. With the myriad factors interwoven in each convertible bond, the analytical process becomes quite involved.

Perhaps the most significant aspect of convertibles is that conversion takes place only upon the holder's request. Conversion occurs only when it is economically advantageous to the holder—when the underlying stock price goes up. Many investors who are new to convertibles don't realize that it is not necessary to *convert* to the underlying common stock to realize a profit. The market price of a convertible varies with changes in the stock price, so the bond can be sold anytime the holder desires.

The two basic components of the convertible (stock value and bond value) can be viewed separately to determine their influence on the price of the convertible bond.

INVESTMENT VALUE (BOND VALUE)

Investment value is the fixed-income component of the convertible. This is determined by calculating an equivalent bond value based on the assumption that the bond is not convertible. The coupon and maturity date are used to decide this value, and over the short term it represents the investment floor.

CONVERSION VALUE (STOCK VALUE)

Conversion value is the equity portion of the convertible bond. It is based on the *conversion price*, at which conversion to stock can be exercised, set by the company at the time the bond is issued. This price in turn determines the number of shares of stock into which each bond can be converted. Conversion value represents the intrinsic value of the bond in stock.

CONVERSION PREMIUM

Conversion premium, often referred to as a parity, is a gauge of equity participation. The difference between the intrinsic (conversion) value and the current market price of the convertible bond is the conversion premium. Conversion premium varies because it changes as the underlying common stock price changes. The trend of conversion premium and coupon rates in the new issue market in recent years provides an insight into how convertibles are priced in the marketplace.

Conversion premium is determined by market forces. The investor must decide whether the conversion premium is considered high or low before purchasing a convertible security. The determinants of the fair value of a convertible will be discussed in Part II.

CONVERSION RATIO

The conversion ratio determines the number of shares of common stock for which a convertible can be exchanged. The conversion ratio is determined upon issuance of the security and is typically protected against dilution. The antidilution clause and conversion ratio are outlined in the securities indenture.

ANTIDILUTION CLAUSE

The antidilution clause protects convertible security holders by allowing the conversion ratio to be raised or lowered under certain conditions. Stock dividends and splits are the most common occurrences that result in an adjustment to the conversion ratio via the antidilution clause.

CALL TERMS AND PROVISIONS

Call terms and provisions are outlined in the securities indenture and are determined at or prior to issuance. The call terms typically indicate under what circumstances the security can be called, the date and the price. Convertible securities often have provisions that are subject to the underlying stocks price. For example, the convertible security cannot be called for three years from issuance unless the stock price exceeds 150 percent of the conversion price for 30 consecutive days.

PAR VALUE

Par value is the face value of the security. Bonds are typically issued at $1,000 par value, and interest on bonds is stated as a percentage of par value. Preferred stocks have par values, and their dividends are also expressed as a percentage of par value.

Although we have explored convertible bonds thus far, convertible preferred stocks have similar characteristics. The holder of a convertible preferred stock also has the right to convert to a specified number of shares of the underlying common stock at any time. The relationship between changes in stock price and convertible price is the same for both convertible bonds and convertible preferred stocks.

Convertibles are brought to the market throughout the years at various levels of stock prices and different interest rate structures. Therefore, individual convertible securities are at many different conversion premium and yield levels. The new issue market gives investors an indication of the various differences in these levels over time.

CONVERTIBLE SECURITIES QUOTATIONS

Convertible bonds and convertible preferred stocks are quoted in the financial journals. Unlike the European financial press, which lists convertibles in a separate section, in the United States, convertibles are mixed in with the other securities, making it a bit difficult for investors to locate specific securities. Convertible bonds can be either listed on the New York Stock Exchange (NYSE), American Stock Exchange (AMEX) and regional exchanges or traded in the NASDAQ over-the-counter market. Convertible bonds listed on the exchanges are distinguished from non-convertible corporate bonds by the designation of "cv" in the current yield column. Figure 2.1 shows the listing for IBM convertible bonds. It identifies the specific issue along with the name of the company, the coupon rate and maturity date. Like all corporate bonds, convertible bonds are quoted as a percentage of par. Therefore, the $1,000 par value is always quoted as 100. The IBM convertible bond closed at $121^1/_4$, or $1,212.50 per bond. The percentage of par pricing convention will be used throughout this book.

Like straight preferred stocks, convertible preferred stocks are listed on the stock pages in the financial press. Unlike the bond listings, there is no way to distinguish between convertible preferreds and straight preferreds. All preferreds are identified by the dividend rate. If there are multiple issues by a company, a letter designation is used. In figure 2.2, Baxter Labs has two preferreds listed: the preferred A with a $2.96 dividend and the preferred B with a $3.50 dividend. There is nothing to indicate that the preferred B is a convertible preferred.

FIGURE 2.1

THE WALL STREET JOURNAL FRIDAY, SEPTEMBER 18, 1987

NEW YORK EXCHANGE BONDS

Thursday, September 17, 1987

Bonds	Cur Yld	Vol	High	Low	Close	Net Chg
IBM 9³/₈04	9.7	122	96³/₄	96¹/₂	96³/₄	+¹/₄
IBM 7⁷/₈04	cv	584	122	120	121¹/₄	+¹/₄
IBM 10¹/₄95	9.9	29	104¹/₄	104	104	−³/₈
IPap dc5¹/₈12	--	20	50⁵/₈	50⁵/₈	50⁵/₈	--
IntRec 9s10	cv	10	80¹/₂	80¹/₄	80¹/₄	−1³/₄
Intnr 10¹/₂08	cv	86	126¹/₈	124¹/₂	126	−1¹/₂
viJnM 7.8504f	--	140	112¹/₂	111¹/₂	112¹/₂	--
viJnM 9.7s85mf						

Volume is indicated in the financial press along with the current quotation. For the convertible preferred market this is a meaningful indication of the number of securities traded in that specific issue. However, the volume given in the bond pages does not necessarily reflect the actual volume of bonds that have traded. The New York Stock Exchange's nine-bond rule requires that orders for nine bonds or less be sent to the floor for one hour to seek a market. Bond trading, which is largely an institutional activity, tends to be inactive on the NYSE, so most bond trades are handled in the over-the-counter market. Most convertible bond trading is done away from the exchange in a very active dealer market. Investors trading convertibles must deal with brokers who are knowledgeable and have access to this dealer network.

For this reason and others, price quotes in the financial press are not always reflective of the actual market for a particular convertible security. This fact is important not only when buying or selling convertibles, but also in determining current market prices for portfo-

FIGURE 2.2

THE WALL STREET JOURNAL FRIDAY, SEPTEMBER 18, 1987

NEW YORK STOCK EXCHANGE COMPOSITE TRANSACTIONS

Thursday, September 17, 1987

Quotations include trades on the Midwest, Pacific Philadelphis, Boston and Cincinnati stock exchanges and reported by the National Association of Securities Dealers and Instinet

52 Weeks High	Low	Stock	Div	Yld %	P.E. Ratio	Sales 100's	High	Low	Close	Net Chg
20⅝	14⅜	BaryWr	.60	3.3	21	127	18⅞	18¼	18¼	−½
10⅛	4½	BASIX	.141	2.8	—	557	5	4¾	5	+⅜
44⅞	17¼	BatlMt	.10	.3	45	1144	35	34⅝	34¾	−⅜
49⅝	35	Bausch	.86	1.9	18	213	45⅜	45⅛	45⅛	—
28¾	15½	Baxter	.44	1.6	13	8069	28½	27⅝	27⅞	−⅜
50⅞	45⅜	Bax pfA	2.96e	5.8	—	326	50⅝	50½	50⅝	+⅛
91¼	59⅝	Bax pfB	3.50	3.9	—	69	91	89¾	90⅞	+⅝
33¼	21¾	BayFin	.20	.9	—	21	22¾	22⅜	22⅜	−⅝
30⅜	22½	BayStG	1.52	6.4	9	81	24¼	23¾	23¾	−⅝
22⅞	14½	BearSt	.48b	2.8	7	2045	17⅞	17¼	17⅜	—

lio evaluation. The professional services that sell prices to consultants for portfolio evaluation often misprice convertibles. Convertibles need to be priced carefully because their value can change without a bond being traded. The convertible price is partially determined by changes in the underlying common stock. If the stock has made a significant change, the convertible's true value has changed whether or not bonds have traded.

COMMISSIONS

Commissions for convertible bonds are determined on a competitive, negotiable basis and vary from firm to firm. Most bonds are sold on a principal basis, meaning that convertible dealers are making markets and trading from their own account. Whether they are selling to investors at a profit or loss from their own account becomes irrelevant. What matters is that the price being traded reflects the current market price of the security. The actual commissions on principal trades are not easily determined. Agency trades are trades in which a firm merely acts as a broker and has arranged the transaction between buyer and seller. These commissions are indicated on the confirmations of sale or purchase and vary with the number of bonds being traded. Convertible bond commissions usually fall under the corporate bond commission schedule.

Commissions as a percentage of assets are usually far less with convertibles than with similar common stock strategies. Therefore, investors employing convertibles as an alternative to common stock investing will substantially reduce their trading costs. With convertibles it is especially important to have knowledgeable brokers executing the trades. Proper execution, a feel for the market and a knowledge of the inventory flows in the dealer network are more important factors in successful trading than discounted commissions.

MARGIN REQUIREMENTS

Convertible securities can be purchased on margin. A margin account at a brokerage firm allows customers to buy securities with money borrowed from the broker. Margin accounts are by governed Regulation T of the Federal Reserve Board, by the National Association of Securities Dealers (NASD), by the New York Stock Exchange and by individual brokerage house rules. The current requirement for buying convertible securities on margin is 50 percent. There are special convertible arbitrage circumstances where the margin requirement is reduced to as little as ten percent. Utilizing margin in convertible trading will be discussed in detail under convertible strategies.

TAX TREATMENT OF CONVERTIBLES

The current tax treatment for convertibles is a result of the Tax Reform Act of 1986. Prior to that act, many investors were under the impression that convertibles were not a suitable investment for the individual investor because of the favorable treatment given to capital gains. They reasoned that since convertible bonds' current yield would be taxed at the high individual rates of the time convertibles would not take advantage of the 60 percent capital gains deduction. They were mistaken, though. Convertible strategies have been used effectively in the past to make the most of the tax code. In fact, the Tax Reform Act of 1986 closed off many of the techniques professional convertible traders once used to reduce, eliminate or postpone taxes.

Convertible investing in general benefited from the new tax bill because it eliminated the distinction between income and capital gains for all practical purposes. Income and capital gains are now taxed at the same rate, so investment decisions can be based on total return. This is a tremendous boon to investors because errors often occur when investors trade securities seeking to gain some tax advantage. By creating an even playing field for income and capital gains, the new tax bill benefits individual investors specifically and the capital markets in general. No longer are investment decisions based solely on a loophole in the tax code. The efficiency of the capital market in employing investor funds will contribute to the growth of the economy over the long term, assuming that the tax code remains stable.

For those seeking capital gains or income, convertibles are a suitable investment from a tax treatment point of view. Investors must be aware of several differences in the tax treatment of convertibles.

Capital Gains

Convertibles, like other securities, are taxed as capital gains. Although there is currently no distinction between short-term and long-term gains, records must be kept showing the holding period. Any trade closed in less than one year is considered a short-term capital gain.* It is not a taxable event when the convertible security is converted to the underlying common stock. In that case, the holding period of the stock began when the convertible security was purchased.

One way to capture the accrued interest on the convertible bond and still effect a sale of the bond prior to the payment date is to sell an equivalent number of stock short against the convertible bond. Much like being short against the box, this technique has the advantage of locking in the profit and obtaining the accrued interest. It is used when the convertible market price is slightly below the conversion price of the convertible. This often happens when convertibles trade in ranges

---

*Note: Applies to securities purchased after December 31, 1987. For securities purchased prior to January 1, 1988 the capital gains period is six months.

above 150. Many bond specialists feel they're entitled to a risk-free profit for handling this transaction. A bondholder can prevent this by simply selling the stock short (no uptick is required because conversion will be made) and holding the short sale until the interest payment date. At that time he would convert and deliver against the short sale. For tax purposes, the short sale constitutes the actual selling date and determines the holding period.

Interest

Convertible bond coupon interest is taxable income to individual and corporate investors. Like all corporate bonds, convertibles trade with accrued interest. Domestic convertible bonds typically pay interest twice a year, while most Euroconvertible bonds pay interest once a year. Individual investors must be careful in determining the amount of interest paid at the end of the year for tax purposes. A problem often arises in computing the amount of interest received and the amount reported. For example, if an investor purchased a convertible bond for a settlement date of December 28, which pays interest on June 30 and December 30, the investor would pay accrued interest from June 30 until December 27. On December 30, the investor would receive the full six months' interest. The actual interest earned is the difference, which amounts to three days' interest. However, the investor receives, either from the company or the stockbroker, a 1099 tax statement with the full six months' interest, which is also reported to the Internal Revenue Service. To prevent paying taxes on the unearned interest portion, the accrued interest paid must be shown as a deduction from the total interest received.

ORIGINAL ISSUE DISCOUNT

Convertible bonds may be issued at a discount from par value. The par value is normally 100 ($1,000), but some issues are brought to the market at a discount from par value, giving investors a built-in capital gain if the bond is held to maturity. The most extreme case of this issue is the zero coupon bond that is originally issued at 25, pays no interest and matures at 100.

The tax treatment of original issue discount bonds is complicated because the Internal Revenue Service assumes a certain rate of appreciation of the bond every year until maturity. Investors pay taxes on this assumed interest on an annual basis, even though interest won't be ceived until maturity. If the bond is sold prior to maturity and for an amount greater than the cost basis, a capital gains tax or a tax at the ordinary income rate is due.

Comments on Commissions, Taxes and Margin

The frequency of changes in the tax code, margin requirements and the variability of commission rates among brokers place the previous discussion in a state of flux. Investors can obtain current information on commissions and margin requirements from their broker, but they should seek expert advice in handling complex tax calculations.

The effect of taxes and commissions will be ignored in the remainder of this book. Commissions for executing transactions are disregarded in the sections on convertible strategies because an all-inclusive statement as to their amount cannot be made. However, investors must take these factors into account in evaluating an opportunity.

ANALYZING CONVERTIBLE SECURITIES

A convertible program requires complex analysis. It includes examining fundamentals, credit data and technical financial measures of the underlying company. It encompasses the use of the mathematical measures of stock and bond risk as well as basic security analysis. This information yields a risk/reward analysis of the convertible security. The following sections detail how investors can evaluate and effectively use these financial instruments.

PART
II

Convertible Evaluation

3

Basics of Convertible Evaluation

The concept of a convertible bond (a corporate bond with the option to convert to the underlying common stock) is easy for investors to grasp. This has led some investors to rely on simple rules of thumb in selecting convertibles. Examples of such rules are: "Only buy converts when the conversion premium is below 20 percent," or "Only buy when the time to break even is less than three years." However, the analysis of convertibles is not that simple. Strategies based upon simplistic rules can only result in disappointing performance, which, at best, is probably equivalent to an unmanaged random selection approach. The proper selection of convertibles requires the analysis of various factors.

The convertible bond has three main parts: its straight bond value (bond investment value), its stock value (conversion value) and its fair or normal price. The fair price value is then compared to the market price to determine profit opportunity and market advantage. All of those factors are interdependent, and each must be considered for a proper evaluation of a convertible security. In this chapter we begin the process of evaluating convertibles by dissecting the convertible bond into its various parts.

INVESTMENT VALUE OF A CONVERTIBLE SECURITY

The investment analysis of a convertible begins with determining its investment value. The investment value of a convertible bond is its value as a bond if it were not convertible. This value is dependent upon the same factors found in any straight corporate bond. These include the financial stability of the company, the type of bond (collateral or debenture), the coupon and maturity date, sinking fund requirements, whether it's callable by the company and, of course, its yield to maturity. The market value of a straight bond fluctuates with any changes in these factors. Figure 3.1 indicates the relationship between the common stock price and market price of the bond investment value.

This relationship is shown graphically as a horizontal line for normal price fluctuations and then for a not-so-normal price deterioration sloping to zero in figure 3.1. With the convertible value shown on the vertical axis and the stock price shown on the horizontal axis, the effect of changes in the variables is determined easily. Over a wide range of stock prices, that investment value is a horizontal line. The financial stability of the company and most of the other bond quality factors do not usually change, so normal fluctuations in the underlying stock price will not change the investment value.

Only when the stock begins to approach zero, with the obvious probable cause being a not-so-normal deterioration of financial fundamentals, it is obvious that the convertible bond must also approach zero. As the common stock increases in value, the bond investment value is not affected. In determining investment value, most investment services assume that the investment value remains constant over relatively short periods of time, so it appears as a horizontal line on the graph.

The assumption is based on studies which conclude that fluctuations in stock prices over short periods of time are random occurrences that are nearly impossible to predict. Over the intermediate to long term, the economic basis to the market takes hold and influences the trend of stock prices. Market risk factors, whether they be short-term, seemingly random moves or longer-term moves caused by significant general economic factors, can cause prices of common stock to vary a great deal. When the stock declines in value based on overall negative market sentiment, it should not influence the investment value. These market factors, referred to as systematic risk, will not influence the

---

FIGURE 3.1   Investment Value

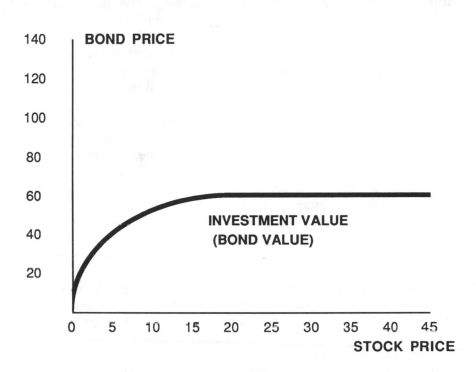

bond value over the short run. Under this assumption, the investment value provides an investment floor below the convertible market price. This provides the essential safety element in convertible bonds. Convertible bonds should always be more valuable than income-equivalent non-convertible bonds. Therefore, the convertible bond will not fall below its investment value.

However, there are a number of factors that do influence the investment value of a convertible security. If the common stock declines due to company factors (unsystematic risk), poor earnings or other causes, the bond investment value *will* be influenced. As the stock declines, the investment value also declines, reflecting the possibility that the company may not be able to pay the coupon or principal of the bond. If the value of the firm were to become zero, the bond investment value would also approach zero. Figure 3.1 illustrates this relationship as the horizontal line becomes a sloping curve and terminates at the zero value along with a stock price of zero. Although studies show that company factors have a smaller influence on stock prices, dramatic changes in the fundamentals of a company will have an immediate effect on the bond investment value. Investors who ignore these fundamentals in evaluating convertibles will be at a distinct disadvantage in the marketplace.

In approaching the mathematical analysis of convertible securities, it's convenient to look at the investment value over the short term under the assumption that the financial stability of the company does not change. This rests on the assumption that any fluctuation in stock price is due to general market sentiment. These price moves are difficult to predict on a consistent basis. Technicians in the financial community would, of course, disagree, but for our purposes we will side with the academic community and not make any judgment on price movements of individual stocks or market indexes based on technical analysis.

The investment value over the long term *does* fluctuate over time, but it must increase to par value at the time the bond matures. Therefore, as time passes the investment value gradually rises to par value, regardless of how the common stock is changing.

The main problem with the assumption of a stable investment value over the short term is that long-term interest rates will affect investment values. As interest rates increase, the investment value will decline; and as interest rates decrease, the investment value will rise. The investment value fluctuates in tandem with the yield to maturity of straight corporate bonds that are similar in quality. These relationships are discussed at length in chapter 4.

Although these factors influence the investment value of the convertible bond, they may not influence the market price. The investment value may move up and down, but the market price of the convertible bond remains relatively stable. Changes in interest rates are just one of the factors that may affect market price at any given moment. If the stock is increasing in value as interest rates are rising, the convertible is being driven by its equity component rather than its fixed-income value, so it will also rise. This occurred in the first six months of 1987. Interest rates rose, causing non-convertible bonds to decrease in value, while convertibles generally increased in value, being pulled along by a strong stock market.

It is important to calculate investment value because it provides a floor for the market price of the bond. A proper estimate of the investment floor is critical in evaluating a convertible security, for it becomes the minimum value below which the convertible bond should not fall, regardless of how the common stock is fluctuating, and it influences all other calculations in the mathematical analysis of convertibles. Because investment value is the hinge to which all other calculations are connected, it's important to understand how various factors affect bond investment value. Chapter 4 discusses this topic in detail.

INVESTMENT VALUE PREMIUM

An important measure of the basic value of the convertible is its premium over investment value. This is determined by calculating the difference between the market price and the investment value, expressed as a percentage. This value is important because it determines downside risk and is a number that can be monitored as market prices of convertibles change. The higher the investment premium, the more susceptible the convertible market price is to a decline in the underlying common stock.

CONVERSION VALUE

The other important aspect of a convertible security is its value in common stock. The conversion value of a convertible bond is the value of the bond if it were immediately converted to common stock. In figure 3.2, the diagonal line indicates the conversion value. For any stock price, the conversion value is found by multiplying the given stock price times the stated number of common shares received per bond. The number of shares per bond is stated as the *conversion ratio* and is set at the time the bond is issued. Like the bond investment value, the conversion value is a minimum value. The market price should not fall below the conversion value because the specialists and market makers quickly take advantage of the situation. If the bond price were below the conversion value, the arbitrager would buy the bond and simultaneously sell an equivalent number of shares of the underlying common stock. The difference between these two values would be a risk-free profit to the arbitrager. Traders sometimes refer to this as "lunch money." The question becomes, How many times a day would a trader take a small, risk-free profit? The answer is, All day long! Because of

---

FIGURE 3.2   Conversion Value

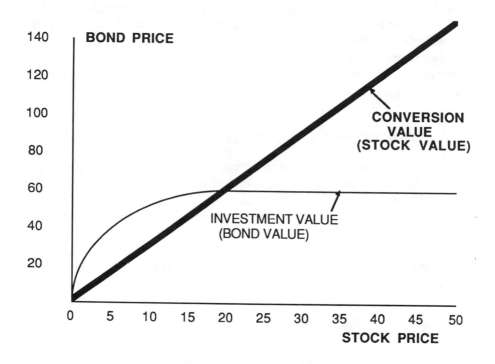

---

this, conversion value, like investment value, becomes a minimum value, below which the convertible's market price cannot fall.[1]

The number of shares the bond converts to stock is determined at the time of issue by the issuing company and stated in the trust indenture and prospectus. Confusion often arises among investors because the conversion ratio is not readily available. At the time of issue, the offering prospectus indicates the equivalent common stock price, which equals the par value of the bond. This is called the *conversion*

---

[1]Upon conversion, any accrued interest is loss. The arbitrager must take that into account in determining the profit opportunity.

FIGURE 3.3   Conversion Ratio

$$\frac{\text{PAR VALUE}}{\text{CONVERSION PRICE}} = \text{CONVERSION RATIO}$$

---

price and is meaningful if the bond were to remain at par. Investors often focus on the conversion price when they should be paying attention to the conversion ratio. From the moment the bond is brought to the market it trades either above or below par value, depending on market forces. Since the conversion ratio remains the same whether the bond is at par or not, that is the more important number for investors. The conversion ratio is determined by dividing the par value by the conversion price as shown in figure 3.3.

For example, if the common stock price at which the bond can be converted is $40, then each convertible represents 25 shares of stock (par value of $1,000 divided by stated conversion price of $40 − 25). This is the *conversion ratio*. The conversion ratio is a more relevant number than the conversion price because it can be used to determine the conversion value since the convertible's market price varies from par. Figure 3.2 depicts the stock value of the convertible by plotting the conversion value line. *Conversion value* is determined by multiplying the conversion ratio times the market price of the common stock.

The conversion ratio is usually adjusted for stock splits and dividends. The initial conversion ratio in our example was 25 shares of stock per each convertible bond. The conversion ratio would be adjusted to 27.500 following a ten percent stock dividend. Although convertible bondholders are not protected against normal cash dividends, in some cases they are protected against dividends that result from a spin-off of assets.

THE IDEAL CONVERTIBLE BOND

To illustrate the relationship between the conversion value and the investment value of the convertible bond, we will disregard many of the

FIGURE 3.4   Ideal Convertible Bond

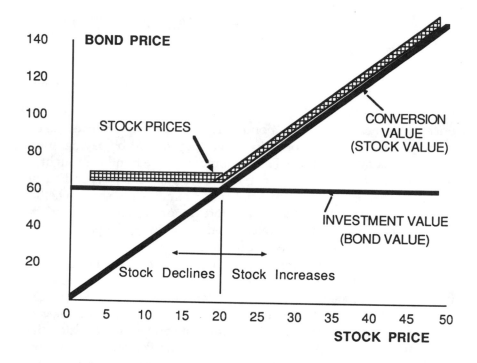

realities of the marketplace. Figure 3.4 shows the relationship between stock price movement (horizontal axis) and its effect on the convertible bond's market price (vertical axis). The arrow indicates the ideal price at which this convertible bond may be purchased. At that price, if the stock increases in value, the convertible bond value will increase at exactly the same percentage. On the other hand, if the common stock were to decline in value, the convertible bond would move along the investment value and maintain its market value. The price movement is indicated by the hatch area in figure 3.4.

In this simplified example, the convertible bond is obviously a superior buy because it offers the same upside potential as the common stock with none of the downside risk. The real world, of course, will

FIGURE 3.5   Convertible Bond

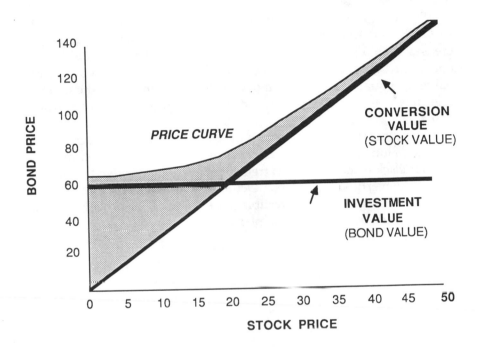

not allow investors such easy profit opportunities. In the financial marketplace there is a trade-off between the safety of the bond investment value and the opportunity of the conversion value. How much an investor is willing to pay for that trade-off becomes the most complicated aspect of convertible investing. A measure of that value is the security's conversion premium.

CONVERSION PREMIUM

The underlying stock value of the convertible bond was determined to be its conversion value. Since the bond is more secure and generally pays a higher interest than the dividend on the common stock, the convertible bond buyer pays a premium over conversion value. Conversion premium is the difference between market price and conversion value, expressed as a percentage. Market forces determine the amount of premium that a particular convertible may command in the marketplace.

Figure 3.5 depicts a typical convertible price curve, with the shaded area denoting conversion premium. Notice that as the stock increases in value, conversion premium gradually decreases until it becomes zero. At that point, the convertible market price and conversion value are equal. As the common stock declines in value, the convertible gains conversion premium because it is approaching its investment value.

The convertible price curve is based on exactly how much conversion premium a particular convertible security would command at various stock prices. It is an extremely important consideration in evaluating convertible securities. Detailed mathematical formulas are needed to estimate the convertible price curve. That process is examined in detail beginning in chapter 5.

4

Types of Convertible Securities

CONVERTIBLE BONDS

So far we have discussed the typical convertible bond, a debenture with a $1,000 par value upon which the company is obligated to pay semiannual interest and the principal upon maturity. Restrictions are often placed on the corporation and are stated in the trust indenture. The corporation and its investment banker define the terms and the type of security to be issued. Market conditions at the time of the offering become the most important factor in determining whether investors will accept the terms of the convertible security.

There are a number of reasons why corporations issue convertible bonds. First, like any corporate bonds, debt financing provides a major tax advantage. Interest payments are considered expenses and are deducted from profit before calculating the corporation's tax liability. Each dollar of interest paid reduces profit by a like amount. This reduces after-tax profits by less than a dollar, whereas a dollar of dividends reduces after-tax profit by a dollar. Therefore, debt financing can be cheaper to the issuing company.

Convertible bonds also provide a means by which corporations can reduce interest cost. Convertible bonds typically provide a saving of two percent to four percent less in interest cost than a straight bond. In the late seventies and early eighties, when interest rates on BBB cor-

FIGURE 4.1 New Offerings of Convertible Bonds (Number of Issues)

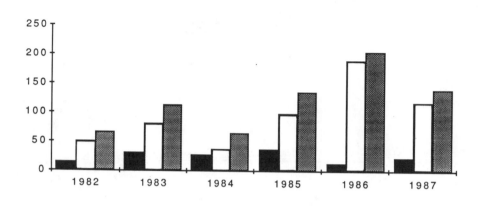

SOURCE: *Investment Dealers' Digest. Information Services, An Extel Financial Company.*

porate bonds were in the mid-teens, this was an important incentive for corporations to issue convertibles.

In addition to the high interest rate environment, there was a general perception that equity prices were low by historical standards. Convertibles gave the issuing corporation a way to sell stock at a premium over the current market price. Convertibles have always been used more extensively in uncertain times. The energy crisis of the early seventies, the accompanying double-digit inflation and the extreme volatility of the stock and bond markets of the eighties all contributed to the increasing interest in convertible securities.

Convertible bonds are usually subordinated debt, but not always. Subordinated debt is just one instrument corporations have used to meet their financing needs. Corporations' financing needs and the financial instruments they choose are dependent on what appeals to investors. At any given time, an issuer may find certain financial

---

FIGURE 4.2   New Offerings of Convertible Bonds

(Dollar Amount Public Offerings)

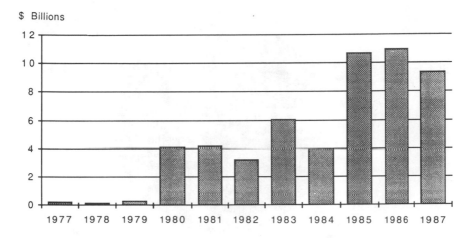

SOURCE: *SEC Monthly Statistical Review.*

instruments more attractive than others. Before 1977, bank debt and insurance company private placements were in vogue. In 1972, 1980 and 1983, when interest rates subsided and equity markets rose, convertible bond issuance increased. In 1977, high-yield bonds became popular securities, in part because equities were depressed. Thus, capital was raised in the form that made the most sense at that time.

Growth of the convertible market is indicated by the number of new issues coming to the market since 1982, as shown in figure 4.1. Issues of both investment grade and below investment grade contributed to the record levels attained in 1986 and 1987. Although the number of investment-grade issues coming to the domestic market has remained relatively stable throughout the years, investment-grade issues from other sources have increased. The Eurobond market has shown a marked increase in the number of investment-grade issues and new issues resulting from mergers.

FIGURE 4.3   Convertible-Market Value

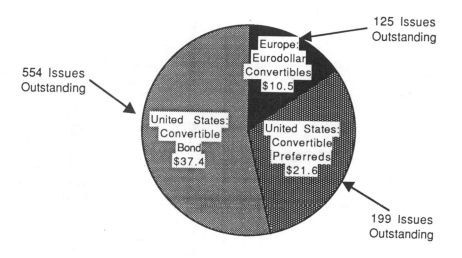

Market Value - $69.5 Billion - 878 Issues

125 Issues
Outstanding

Europe:
Eurodollar
Convertibles
$10.5

554 Issues
Outstanding

United States:
Convertible
Bond
$37.4

United States:
Convertible
Preferreds
$21.6

199 Issues
Outstanding

The actual dollar amount may be more reflective of what has occurred in the growth of the convertible bond market in recent years.
Figure 4.2 shows that before 1980 the convertible new issue market
was inactive, with a small number of new issues replacing those that
had either been called by the company or converted to stock by investors. The new issue market has grown tremendously in the eighties, reflecting the expansion of our capital markets and the rising interest in
convertible securities.

Eurodollar convertibles are those issued by U.S. companies and
convertible into domestic common stocks. This has expanded the universe of convertibles, with 125 issues outstanding as of June 1987. Estimates of this market may be imprecise because some convertibles may
be held while others may be called or converted to common stock.
Therefore, as stock prices rise, the convertible issue may dwindle in
size. As the globalization of the financial markets continues, the issu-

**FIGURE 4.4   Industry Sector Distribution
Convertible Bond New Issues: 1982–1987**

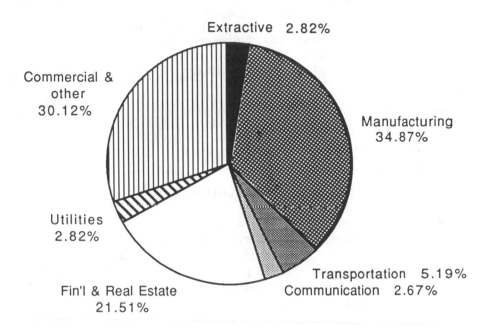

Extractive 2.82%

Commercial &
other
30.12%

Manufacturing
34.87%

Utilities
2.82%

Transportation 5.19%
Communication 2.67%

Fin'l & Real Estate
21.51%

SOURCE: *SEC Monthly Statistical Review*, December 1987.

ance of convertibles worldwide should expand the market further. Figure 4.3 shows the estimated total market value of convertibles outstanding by domestic companies.

As indicated in figure 4.4, convertibles are issued by many different industries. Although the growth of the convertible market in recent years has allowed convertible portfolios to become more diversified, some industry sectors use convertibles much more than others. Industry representation in the convertible market is fluid and dependent on each sector's financing needs. Convertibles often seem to be issued in bunches when a whole industry expands. One case in point is the hospital care group. Many companies in that industry, from blue chips to secondary companies, issued convertibles in large numbers during the late seventies. Investors who purchase convertibles predominantly in the new issue market sometimes see their portfolio become heavily weighted in a particular industry group.

FIGURE 4.5   Convertible Debt Offerings Highlights

	Number of Issues		Market Value (millions)	Average Coupon %	Average Conversion Premium %
	Total	Percent Investment Grade			
1982	67	23.9	3172.6	10.2	21.2
1983	113	27.4	6056.6	9.2	19.1
1984	66	42.4	4078.7	9.6	19.1
1985	137	27.7	10283.0	8.7	19.6
1986	207	6.8	10966.6	7.4	21.3
1987	148	16.9	9793.7	7.2	22.2

SOURCE: IDD Information Services, An Extel Financial Company.

REVIEWING THE NEW ISSUE MARKET

Generally, new convertibles carry a conversion price 15 percent to 25 percent over the price of the underlying common stock when they are brought to market. In addition, they often carry an interest rate two percent to four percent less than that of a straight corporate bond issued by the same company. Figure 4.5 indicates new issues that have been brought to the market from 1982 through 1987.

The average coupon rate of all convertible new issues during the six-year period ranges from 7.2 percent in 1987 to 10.2 percent in 1982, reflecting the lowering of long-term corporate bond rates in recent years. Coupon rates of convertibles follow the corporate bond market, and this relationship has remained relatively constant throughout the years.

However, the level of conversion premiums has not remained constant. The conversion premium in the new issue market trended upward in the bull market phase of the eighties. This trend is indicated in figure 4.5. During 1987, conversion premium averaged 22.2 percent, the highest in recent years. While the average coupon rate has been decreasing, reflecting the lowering of long-term corporate bond rates, the conversion premium of new issues has been increasing. This led some analysts to conclude that the new issue convertible market was overpriced and should be avoided. However, before making that broad generalization, the new issue market needs to be examined more carefully.

It is convenient to consider two broad sectors of the convertible market—*investment-grade convertibles*, those rated as investment

FIGURE 4.6   Conversion Premium and Coupon Rate

	Investment Grade		Below Investment Grade	
	Coupon Rate	Conversion Premium	Coupon Rate	Conversion Premium
1982	9.1%	16.5%	10.2%	21.8%
1987	6.5%	23.4%	7.3%	22.1%

SOURCE: IDD Information Services, An Extel Financial Company.

grade quality, BBB or better, by Standard & Poor's, and *aggressive convertibles*, those rated below investment grade. Since the convertible market reflects what is happening in the stock and bond market, it is better to look at these sectors of the market rather than at broad generalizations about the total convertible market.

Figure 4.5 shows the number of new issues that have come to the market on an annual basis since 1982. This chart also indicates the portion of the total that was rated investment grade or low risk. In 1986 and 1987, there was a distinct decrease in the issuance of investment-grade convertibles. Only 25 were issued during 1987, as compared to 123 issued with ratings below investment grade.

The influence of market sentiment is clearly visible on closer examination of conversion premium levels. In 1982, the traditional relationship regarding conversion premium and coupon rate existed. The conversion premium for an average new convertible issue of investment grade was 16.5 percent, with a coupon of 9.1 percent. New issues of below investment-grade convertibles that year averaged 21.8 percent, with a coupon rate of 10.2 percent. In 1987, the average coupon was 6.5 percent, with an average conversion premium of 23.4 percent. The two years are highlighted in figure 4.6.

Investors in 1987 seemed willing to pay a higher conversion premium for investment-grade convertibles than below investment-grade convertibles. This curious relationship led observers to question whether investors may have been overpaying for those investment-grade issues. The relationship that existed in 1982 was more customary. Conversion premiums on investment-grade convertibles were well below those of the higher-risk, below investment-grade issues. Investors expect to receive a higher coupon rate on below investment-grade convertibles and are usually willing to accept a higher conversion premium. This is because those stocks have more volatility, higher risk and, therefore, greater price movements. Presumably, common stocks of these smaller companies have greater growth prospects, so the conversion premium of their convertibles could be made up more quickly than with a staid blue-chip stock.

The convertible market is not an island; it reflects the dynamics of the financial marketplace. The blue-chip market during that period was anything but staid. The high-quality sector of the stock market continued to outpace the more risky growth areas. The demand for investment-grade convertibles was reflected in higher conversion premiums. Conversion premium levels have always ebbed and flowed depending on market sentiment. In a bullish environment, the enthusiasm of the market boosts premium levels. When market sentiment changes, premium levels can decrease very rapidly. The investment-grade convertible new issue market may have seemed overpriced by historical standards, so managers should have been wary.

On the other hand, the market sentiment among investors for the aggressive sectors of the market did not match the enthusiasm of the blue-chip sector. The conversion premium level for below investment-grade convertibles remained relatively stable over those years. These issues seem to be fairly priced, and occasionally underpriced, providing some value for investors. Methods to identify these opportunities are discussed in detail in chapter 6.

Those investing primarily in the new issue convertible market must be very selective and may be disappointed over time because the best opportunities in the convertible market occur in the after-market. However, selecting convertibles in the after-market becomes more complicated. Attention must be given not only to the level of conversion premium, but to the call features, the yield to maturity, the bond value and, of course, the growth prospects of the underlying common stock. Many of those factors are also important in selecting new issues, but they do not vary a great deal from issue to issue. Because of its ample supply, it may be easier to use the new issue market to build a convertible portfolio, but a properly balanced convertible portfolio must take other variables into account as well. By selecting convertibles in the after-market, investors can take advantage of occasional inefficiencies, which allow them to purchase convertibles that are underpriced and undervalued.

The most exciting feature of the new issue convertible market is its tremendous growth. In the past, many large investors, like pension funds, were hesitant to participate in the convertible market because of its relatively small size. Today, the convertible market is expanding and providing ample opportunities for even large institutional investors.

The convertible market now represents the complete spectrum of the stock market—from New York Stock Exchange blue chips to aggressive high-technology issues to more speculative OTC stocks and energy sectors on the American Stock Exchange. Health care, electronics, computers and airline industry groups are also represented by convertibles.

Merger activities have also catalyzed the convertible market. Perhaps the best recent example of a change in investor perception of convertibles is IBM's acquisition of Rolm Corporation, a leading telecommunications company. In November 1984, IBM's exchange offer for Rolm resulted in a $1.25 billion convertible bond issue, the largest of that time. Rolm shareholders received IBM convertible bonds. The more recent merger between Sperry Rand and Burroughs, now called Unisys, resulted in the largest convertible offering thus far. The exchange of securities between the companies was accomplished by a $1.425 billion offering of a $50 par value, $3.50 convertible preferred. The attention the IBM convertible and Unisys have brought to the convertible market should dispel the misconception that convertibles are issued only by marginal companies in dire financial straits.

In later chapters we will analyze methods that can be used to follow the new issue market and more accurately reflect the over- and underpriced valuation for the various sectors of the convertible market.

CONVERTIBLE PREFERRED STOCKS

Convertible preferred stock, like non-convertible preferred stock, is a class of capital stock of a corporation. The dividend rate is specified and declared by the board of directors, usually on a quarterly basis, and has preference over common stock in dividends and liquidations of assets. Preferred stocks are usually cumulative in that if the dividend is not declared, it accumulates in arrears. Convertible preferred stock has a specified rate at which the preferred stock can be converted to the common stock at the holder's option. After expiration of call protection, the company has the option of redeeming the issue at the stated par value.

Exchangeable convertible preferred stock gives the company the additional option of exchanging the convertible preferred stock for convertible bonds. The terms of the exchange are stated at the time of issue and are at the original fixed-income rate of the preferred stock. The company has the advantage of changing a non-deductible dividend cost to a tax-deductible interest expense. It may have issued the preferreds at a time when its balance sheet would not allow it to take on more debt. The exchangeable preferreds give the company additional flexibility to exchange equity for debt in the future.

CONVERTIBLE MONEY MARKET PREFERREDS

Convertible money market preferreds are not of interest to convertible investors because they are not convertible into common stock. They are an alternative to money market instruments for corporations. They are converted to a fixed number of dollars by varying the number of shares received by the holder. This is a fail-safe method for the holder to receive par value. Corporate investors use this vehicle as a short-term money market instrument to take advantage of the 70 percent dividend exclusion rule.

EXCHANGEABLE CONVERTIBLE BONDS

Convertible bonds may be issued by one company and converted into stock of another company. This situation can occur if a company has acquired a large block of a company's common stock and wants to sell. By issuing a convertible bond on that block of stock, the corporation receives the proceeds immediately and may dispose of the stock at a premium above the current market value. The corporation does not establish a taxable event because it still owns the stock and therefore postpones any tax liability until the convertible bonds are actually converted. This may take a number of years, during which time the corporation has full use of the proceeds.

The postponement of tax payments is an incentive for corporations to issue exchangeable convertible bonds. The risk to the corporation is that the stock may decline below the conversion price and not be sold. The advantage to the investor is that some interesting convertible opportunities occur. The convertible bond rating is dependent upon the issuing corporation rather than the common stock into which it can be converted.

For example, IBM owned a block of Intel common stock for which it issued an exchangeable convertible bond. The investor purchasing this bond had the credit obligation guaranteed by IBM but the stock performance of Intel Corporation, a volatile growth company in the microchip industry. This convertible bond carried a coupon of 6.375 percent, was convertible into 26.143 shares of Intel common stock and was rated AAA by Standard & Poor's. When Intel's common stock rose to $60 per share in October 1987, the convertible had an intrinsic value of $1568.86.

Although limited to a handful of issues, exchangeable convertibles offer some interesting investment opportunities. Because the bonds are identified by the issuing company rather than the stock they are converted into, these issues often go unnoticed by investors.

WARRANTS

Warrants are options to buy the underlying common stocks at a specific price over a specific time period. Warrants are similar to call options on stocks except that they are issued by the corporation and remain in effect for longer periods of time. They typically come into being as part of a unit attached to a corporate bond offering but are detachable after a short time. The value of the warrant depends on its terms, notably its exercise price and the time to expiration.

The *exercise price* of the warrant is determined at the time of issue. The investor exercising the warrant has the right to purchase the underlying common stock at the stated exercise price. Since most warrants are issued as part of a unit, the investor may use the straight corporate bond that was part of the unit in lieu of cash to exercise the warrant. The bond is called a "usable bond," and its value is important in determining the *effective exercise price* of the warrant. Since the bond can be used in lieu of cash, any purchase of the bond below par would effectively reduce the exercise price of the warrant. For example, if the usable bond is trading at 80, representing a 20 percent discount, the warrant exercise price should also be reduced by 20 percent. The effective exercise price is quite an important consideration in evaluating the warrant.

Warrants, like stock options, are purchased by speculators because of their high leverage. The investor is able to control large quantities of the underlying common stock with a relatively small investment. Whether they can be used successfully depends on the evaluation process and the strategy. Conservative investors may combine warrants with fixed-income securities to create synthetic convertibles.

SCORES AND PRIMES

In 1983, A. Joseph Debe of Americus Shareowner Service Corporation developed the concept for the Americus Trust. A special ruling by the Internal Revenue Service and The Securities and Exchange Commission permitted the trust in selected issues. These trusts separated the dividend yielding component of common stock from its capital appreciation component. Although slow to catch on, they contained some interesting opportunities for convertible investors. They take in from investors blue-chip stocks such as American Express, Coca-Cola and Exxon in return for a trust unit that separates the income portion, called *PRIME*, from the capital gain portion, called *SCORE*.

The trust gives PRIME the right to all dividends (less a small fee) over the five-year life of the trust, plus an additional amount of stock at expiration, which is fixed by the *termination claim*. SCORE holders receive any appreciation above the specified termination claim amount at expiration. Figure 4.7 shows some of the specifics of the trust units.

There are a number of investment strategies that can be used with SCOREs and PRIMEs. They offer a way to apply convertible investment techniques to the blue-chip market and can be evaluated much like warrants.

ZERO-COUPON CONVERTIBLES (LYONS)

Liquid yield option notes (LYON) combine zero-coupon bonds with a stock play. Created by Merrill Lynch in 1982, LYONs are corporate zero-coupon bonds with the right to convert to the underlying common stock. An additional important feature is that the investor has the right to put back (sell back) the bond to the company at a specified price listed in a schedule at the time of issue. This feature protects the investor against a sharp increase in interest rates, which would cause a long-term zero-coupon bond to fall in value. The company typically has the right to call the bonds for cash in five years. The determination of the LYON's investment value must take the put feature into account and is discussed in detail in chapter 5.

EURODOLLAR CONVERTIBLE BONDS

Many of the largest domestic companies have issued convertible bonds in the Eurobond market. These bonds are dollar-denominated and are

FIGURE 4.7   Americus Trust PRIME/SCORE

COMPANY	MAXIMUM SIZE*	TERMINATION DATE	CLAIM	AMEX SYMBOLS** UNITS	PRIMES	SCORES
American Express	7.5	8/24/92	50	XPU	XPP	XPS
American Home Products	7.5	12/20/91	90	HPU	HPP	HPS
American Tel/Tel Series 2	10.0	2/14/92	30	ATU	ATP	ATS
Amoco	10.0	3/30/92	105	AOU	AOP	AOS
Atlantic Richfield	10.0	7/01/92	116	RFU	RFP	RFS
Bristol-Meyers***	5.0	2/14/92	110	BYU	BYP	BYS
Chevron	10.0	7/01/92	75	CVU	CVP	CVS
Coca-Cola	5.0	7/15/92	56	KKU	KKP	KKS
Dow Chemical	7.5	5/18/92	110	DOU	DOP	DOS
DuPont	10.0	3/27/92	110	DPU	DPP	DPS
Eastman Kodak	7.5	4/15/92	92	KDU	KDP	KDS
Exxon	5.4	9/20/90	60	XNU	XNP	XNS
Ford	10.0	6/30/92	104	FCU	FCP	FCS
General Electric***	10.0	5/11/92	140	GNU	GNP	GNS
General Motors	10.0	6/30/92	107	GCU	GCP	GCS
GTE	7.5	7/15/92	44	LDU	LDP	LDS
Hewlett-Packard	10.0	7/27/92	90	HLU	HLP	HLS
IBM	10.0	6/30/92	210	BZU	BZP	BZS
Johnson & Johnson	7.5	6/30/92	118	JNU	JNP	JNS
Merck	3.5	4/14/92	200	MKU	MKP	MKS
3M***	2.5	3/25/92	156	MMU	MMP	MMS
Mobil	10.0	6/30/92	60	MBU	MBP	MBS
Philip Morris	5.0	7/27/92	110	HMU	HMP	HMS
Proctor & Gamble	7.5	6/01/92	105	OGU	OGP	OGS
Sears Roebuck	10.0	7/15/92	64	RSU	RSP	RSS
Texaco	10.0	6/30/92	70	TCU	TCP	TCS
Union Pacific	5.0	4/15/92	87	UPU	UPP	UPS
Xerox	3.5	7/15/92	97	XXU	XXP	XXS

*   Millions of units.
**   "PRIME" stands for "Prescribed Right to Income and Maximum Equity";
     "SCORE" stands for "Special Claim on Residual Equity."
*** Because of a stock split subsequent to creation of the trust, each unit repre-
     sents two shares.

SOURCE: Alex. Brown & Sons, Inc.

similar to the convertible bonds issued in the United States. Because
the bonds are not registered with the Securities and Exchange Commission, they cannot be purchased by U.S. investors until they have become seasoned. The seasoning period is usually 90 days. Over 140
domestic companies have issued Eurodollar convertibles over the last
20 years, most of them since 1981.

Although the issues have been smaller in size than domestic issues, Texaco raised $1.5 billion by issuing two convertible Eurobonds in 1984. Most of these issues are offered by foreign finance subsidiaries that are set up to market the issues. The payment of interest and principal is guaranteed by the parent company, making the Eurobonds as safe as domestic issues.

There are some differences that investors should be aware of. Eurodollar convertibles generally pay interest annually instead of semiannually. Upon issuance, both the coupon and the conversion premium are lower than their U.S. counterparts, and many carry special features. Foreign investors viewed convertibles as a direct alternative to the purchase of common stock, so they were usually more interested in convertibles with greater equity participation. Eurodollar convertibles are generally issued with shorter maturities and without sinking funds. Many issues have put features that allow investors to sell the bond back to the company at a price above par in five years. Others carry absolute call protection and short maturities that are unavailable in the domestic market. Since many of the Eurodollar convertibles are issued by companies that do not have corresponding domestic issues, the Eurodollar convertible market offers wider investment alternatives.

Investing in Eurodollar convertibles can be difficult for investors because many brokers are not equipped to handle the transaction. The brokers that are members of Euro-clear handle such trades as routinely as any domestic issue. Because of the difficulty in executing the transaction and the difference in terms, Eurodollar convertibles can be overlooked by investors and are often attractively priced.

CONVERTIBLES WITH PUT FEATURES

Investors in the Eurobond convertible market seemed hesitant to purchase bonds with long maturities. This is undoubtedly due to the European experience of inflation and the disastrous effect it can have on long-term bond investments. To allay this fear, many convertibles are issued with a put feature that allows the bondholder to sell the bonds back to the company at par or a premium above par prior to maturity. The Euroconvertibles usually can be put back to the company in three to seven years, so if the company's common stock does not rise in value over the life of the put, the investor is guaranteed a minimum return on investment. These minimum returns are usually in line with short-term money instruments at the time of issue.

An example of this was the Eurobond offering on February 12, 1987, by Wyse Technology of $45 million, six percent convertible subordinated debentures due February 25, 2002. The prospectus stated that "each debenture may be redeemed, as a whole or in part, in increments of $1,000 on February 25, 1994, at the option of holders thereof at 100 percent of the principal amount to be redeemed plus interest accrued to the redemption date."[1]

The average maturity of most convertible bonds is long term, approaching 20 years. This makes convertibles with put features valuable because of their shorter maturities and lower interest rate risk.

SYNTHETIC CONVERTIBLES

A synthetic convertible is created by combining separate fixed-income securities with equity securities. Whereas a convertible security combines a fixed-income vehicle with a non-detachable warrant, a synthetic convertible achieves the same effect by putting together the fixed-income and equity parts. These types of securities are often issued as a unit. The unit is sold to the public as a straight bond with warrants attached. In the after-market, the straight bonds and the warrants can either be purchased as a unit, therefore becoming the equivalent to a convertible bond, or separately. The bond portion will trade on a yield basis as a fixed-income security, while the warrant will trade as an option to buy the common stock at a predetermined exercise price.

Since both parts trade separately in the market, the aggressive investor may simply buy the warrants to speculate on a common stock price increase. Other investors, to create the attributes of a convertible bond, would purchase both the straight bond and the warrant. An investor can purchase the bond component as part of a fixed-income portfolio. These bonds should be more valuable for a fixed-income investor than similar rated bonds because there is always the possibility that they will be used for conversion of the warrants, causing an increase in value.

A variation on this theme is to create synthetic convertibles from stock options and SCOREs. In this case, the fixed-income component

---

[1]Prospectus dated February 12, 1987. Wyse Technology, $45,000,000, 6% Convertible Subordinated Debentures Due 2002. These securities were not offered in the United States or to any person who is a citizen, national, or resident thereof. U.S. citizens may purchase bonds after the seasoning period.

does not necessarily relate to the call option or warrants. Money market funds, Treasury bills and other corporate bonds could be combined with call options and warrants to create the synthetic convertible. Whether or not this is an advisable strategy will be discussed in Part III.

CONVERTIBLES WITH RESET FEATURES

Reset features are used as sweeteners to help troubled companies sell their bonds. The reset feature allows for the adjustment of the coupon rate, conversion ratio or maturity date should certain stipulated events occur. For example, this feature could be used to protect the bondholder's value if the stock has not performed as well as expected. Increasing the conversion ratio or the coupon would bolster the value of the bond. Obviously, these bonds are lower-grade speculative issues.

A deal structured by Drexel Burnham Lambert for United Artists Communications gave investors the protection of a reset and guaranteed the issuer long-term financing. After a fixed period of time, the bonds are evaluated by an independent investment banker to determine a coupon rate that will allow the bonds to trade at 101 plus accrued interest. This adjustment to the coupon rate prevents the investor from losing principal should the stock not perform as expected. It also prevents losses due to rising long-term interest rates because the reset occurs in only three years. However, since many companies that issue these types of bonds are highly leveraged, the financial status of the corporation must be considered very carefully.

From the corporate viewpoint, the company saves interest rate costs and maintains long-term financing. This is important to an emerging company because it can have its financing remain secure and allow the terms of the financing to float with market conditions. In the case of United Artists, the company's cost of financing would be $6^3/8$ percent for three years. It could choose instead to maintain the fixed-rate financing with a higher coupon for the life of the maturity. Conversion premium on this issue was a high 31 percent, which also benefited the company.

CONVERTIBLE STOCK NOTES

Another variation on the convertible theme is the convertible stock note. Instead of paying interest and principal in cash, this note pays in common stock or cash at the issuer's option. It is sometimes referred to as a *pay-in-kind* (PIK) security and is designed to give issuers flexibility in managing cash flow. In cases where these issues are subordinated, most senior lenders view them as equity alternatives. Convertible stock notes are typically issued by troubled companies, so their yield cannot be readily compared to yields on other convertibles. As a group, these bonds trade *flat*, without accrued interest, and their market prices usually reflect an amount representing accrued interest since the last payment date. Even though these types of securities are generally deeply subordinated, issuers are highly motivated to retire them because they are usually their most costly form of capital.

Companies facing bankruptcy often ask creditors to exchange debt for convertible stock notes. Since a company is in dire financial condition when these options are given, the bondholder often has little choice but to accept. Still offers are made in an attempt to negotiate a settlement that will be acceptable to the bondholders. It is important for the convertible investor to evaluate the terms in detail before arriving at a decision to accept the offer.

One case in point is Anacomp. Facing bankruptcy, the company proposed to convertible holders a plan to exchange their $13^7/8$ percent bonds for convertible bonds with a higher conversion ratio and give the company the option of paying the interest in either common stock or cash. The conversion ratio on the new bonds was increased to 250 shares per bond from 57.143. As financial conditions improved and the stock recovered from $2 per share to $4, the new convertible bond with the higher conversion ratio increased from 50 to 100. In fact, as the stock recovered to $8 a share in mid-1987, the new convertible bonds had an intrinsic value of 200. The common stock was still well below its former high. Again, this points out the advantage of being a creditor rather than a shareholder when a company's fortunes change.

The original convertible bondholder of the Anacomp $13^7/8$ percent bond who did not accept the exchange offer did not fare as well. As the company's financial condition improved, the bond price returned to par; however, the high conversion premium and a conversion price of $17.50 left little room for much equity participation. The convertible investor in either case still fared a great deal better than the common stock holder.

As a general rule, exchange offers allowing for increased equity participation should be accepted by convertible bondholders, while offers to exchange convertible bonds for non-convertible fixed-income securities should not be accepted. The latter usually are made with a higher yield factor than that of the convertible to entice investors to accept the offer and give up their equity participation.

While most convertible stock notes had been negotiated as part of bankruptcy hearings, Bear, Stearns and Company managed the first public offering of convertible stock notes in August 1987. The offering for Tosco Corporation was part of the restructuring of $411 million in debt the troubled company owed to a group of banks. Structured as a private deal in December 1986, it carried registration rights that allowed investors to demand that the securities be registered with the Securities and Exchange Commission and offered to the public after a certain period of time. The public offering occurred in August 1987 with $58.5 million face value priced at a discount of $640 per $1,000 note. The notes were convertible into 250 shares of common stock at a conversion price of $4. The notes pay four percent interest a year in stock, or ten shares a year, so that upon maturity they will represent 300 shares. The issuer can call the issue for redemption at any time at 120 percent of principal plus accrued interest.

ASSET-LINKED CONVERTIBLES

In the late seventies and early eighties, the concern about inflation became so pronounced that investors looked to metals to preserve their capital. Convertibles that were linked to metals combined the security of fixed income with convertibility into the precious metal instead of the common stock. The asset-linked convertibles were an extension of the gold-linked certificates used in the past.

Commodities such as gold, silver, crude oil and real estate were linked with fixed income to provide the asset-linked convertible issue. Each issue carried very specific requirements for converting to the commodity. For example, Sunshine Mines issued a 15-year, $8^1/2$ percent coupon convertible bond, convertible into silver at $20 an ounce. This represented a 25 percent premium above the then-current market price of silver. Others were issued by companies linked to oil and real estate.

On June 10, 1987, Eastman Kodak Company issued in Europe a unit consisting of $130,000,000 of nine percent notes due in 1990 with 130,000 gold warrants. Since this offering was not registered with the Securities and Exchange Commission, U.S. investors could not participate in this issue. The warrant entitled the holder to receive an amount in U.S. dollars equal to the excess of the price of one troy ounce of gold over the $470.60 strike price.

These securities were much more popular in the Eurobond market than the domestic market. As inflation leveled off from its peak in the early eighties, the interest in asset-linked convertibles faded.

GLOBAL CONVERTIBLES

In response to expanding world capital markets, a new sector of the Euroconvertible market developed in the first half of 1987. During that period, 21 issues of sterling-dominated convertibles came to the market on the strength of the U.K. equity market, of which 18 are U.K. and three are Australian. Convertibles in the Euromarket are typically issued with low conversion premium and put features.

Many foreign companies have issued convertibles. Japan and West Germany have many issues outstanding, including warrants. The evaluation of international convertibles is further complicated by currency fluctuations.

CONVERTIBLE MORTGAGES

A variation on the convertible theme has been applied to the real estate market. In an attempt to entice investors to finance real estate projects, syndicators often package mortgages with equity participation. Like the public Real Estate Investment Trusts, these private issues have little appeal to convertible investors. Although there is a hint of the hybrid nature of convertible securities, aside from the illiquidity of the investment, equity participation in real estate partnership is usually so slight as to be meaningless. Investors should compare and evaluate those limited partnership units as they would any convertible issue. The most likely finding would be that the issue is extremely overvalued with little chance for an equity participation.

5

Anatomy of a Convertible Bond

Each component of the convertible security must be considered carefully before determining whether it is attractively priced. In this chapter we will discuss the various calculations that must be done along with some of the more commonly used mathematical methods found in many convertible research reports.

CALCULATING BOND INVESTMENT VALUE

The investment value of a convertible bond is the fixed-income value without the convertibility feature. In other words, it is the worth of a straight bond with exactly the same coupon rate, maturity date and quality rating. To determine the bond investment value, the straight bond yield to maturity needs to be estimated. An estimate may be obtained by looking at the yield to maturity of straight bonds with the same Standard & Poor's and Moody's bond rating. The bond investment value is equal to the present value of the interest and principal payments discounted at the straight bond yield through the maturity of the bond.

The present value of the series of interest payments and the par value received upon maturity is the actual value discounted at an appropriate rate of interest. The discounting reflects the productivity of capital and the risk premium. For example, figure 5.1 indicates the cal-

---

FIGURE 5.1   Bond Investment Value Calculation

Years	(1) Present Value Payment	(2) Present Value Factor* at 10%	(1) × (2)
1–20	$80	8.514	$681.12
20	$1000	0.149	149.00
Bond Investment Value (Sv(t))			$830.12

$$Sv(t) = \sum_{t=1}^{n} \frac{C}{(1+r)^t} + \frac{P}{(1+r)^n}$$

P = par value
r = discount rate
C = coupon rate
n = number periods to maturity

*Obtained from interest tables.

---

culation using standard interest tables of an eight percent, 20-year bond.[1] In this case, a ten percent discount rate is used to determine the investment value of $830.12. The discount rate is the estimate of the yield to maturity of a non-convertible bond of similar quality.

Once the yield-to-maturity factor is known, the bond investment value can be determined easily. A calculator with financial functions can accomplish this by using the par value at maturity as the FV (future value), coupon rate (payment) and years to maturity (n time periods) to solve for bond investment value (PV, present value). A more serious problem comes in estimating the discount rate to use. In most cases, the bond ratings of Standard & Poor's and Moody's will suffice. However, ratings are not very responsive to changing financial fundamentals, and the lag can cause significant errors in estimating the discount rate. Studies indicate that bonds accomplish most of their price

---

[1]Interest tables are found in most investment textbooks. Computer spread sheets and financial calculators also provide a convenient means to quickly access present value formulas and determine investment value.

change reactions about one year before their ratings change.[2] There even have been occasions where a company has filed Chapter 11 proceedings but the bond rating has not yet been changed. Attention to creditwatch news and other fundamental information on the company is critical in monitoring investment values. The market quickly assesses investment value in response to news items.

Since market sentiment plays an important role in the assessment of the convertible's bond risk, monitoring the prices of straight debt issues of the underlying company can be helpful in selecting the proper discount rate. Often the apparent deterioration of the creditworthiness of an issue will not be reflected in the convertible price because the common stock may be rising. This may seem unusual at first glance, but it is not unusual for companies to take on additional debt when business is on an upswing. The stock price is reflecting the increase in business, while the bond value is reflecting the increase in the debt/ equity ratio. While ratings lag, astute bond traders quickly reprice the straight debt reflecting the higher credit risk. By monitoring the straight debt the investor is able to adjust the investment value of the convertible long before the rating changes.

In the case of investment-grade convertibles, bonds rated BBB or better, investment values can be estimated conveniently through the bond rating mechanism. The same company often issues straight bonds that can be used to estimate the discount rate in the bond investment value. For investment-grade issues, bonds of other companies with similar ratings can also be used to determine the discount rate.

Figure 2.3 in chapter 2 showed the IBM convertible bond listed in the financial pages along with two non-convertible bonds. The 9.375 percent coupon due to mature in 2004 is similar in maturity date to the 7.875 percent coupon on the convertible bond, also due to mature in 2004. Using a Hewlett-Packard HP 12C financial calculator, we find that the yield to maturity for the 9.375 percent coupon straight bond is 9.77 percent. Using the 9.77 percent as the discount rate, we find that the convertible bond's investment value is 84.58. Using similar bonds to determine the discount rate has the advantage of quickly reflecting changes in market sentiment. A great deal of confidence can be placed

[2]Mark I. Weinstein, "The Effect of a Rating Change Announcement on Bond Price," *Journal of Financial Economics* 5 (December 1977): 159–68.

in the estimate of the investment value of this particular highly liquid convertible bond.

Not all bonds are as easy to estimate as IBM. In general, whether the investment value acts as the investment floor of the convertible in declining markets depends on the accuracy of the investment value estimate. Great care should be exercised in determining this important value.

MEASURING INVESTMENT VALUE RISK

Selecting the appropriate measure of risk is one of the most difficult decisions the convertible investor must make. Many practitioners ignore this process and simply rely on published bond ratings to evaluate the risk of bond investment values. Others assume no changes in interest rates to simplify the analytical process.

Simplifying the process by ignoring interest rates and fundamentals may work most of the time; however, the investor using that approach should be mentally ready to accept an inordinate number of decreasing ratings or even bankruptcy situations in the portfolio.

The proper measure of risk is needed to reflect the uncertainty of achieving the expected return. Without measuring all known risk factors, the implied assumptions that the analysis is based on can be completely misleading. In addition, convertible bonds are generally subordinated debentures, so they have lower ratings. Lower ratings imply higher risk, not merely higher yields.

DEFAULT RISK OF CONVERTIBLES

The discussion of investment value is not complete without reviewing the most serious consequence that can occur to a convertible bondholder: default. Default losses are rare, but they do occur from time to time. Figure 5.2 indicates public defaults of both straight bonds and convertible bonds by industry sector. The concentration of defaults in industry sectors, namely steel and energy issues, reflects troubled times in these segments of the economy. It also indicates that industry factors are very important in determining default risk. Although convertibles on average have a higher default rate than non-convertible bonds, there is not a significant difference.

Although figure 5.3 includes both non-convertible and convertible debt, it is useful to review the rating distribution of defaulting issues

FIGURE 5.2 Public Defaults by Industry Sector: 1970–1986 (millions of dollars)

	Number of Companies	Straight Debt	Percentage of Total Straight	Convertible Debt	Total in Default	Percentage of Total
Industrial						
Retailers	15	$ 556.74	7.14	$ 211.87	$ 768.61	7.70
General Mfg.	23	2301.49	29.53	331.64	2563.73	25.68
Elec./Computer & Comm.	22	200.79	2.58	413.58	614.37	6.15
Oil & Gas	29	1581.09	20.29	449.65	2030.74	20.34
Real Estate-Const., Supplies	13	103.93	1.33	126.55	230.48	2.30
Misc. Industries	18	570.30	7.32	177.68	747.98	7.49
TOTAL	120	$5314.34	68.19	$1710.97	$ 6955.91	69.66
Transportation						
Railroads	9	$1260.22	16.17	$31.10	$ 1291.32	12.93
Airlines/Cargo	7	211.81	2.72	122.81	334.62	3.35
Sea Lines	4	243.00	3.12	123.10	366.10	3.67
Trucks/Motor Carriers	3	48.31	.62	9.75	58.06	.58
TOTAL	23	$1763.34	22.63	$ 268.76	$ 2050.10	20.53
Finance						
Financial Services	11	$ 436.09	5.60	$ 164.04	$ 600.13	6.01
REITs	12	279.71	3.58	99.46	379.17	3.80
TOTAL	23	$715.80	9.18	$ 263.50	$ 979.30	9.81
TOTAL	166	$7793.48	100.00	$2261.23	$10054.71	100.00

SOURCE: Edward I. Altman, *Financial Analysts Journal* 43, no. 4 (July/August 1987): 21.

FIGURE 5.3 Rating Distribution of Defaulting Issues at Various Points Prior to Default: 1970–1986

Original Rating	AAA	AA	A	BBB	BB	B	CCC	CC	TOTAL
Number	0	3	11	29	26	79	33	1	182
Percentage	0.00%	1.65%	6.04%	15.93%	14.29%	43.41%	18.13%	0.55%	100.00%
Rating One Year Prior	AAA	AA	A	BBB	BB	B	CCC	CC	TOTAL
Number	0	0	2	11	29	81	67	9	199
Percentage	0.00%	0.00%	1.01%	5.53%	14.57%	40.70%	33.67%	4.52%	100.00%
Rating Six Months Prior	AAA	AA	A	BBB	BB	B	CCC	CC	TOTAL
Number	0	0	2	3	11	77	95	15	203
Percentage	0.00%	0.00%	0.99%	1.48%	5.42%	37.93%	46.80%	7.39%	100.00%

SOURCE: Edward I. Altman, *Financial Analysts Journal* 43, no. 4 (July/August 1987): 22.

prior to default. Notice the jump in the default rate from the medium-grade BB category to the B ratings. The original rating of bond issues that eventually default is also of interest. These fallen angels can be troublesome to investors who rely on rating alone to determine investment value of convertibles.

An awareness of the probability of default regarding convertible issues is an important consideration in determining investment value. Although default rates of convertible and non-convertible issues are similar, the price declines are more dramatic for convertible issues. The average price decline of a defaulting bond issue from January 1 of the defaulting year until the end of the defaulting month was 40.1 percent for 195 defaulting issues between 1970 and 1986. Of the 195 issues, 49 were convertibles, and out of the top ten losers, seven were convertibles.

If an investor is holding a convertible issue and a default is announced, is it better to sell immediately or try and ride it out? Although most issues drop in price prior to the actual announcement, reflecting financial deterioration of the company, there is still a significant drop in price around the announcement date. For example, Interstate Department Stores' convertible issue had the dubious distinction of registering the largest one month decline after the default announcement, dropping 89.4 percent. In 18 of the 195 cases of defaulting bonds, bond prices actually rose in the month the default was announced. In fact, the three that rose the most were convertible issues, and in ten cases there was no price change.[3]

work. Monitoring the financial condition of the company is a necessary procedure in updating investment values. Relying on rating services alone to calculate investment values is not sufficient to prevent investment errors. The answer to the question, Is it best to sell or ride out a defaulted convertible issue? is to sell. However, investing in defaulted convertible issues can be extremely profitable. Interstate Department Stores' bankruptcy had a happy ending in that the company later became tremendously successful as Toys "R" Us. The Anacomp defaulted convertible issue rallied from 50 to nearly 200 in two years as the company came out of bankruptcy. Finding convertible issues *after* the terms have been negotiated is a much better strategy than holding and hoping for favorable treatment throughout the bankruptcy proceedings.

---

[3]Edward I. Altman, *Financial Analysts Journal* 43 (July/August 1987): 23.

It is important for convertible investors to realize that high yield alone cannot compensate for lower quality. Given today's mathematically oriented investment analysis, it is well to remember that it may take years to compensate for the loss of principal value that can occur in the event of default. In the classic work, *Security Analysis*, Benjamin Graham observed that "deficient safety cannot be compensated by an abnormally high coupon rate alone."[4] The additional reality of the marketplace is that lower-quality bonds are much more susceptible to price breaks on changing fundamentals of the company. This is why many convertible investors and managers run into trouble. Many of them view a high-grade convertible bond in the same light as a lower-grade convertible, with the only adjustment being a yield differential. Common sense tells us that the same formula cannot be used to evaluate an IBM convertible bond and a convertible bond of an unseasoned lower-quality issue. Since the companies are not readily comparable, neither are their securities. Investment-grade issues must be compared to issues of the same quality.

The good news in the lower-grade market is that although convertible bonds seem to have a higher default rate than corporate bonds in general, the actual instances of default are comparatively rare. The convertible investor can prevent such disasters from occurring by assuming an active role in managing the portfolio. Most defaults are issuer and industry related, a risk that can be reduced by proper diversification. Poor economic conditions can heighten the threat of default, so investors tend to avoid lower-quality issues in poor economic times. This widens the yield spread between high- and low-quality issues. The market generally announces its concern over pending default by sharp price breaks and a continual stream of bad news. To ignore these warnings is poor portfolio management, whether investing in convertibles, stocks or straight fixed income.

The controlling of default risk in convertible bonds begins with the categorization of convertibles between quality levels. For investment-grade convertible securities, the bond ratings usually accomplish just that. Extra care must be taken in estimating investment value of below investment-grade convertible securities.

---

[4]Benjamin Graham, D.L. Dodd and S. Cottle. *Security Analysis, Principles and Techniques.* 4th ed. (New York: McGraw-Hill, 1962), pp. 310.

INVESTMENT VALUE FOR BELOW INVESTMENT-GRADE SECURITIES

To estimate the investment value in the high-risk sector of the convertible market is much more difficult. The returns of lower-quality bonds are more closely correlated to the returns on common stocks because the level of concern about default varies with the same factors that drive the stock market. For example, during the stock market crash of 1987 a divergence occurred between investment-grade and below investment-grade securities. Even though interest rates declined slightly during those hectic weeks, the investment values of below investment-grade issues plummeted as a "flight to quality" occurred. What is needed is a method by which the convertible investor can categorize convertibles into various risk classes. Only then can the convertible investor match convertibles to investment objectives.

This is an important distinction in convertible investing. There has been a tendency to group all convertibles together and to use evaluation methods that ignore risk classes. For many investors, the extra return is acceptable for incurring greater default risk. Those investors need clearer guidelines that correlate risk tolerance levels with investment objectives. The investment policy statement of pension funds should address this very important issue.

When discussing relative risk, a clear understanding of risk measures is needed. For example, the convertible bond on a high-risk stock would always have less risk than the underlying common stock. Therefore, if the investment guidelines called for participation in the high-risk sector of the stock market, a convertible bond with a CCC S&P rating might be appropriate.

The categories of convertibles suggested below have two benefits. They can help investment counselors develop risk tolerance guidelines for their clients. They also provide an important ingredient in the analytical process so that convertible issues can be compared properly.

BOND INVESTMENT VALUE RISK CLASSES

Investment value risk classes are based on several factors. These factors culminate in a bond investment value class that will respond quickly to changing market conditions. Several items respond quickly to market conditions, while others are a function of historical data.

Investment value yield to maturity should be adjusted for the most current credit information available. Often, rating services lag changes to the creditworthiness of the bond. Therefore, investors must change investment value yields to reflect that information. Calamos Convertible Evaluation Service (CCES) does this by applying a CCES grade to each security in a range from one to twenty. This allows for a finer adjustment to the yield to maturity investment value calculation, than by simply relying on misleading financial ratings.

CREDIT ANALYSIS OF CONVERTIBLE SECURITIES

Credit analysis plays a significant role in analyzing convertible securities. As discussed earlier, the investor must determine the appropriate discount rate factor to calculate the straight bond value component of the convertible security. The investment value provides the cushion for the convertible when equity prices fall.

The key factors in determining the credit risk of a convertible security are outlined below. They are the same factors that a bond analyst might use in determining the risk of straight fixed-income instruments. Here the convertible analyst puts on the bond analyst hat and looks only at the convertible's fixed-income attributes.

1. *Industry Risk*—competitiveness, growth, government regulations, cost factors, operating coverage, cyclical nature of the business and the issuer's position within the industry
2. *Financial Considerations*—conservativeness of accounting practices, financial goals and policies of the company
3. *Profitability Ratios*—return on equity, profit margins, earnings growth, coefficient of variations for return on earnings and coefficient of variation for earnings per share
4. *Financial Ratios*—debt to equity, interest coverage ratios, operating income to sales, equity turnover, net income total assets, working capital to total debt, debt in payback period and total debt as percent of capital
5. *Management Considerations*—operating track record, change in key personnel, depth of management, cost control effectiveness, innovativeness and labor relations
6. *Other Considerations*—issue size, subordination of the issue, size of the firm, financial flexibility, future capital needs and product diversification

FIGURE 5.4   Yield-to-Maturity Examples

Bonds with a 9% Coupon			
Yield-to-Maturity	7%	9%	11%
Price change of			
9%: 25-year bond	$1,233	$1,000	$832
Price change of			
9%: 15-year bond	$1,182	$1,000	$856
Bonds with a 5% Coupon			
Yield-to-Maturity	7%	9%	11%
Price change of			
5%: 25-year bond	$767	$607	$495
Price change of			
5%: 15-year bond	$818	$678	$569

It is always important to compare the considerations and ratios with industry averages. The trend and variation in ratios may be as important as the ratio itself. The company's future capital needs and goals also must be considered. Our purpose in this book is not to discuss fixed-income credit analysis in depth, but to alert the investor to the importance of these factors in analyzing the convertible's investment value.

INTEREST RATE SENSITIVITY

An advantage of using the yield-to-maturity concept is that it equalizes various coupons and maturity dates. Changes in yield-to-maturity values can then be easily related to changes in bond investment value. There is an inverse relationship between the level of interest rates and the convertible's investment value.

Figure 5.4 indicates how the investment value is changed by changes in interest rates. For example, if a convertible bond with a nine percent coupon and a 25-year maturity was issued when long-term interest rates were 11 percent, its investment value would be $832. If long-term interest rates declined to nine percent, the investment value would be at par. Figure 5.4 illustrates several coupons and maturity dates to show their influence on the investment value of the convertible security.

DURATION ANALYSIS

Duration analysis is used by fixed-income analysts to better measure how bond values, and in our case convertible investment values, change with changing interest rates. Duration analysis is valuable because it not only takes into account the coupon rate and the maturity date, but it time weights these cash flows. Bond price volatility is related to the length of time over which the instrument matures, but it is not so much related to the final maturity date, when the principal comes due, as it is to the series of payments over the life of the bond.

There has been a renewed interest in the concept of duration in recent years as interest rates became volatile. Adjusted duration formulas have been used to provide a time-based measure which can be matched against the same time measure of liabilities, thereby reducing reinvestment risk. Financial analysts use these immunization techniques in managing fixed-income portfolios. Our interest is to apply duration analysis to estimate the sensitivity of interest rate changes on the convertible security's embedded investment value and its market price.

Duration[5] is the weighted average time to full recovery of principal and interest payments. The time of each payment is weighted by the present value of that payment, with the largest payment occurring at the time the bond matures.

$$D = \frac{\sum\limits_{t=1}^{n} C_t(t)/(1+i)^t}{\sum\limits_{t=1}^{n} C_t/(1+i)^t}$$

where: t = time period
C_t = coupon and/or principal payment
i = market yield

Holding all other variables equal, higher yielding bonds will have lower duration than bonds with lower yields. A bond with a longer term to maturity will have a higher duration than one that will mature

---

[5]Frederick R. Macaulay, "Some Theoretical Problems Suggested by Movements of Interest Rates, Bond Yields and Stock Prices in the United States Since 1856" (New York: National Bureau of Economic Research, 1938).

in a shorter period. For coupon-paying bonds, the duration number will always be less than the number of years to maturity. For zero-coupon bonds, the duration number will equal the number of years to maturity. Duration of a perpetual bond approaches a number equal to one divided by the coupon. This can be used as the duration of a preferred stock.

Duration can be adjusted to determine investment value sensitivity to interest rates. The investment value adjusted duration (D adj) number will indicate how much the investment value will change for a one percent change (100 basis points) in interest rates. If the adjusted duration is ten and interest rates fell one percent, the investment value would rise by ten percent.

$$\text{Adjusted Duration (D adj)} = \text{Duration (D)} / (1 + Y)$$
$$\text{Where } Y = \text{yield}$$

To determine the duration of the convertible's investment value, present value calculations are accomplished as indicated in figure 5.5. The discount rate of 9.5 percent is used because a non-convertible bond of similar quality would have a yield to maturity of 9.5 percent. The duration is the time weighted present value of the series of payments and is equal to 9.4 years. To determine interest rate sensitivity, duration value is adjusted by dividing it by one plus the yield. In this example the *adjusted duration* is 8.59, indicating that if long-term interest rates were to increase by one percent (100 basis points), this bond would decrease in value by 8.59 percent.

Duration Analysis Applied to Convertibles

Up to now we have been estimating the effect of interest rates on the investment value of the convertible bond ignoring the equity component. The equity component of the convertible bond may dampen the interest rate sensitivity of the convertible depending on how much equity participation the bond has. Convertible bonds that are trading high above their investment value will be less sensitive to interest rates than bonds that are trading close to their investment value. It is best to determine both the interest rate sensitivity of a convertible bond price and its investment value.

We have accomplished this by applying duration analysis to convertibles. The mathematics and the methodology of duration analysis are detailed in Appendix A. Out of our studies a short-cut method has

---

FIGURE 5.5   Computation of Convertible's Interest Rate Sensitivity

---

Security Data: IBM 7.875% due November 21, 2004

Market price (Cv(t)) = 104
Stock = $118.00 per share
Current yield (CY) = 7.57%
Conversion premium = 35.43%
Investment value yield-to-maturity (Y) = 9.5%

Year	Payments	PV at 9.5%	PV of Payments	PV as % of Price	PV of Pymt. Time Weighted
1988	78.7500	0.9133	71.9224	0.0830	0.0830
1989	78.7500	0.8341	65.6854	0.0758	0.1516
1990	78.7500	0.7618	59.9918	0.0692	0.2076
1991	78.7500	0.6957	54.7864	0.0632	0.2528
1992	78.7500	0.6354	50.0377	0.0577	0.2886
1993	78.7500	0.5804	45.7065	0.0527	0.3164
1994	78.7500	0.5301	41.7454	0.0482	0.3371
1995	78.7500	0.4842	38.1308	0.0440	0.3519
1996	78.7500	0.4423	34.8311	0.0402	0.3617
1997	78.7500	0.4040	31.8150	0.0367	0.3670
1998	78.7500	0.3690	29.0588	0.0335	0.3688
1999	78.7500	0.3371	26.5466	0.0306	0.3675
2000	78.7500	0.3080	24.2550	0.0280	0.3638
2001	78.7500	0.2813	22.1524	0.0256	0.3578
2002	78.7500	0.2570	20.2388	0.0233	0.3502
2003	78.7500	0.2348	18.4905	0.0213	0.3413
2004	1078.7500	0.2145	231.3919	0.2670	4.5382
			866.7863	1.0000	9.4054

Investment value (Sv(t)) = 886.79
Duration (D) = 9.41 years

Investment Value
Interest Rate Sensitivity: Adjusted Duration (D adj.)

$$D \text{ adj.} = \frac{D}{1+Y} \qquad\qquad 8.5894 = \frac{9.4054}{1.095}$$

Convertibles Interest Rate Sensitivity: (Dcv)

$$Dcv = D \text{ adj.} \left(1 - \frac{C/I}{2}\right) \qquad 4.7844 = 8.5894 \left(1 - \frac{\dfrac{767.9440}{866.7863}}{2}\right)$$

NOTE: (1) Duration calculated assuming annual interest payments.
(2) Present value (PV) factors obtained from interest rate tables.

been developed that allows investors to quickly determine the interest rate sensitivity of a convertible bond. The formula for the convertible bond's interest rate sensitivity (D^{cv}) is:

$$D^{cv} = D \text{ adj.} \left(1 - \frac{C/I}{2}\right)$$

C = Conversion value   I = Investment value

Figure 5.5 indicates the use of the formula for the adjusted duration of the convertible, given as 4.78 for that example. Notice that this convertible has less interest rate sensitivity than that of its investment value, reflecting the influence of the equity component of a convertible bond.

For convertible investors the (D_{cv}) becomes a valuable tool to measure the convertible's vulnerability to changing interest rates. It can also be used by investors who want to use interest rate forecasting as part of the investment management process.

DETERMINING INVESTMENT VALUE FOR ZERO-COUPON BONDS

LYONs combine the concept of a zero coupon with convertibility and a put feature. Each factor must be considered in determining the bond investment value of these convertibles.

The National Medical Enterprises, Inc. LYON is a zero-coupon bond with a maturity of 18 years at the time of issue. Its investment value would be the present value of the par value discounted at the appropriate equivalent bond rate. The price to the public of a National Medical Enterprises, Inc. LYON represented a yield to maturity of 7.5 percent per annum (computed on a semiannual bond equivalent basis) calculated from the date of issue.

A put feature was added in the prospectus stating that "each LYON will be repurchased by the company at the option of the holder on December 31, 1988, and on each December 31 thereafter prior to maturity at repurchase prices as set forth in this prospectus." The holder of the bond could put the bonds back to the company as early as December 31, 1988. Therefore, the investment value must be adjusted to take into account the repurchase price.

An appropriate discount rate as determined by bond ratings would be ten percent. Therefore, the investment value at the time of issue is

---

FIGURE 5.6   National Medical Enterprises, Inc.

LYONs-Repurchase Price
The Repurchase Price payable to the holder of a
LYON demanding repurchase thereof shall be as follows:

Repurchase Date	Repurchase Price	Yield to Holder (1)	Investment Value (2)
12/31/86	N/A	N/A	$245.25
12/31/87	N/A	N/A	265.16
12/31/88	$296.75	6.00%	289.45
12/31/89	320.84	6.50	319.02
12/31/90	350.23	7.00	343.39
12/31/91	386.01	7.50	369.63
12/31/92	415.50	7.50	397.87
12/31/93	447.25	7.50	428.27
12/31/94	481.42	7.50	460.99
12/31/95	518.21	7.50	496.21
12/31/96	557.80	7.50	534.13
12/31/97	600.42	7.50	574.94
12/31/98	646.30	7.50	618.87
12/31/99	695.68	7.50	666.16
12/31/00	748.83	7.50	717.06
12/31/01	806.05	7.50	771.84
12/31/02	867.64	7.50	826.45
12/31/03	933.93	7.50	909.10
12/04/04	1,000.00	7.50	1,000.00

(1) Yield to holder is per annum as computed on a semiannual bond equivalent basis.
(2) Discount Rate = 10%, two years to each put.

---

estimated to be $245.25. Figure 5.6 lists the schedule of repurchase prices as stated in the prospectus.

Figure 5.7 indicates the LYON's repurchase price graphically over time and shows the relationship of the purchase price to the investment value. Investment value in this case is estimated by the present value for two years at a discount rate of ten percent. As interest rates change over time, the discount rate should also be updated.

Since the holder can receive $296.75 on December 31, 1988, the investment value becomes the present value of that amount discounted at an appropriate short-term rate commensurate with the risk level of that issue. An appropriate rate might be ten percent, making the investment value of the National Medical Enterprises, Inc. LYON at the time of issue $245.25.

FIGURE 5.7   National Medical Enterprises, Inc.

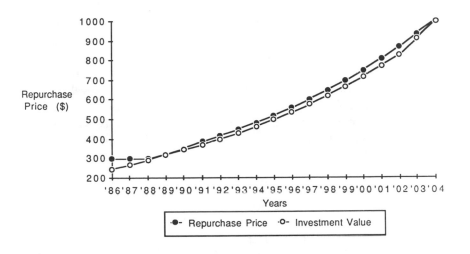

LYONs-Repurchase Price vs. Investment Value*

*Investment Value assumes a 10% discount rate, 2 years to next put.

Merrill Lynch has invented and issued nine LYONs, the latest being offered to the public on February 14, 1986. All contain the put feature. In October 1987, the investment firm of Morgan Stanley proposed an offering of a LYON to revitalize the instrument. The proposed offering was similar to the Merrill Lynch LYONs except for one crucial difference: Morgan Stanley eliminated the put feature. The trade-off was that the maturity has been reduced to seven years.

CALL PROTECTION FOR CONVERTIBLES

Call protection for convertibles is provided to guarantee the holder of the convertible bond a minimum income before the company has the right to call the bonds for redemption. For many years most convertibles did not have call protection. This all changed in 1970. Wang issued a convertible that year, and before it paid a single interest payment, the issue was called. Institutional investors were furious. Although they had participated in the sharp increase in the common stock, which in turn increased the value of the convertible, many felt that the 20 percent premium they paid at the time of issue entitled them to at least a few interest payments. This case and others brought enough pressure on underwriters to demand call protection. Initially, this took the same form that was provided for straight corporate bonds, typically two to three years of full or absolute call protection. This guaranteed the holder at least two to three years of income.

Absolute call protection was short-lived. In 1982, provisional call protection was introduced. This variation provided that the bond could not be called unless the underlying common stock increased to a certain level for 20 or 30 consecutive trading days. This level is typically defined as 140 percent to 150 percent above the conversion price. The underlying common stock would have to increase somewhere between 60 percent and 100 percent before the call could be effected. Most convertibles issued since 1982 have provisional call protection for two to three years.

A trust indenture, like many legal documents, is read most carefully when someone is trying not to abide by its terms. This practice, which convertible traders aptly refer to as looking for the "screw" or "weasel" clause, is becoming alarmingly popular in corporate finance.

For example, in 1983 Wal Mart called a large convertible issue for redemption on the day the full call protection expired, which also was the date on which the last coupon was to be paid. The call made sense because the stock had risen dramatically over the past three years. The enterprising treasurer informed holders that the last coupon would not be paid based on a careful reading of the prospectus, which stated that "conversion rights expire 15 days before the redemption date." The general perception of this statement was to limit the corporation's exposure to a sharp drop in the stock price and thus cause a redemption instead of a forced conversion. The prospectus also stated that "any debenture surrendered for conversion between a record date and the next interest payment date must be accompanied by an amount equal to the interest payable on that date." In effect, the holder, in order to convert, gives up the six-month interest payment. Investors should read a company's prospectus as carefully as its treasurer does.

DILUTION PROTECTION FOR CONVERTIBLES

Since a large part of the value of a convertible is determined by the ability to convert the underlying stock, antidilution protection against corporate maneuvers to jeopardize this value is important. Most convertibles provide for protection against stock splits by adjusting the conversion ratio for the amount of the stock dividend in the proportional amount. If the convertible had a conversion ratio of 30 shares per bond prior to a two for one split, the conversion ratio would become 60 shares per bond after the split. Convertibles with full dilution protection are protected against small stock dividends in the event of spin-offs if the company is acquired by another corporation. Others are protected from diluting the value of the company from issuing stock below book value.

Commonwealth Edison issued a $1.96 convertible preferred with this type of protection. During the seventies it continued to issue stock below book value, so it had to increase the conversion ratio of the convertible preferred stock. The convertible preferred increased in value while the common stock fluctuated in a narrow range.

BONDHOLDER PROTECTION

Unfortunately, full dilution is not guaranteed. The degree of protection varies widely from issue to issue, depending upon the ingenuity of corporate attorneys. Negating the conversion value of convertibles is a common practice in the merger mania of the 1980s. Figure 5.8 shows a number of issues in which unscrupulous corporate managers completely negated the convertibility feature.

Given the tremendous growth of the convertible market and the merger mania, it's not surprising that some problems have arisen over bondholders' rights. Convertible bondholders bought and paid for the right to convert to the common stock for a period of time. The cases have been few but alarming where the convertibility feature has been lost far short of the time that is stipulated in the trust indenture. As shown in figure 5.8, the list is growing and some action is definitely in order.

Action to correct this problem can take several forms. Institutional investors, the major purchasers of new issue convertibles, must apply pressure on investment bankers to add protective clauses to the indenture. This protection could take the form of having the bond immediately called at the next call price plus some conversion premium. After all, the bond was issued by the corporation at conversion premium levels ranging from 20 percent to 30 percent. The conversion premium

---

FIGURE 5.8   Convertible Holders Hard-Hit in Takeovers

Issue	Coupon/ maturity	Conversion price	Takeover price/ Takover Co./ Date	$1,000 bond worth/ convertible into % of debentures	Bond price prior to takeover announcement
Knoll International	9.88%* 8/15/2003	$19.20	$12.00 General Felt Winter, 1987	$625.00	$880.00
Lieberman Enterprises	7.62% 8/15/2005	$21.00	$20.50 Carolco Pictures in negotiations	$976.19	NA
Big Three Industries	8.50% 4/15/2006	$43.50	$29.00 Air Liquids Fall, 1986	$666.70	$980.00
Energy Factors	8.25% 12/15/2005	$24.75	$17.25 Silthe Energies proposal terminated Summer, 1987	$696.96	$870.00
Miles Laboratories	5.25% 4/01/1994	$65.00	$47.00 Rhinechen Labs Winter, 1979	$722.86	NA
Dorchester Gas	8.50% 12/01/2005	$34.48	$22.50 Damson Oil Summer, 1984	$625.55	$720.00
Healthcare USA	8.25% 6/30/2003	$19.80	$13.50 Maxicare Fall, 1986	$681.82	$765.00
Fibreboard	6.75% 10/15/1988	$18.50	$17.00 Louisiana Pacific June, 1978	$918.15	NA
Fibreboard	4.75% 10/15/1993	$31.25	$17.00 Louisiana Pacific June, 1978	$544.00	NA
Sprague Electric	4.25% 10/01/1992	$45.50	$27.50 G.F. Technologies Spring, 1979	$604.40	NA
H.J. Wilson	10.50% 5/15/2002	$21.00	$20.00 Service Merchandise Spring, 1985	$952.38	$950.00
Van Dusen Air	10.50% 8/01/2005	$20.00	$21.00 APL Limited Partnership Winter, 1986	$1,050.00	NA
Fruehauf	8.50% 4/15/2011	$50.00	$49.50 Asher Edelman Fall, 1986	$1,085.00**	NA

FIGURE 5.8   Convertible Holders Hard-Hit in Takeovers (continued)

Issue	Coupon/ maturity	Conversion price	Takeover price/ Takover Co./ Date	$1,000 bond worth/ convertible into % of debentures	Bond price prior to takeover announcement
Grunthal Financial	7.50% 6/05/2011	$10.00	$9.50 Home Group Summer, 1987	$950.00	$1,000.00
Mayflower	7.88% 3/15/2006	$32.50	$29.25 Laidlaw Transportation Summer, 1986	$900.00	$1,000.00
Crazy Eddie	6.00% 6/15/2011	$23.13	$8.00 Entertainment Marketing pending	$345.94	$620.00

* Bondholders' coupon raised to 9.875% from 8.125%.
** Bonds would have been convertible into $990 of debt, but poison pill raised value to $1085.

SOURCE: Froley Revy Asset Mgmt., Inc., Los Angeles; Calamos Asset Mgmt., Inc., Oak Brook, IL. Reprinted with permission. *Pensions & Investment Age*; July 27, 1987.

could be amortized to the first call price and a schedule easily provided for in the prospectus. This would be appropriate for a leverage buy-out or any takeover. The group assuming control should accept the cost of paying fair value for the convertibles regardless of whether it's by a leveraged buy-out or another company.

Another means may be through changes to the Trust Indenture Act. Those of us involved with convertibles should pursue this avenue as a long-term commitment to the convertible market. If these changes were made, would they decrease the number of new issues coming to the market? A corporate treasurer who decides not to issue a convertible because of this added protection is admitting that the corporation is trying to negate the conversion rights in the future. Therefore, such protective clauses should not be detrimental to the issuance of convertible debt.

It is hoped that sufficient means can be brought to bear to protect bondholders and to allow corporations to meet their financing needs through the use of convertible debt.

YIELD ADVANTAGE OF CONVERTIBLE SECURITIES

One of the advantages of convertibles is that they generally offer more income than the underlying common stock. The difference between the current yield of the convertible and the dividend yield of the common stock is the convertible's yield advantage. Since convertibles can be viewed as an alternative to the purchase of common stock, this direct comparison of yield difference is often made. When both the yield advantage and conversion premium are considered, the break-even analysis is used.

BREAK-EVEN ANALYSIS

Before proceeding to the break-even calculations, let's review the following formulas using the example below:

stock price	$30.00 per share
stock dividend	$0.50 per share
convertible market price	100 or $1000
coupon rate	7.00%
maturity date	20 years
conversion price	$36.37

Stock dividend yield = the annual dividend rate divided by the current stock price.

$$\text{Stock dividend yield} = \frac{\text{stock dividend}}{\text{stock price.}}$$

$$1.67\% = \frac{\$\ 0.50}{\$30.00}$$

Convertible current yield = coupon rate divided by current market price of the convertible.

$$\text{Convertible current yield} = \frac{\text{coupon rate}}{\text{convertible market price}}$$

$$7.00\% = \frac{7.00}{100}$$

Conversion price = the price stated in the prospectus at which each convertible security may be exchanged into the underlying common stock.

Conversion ratio = the number of shares for which one bond may be exchanged.

$$\text{Conversion ratio} = \frac{\text{par value}}{\text{conversion price}}$$

$$27.50 \text{ shares} = \frac{1000}{\$36.37}$$

Conversion value = the equity value or stock value of the convertible security.

$$\text{Conversion value} = \text{stock price times conversion ratio}$$
$$\$825.00 \text{ per bond or } 82.50 = (\$30.00)\,(27.50)$$

Conversion premium = the difference between the market price and the conversion value usually expressed as a percent.

$$\text{Conversion premium (\%)} = \frac{\text{convertible price} - \text{conversion value}}{\text{conversion value}}$$

$$21.21\% = \frac{100 - 82.50}{82.50}$$

Dollar premium = the difference between the market price and the conversion value expressed in number of dollars or points.

$$\text{Dollar premium} = \text{convertible price} - \text{conversion value}$$
$$17.50 \text{ points} = 100 - 82.50$$

BREAK-EVEN ANALYSIS

Usually stated in years, break-even is simply the conversion premium divided by the convertible's yield advantage over the underlying common stock. The calculations are accomplished using data from above.

$$\text{Break-even (years)} = \frac{\text{conversion premium}}{\text{convertible yield} - \text{stock yield.}}$$

$$3.98 \text{ years} = \frac{21.21}{(7.00 - 1.67).}$$

The two other common break-even methods are dollar maintenance and equity maintenance.

Dollar maintenance is used in the case of the common to convertible swap done dollar for dollar.

$$\text{Dollar maintenance} = \frac{\text{convertible market price} - \text{conversion value}}{\text{Cvt. coupon} - \left(\dfrac{\text{Cvt mkt price}}{\text{stock price}}\right) \text{stock dividend}}$$

$$3.28 \text{ years} = \frac{100 - 82.50}{7.00 - \left(\dfrac{100}{30.0}\right)0.50}$$

Equity maintenance is used to maintain the exact call on the common in the purchased security, as the one sold.

$$\text{Equity maintenance} = \frac{\text{convertible market price} - \text{conversion value}}{\text{cvt. coupon} - [(\text{stock dividend}) \, (\text{conversion ratio})]}$$

$$3.11 \text{ years} = \frac{1000 - 825}{70 - [(0.50) \, (27.50)]}$$

These methods provide a way of evaluating the conversion premium, but they focus solely on the income aspect of a convertible versus the dividend yield of the common stock. A complete evaluation of a convertible security must take many other factors into account.

The break-even analysis makes sense based on the theory that if the convertible bond did not offer a yield advantage over the common stock there would be little incentive for an investor to hold the bond. Most bondholders would convert to the underlying common stock to realize the higher income flow. Convertibles with a small yield advantage would command very little conversion premium.

In the marketplace, many bonds are converted that probably would not be if a more sophisticated method of evaluation were used. Consider a convertible bond that has a negative yield advantage over the common stock, is trading at a discount from par, offers no conversion premium and is due to mature in the very near future. On a risk/reward basis, this bond is a superior buy to the common stock. If the stock goes up, the convertible also goes up by the same amount, less

---

FIGURE 5.9   Chase Manhattan Risk/Reward Analysis

June 11, 1984

	Market Price			Current Yield
Common Stock Price	41.13			8.9%
Convertible Bond Price	74.00			8.8%

Profit/Loss estimates over the next 12 months					
Stock Change	−50%	−25%	0	+25%	+50%
Stock Investment	−41.1	−16.1	+8.9	+33.9	+58.9
Convert Investment	− 6.0	− 2.0	+8.8	+30.0	+53.0

Conversion Ratio = 17.391 shares of stock per each bond.
Chase Manhattan Corporation 6.5% due July 1, 1996.
Chase Manhattan Corporation convertible's yield to maturity = 10.7%.

---

the small difference in yield. On the other hand, if the stock declines, the bond value will be par at maturity. The investor would be foolish to convert to the stock with such a favorable risk/reward relationship.

Chase Manhattan's six percent convertible bond is a good example of a convertible that has a favorable risk/reward relationship but a negative yield advantage. Consider the situation as it was on June 11, 1984. The common stock of Chase Manhattan was trading at 41^{1}/$_{8}$ with the convertible bond trading at 74. Conversion value was 71.520 (17.391 × 41.125) representing a slight conversion premium of 3.47 percent. Although the current yield of the convertible bond was slightly less than that of the common stock, the convertible offered a tremendous risk/reward advantage. This is shown in figure 5.9, which compares the risk/reward of holding the common stock to that of the convertible bond.

The slight yield advantage that the common stock enjoys would mean very little in a declining market. Notice that if the stock declines, the value of the discounted bond cushions the loss and preserves capital.

Risk/reward is based on upside potential versus downside risk. In this case the common stock investment has slightly more potential, as shown in figure 5.9. For an increase of 50 percent in price, the stock's total return would be 58.9 percent, compared to 53.0 percent for the convertible investment. But, if the stock decreased by 50 percent, the convertible return would be a −6.0 percent, compared to a −41.1 percent from the stock investment. The convertible bondholder achieves a significant reduction in risk. Based on the risk/reward analysis, the convertible is a better investment than the common stock, regardless of the conclusion drawn from the break-even analysis.

The above example illustrates the main drawback of the break-even method. It considers conversion premium and yield advantage, but it can be very misleading and does not provide an adequate way to compare alternative opportunities in the market. Unfortunately, many convertible research reports published by brokerage firms do just that. In an attempt to select one convertible over another, they will rely on the break-even analysis as the basis for selection.

Traders use some general rules of thumb based on break-even analysis. For example, in the new issue market, break-even for investment-grade issues should not exceed five years. For BB to strong B-rated bonds, break-even should not exceed one year past call date. For B and below, call protection should be at least equal to break-even. Traders also use a 200 basis point rule in swapping between the straight bond and the convertible: Swap into the convertible if the yield advantage of the straight bond over the convertible is less than 200 basis points.

Swaps are often initiated based on break-even analysis. A swap, when executed, maintains the exact call on common stock in the purchased security as in the one sold. If the equity maintenance formula is used, additional dollars will be required. Dealers in the convertible market often do swaps to derive arbitrage profits and facilitate trades for their clients. They are also done by investors who are committed to a long equity position in the company and, therefore, will be long either the common stock or the convertible, depending on premium levels and break-even analysis.

The advantage of rule-of-thumb trading is that decisions can be made very quickly. The disadvantage is that the decision is based on limited information and may cause investment errors. As often mentioned, convertible investment decisions require a more thorough evaluation process.

EQUITY RISK MEASURES

In addition to fixed-income risk measures it is necessary to evaluate the equity component of the convertible security. A significant part of the attractiveness of a convertible security is derived from its resulting capital gain potential as the stock increases in value. Fundamental analysis is helpful in selecting the best prospects for growth but is often very subjective. Our discussion will be limited to the more objective statistical risk measures to evaluate the equity component of the convertible security. Two risk measures are generally used to evaluate common stock risk: beta and total variance.

Beta

The common stock beta coefficient is a measure of the stock's systematic (market related) risk. It is the portion of a stock's variance that can be explained by general market movements. A beta of 1.0 indicates the stock is expected to move up or down equally with the market. A stock with a beta of 1.50 is expected to be 50 percent more sensitive to market gyrations. Thus, a high beta stock is expected to move up more quickly than the market averages in rising markets and decline more quickly in periods of declining market averages.

Beta is often considered the only relevant risk of a stock in a well-diversified portfolio because any unsystematic risk (non-market related) can be theoretically eliminated through proper diversification. Stock beta measures can be found by regressing stock price changes (usually weekly) against the market average price changes. Five years of data points are generally used. The beta coefficient on average explains about 50 percent of a stock's total volatility. The value of beta can be significantly increased by computing the weighted portfolio beta for a well-diversified portfolio. This can account for as much as 98 percent of the portfolio volatility.

Convertible's Beta

The equity sensitivity of a convertible is partially attributable to the underlying stock's beta. The convertible's beta is also a function of its conversion and investment premiums. Simply stated, the leverage ratio of a convertible, multiplied by the stock's beta will produce the convertible's beta. Unlike a stock beta, the convertible beta changes as either the stock price or interest rates change. Since the convertible's price will respond differently than the common stock because of its leverage, the convertible will have an upside beta and a downside beta.

To measure a convertible's sensitivity to changes in general market moves, calculate both the upside and downside beta. Figure 5.10 uses the convertible security of a common stock with a beta of 1.2 to determine the convertible's betas. The common stock percentage moves are compared to corresponding moves in the convertible. Since the con-

---

FIGURE 5.10   Calculating Convertible Beta

Stock beta = 1.2
Stock price move %   −50   −25   +25   +50
Expected convertible price move %   −30   −15   +18   +40

$$\text{Downside ratio} \quad = \quad \frac{(-30)+(-15)}{(-50)+(-25)} \quad = \quad .600$$

$$\text{Upside ratio} \quad = \quad \frac{18\ +\ 40}{25\ +\ 50} \quad = \quad .773$$

Downside beta   =   .600 × 1.2 =   .72
Upside beta   =   .773 × 1.2 =   .93

---

vertible would decrease at a 60 percent rate of the stock, its downside beta would also be 60 percent of the common stock beta. This results in a downside beta of .72. The convertible upside beta of .93 is calculated by the same procedure.

The convertible's beta will approach the stock's beta as it rises above its investment value. It will also decrease as the price declines. In effect, in rising markets the convertible's stock market exposure will increase; in falling markets, it decreases and the bond market sensitivity takes hold.

STOCK VARIANCE

The variability of a stock return is the measure of the stock's total risk. The higher the variability of returns, the more likely the stock's actual return will vary from its average or expected return. Thus, the higher the variance, the higher the risk. The stock's historical standard deviation (variance of returns) measures both systematic and unsystematic risk and is, therefore, known as the total risk measure.

Calculating the stock's total risk measure is quite simple, but a large data bank of stock returns must be available. Most academic studies indicate that the most relevant price return information resides in the most recent time period. Investors can estimate the stock's variance and standard deviation for the past year as shown in figure 5.11.

FIGURE 5.11   Estimating Stock Variance

MONTH	CLOSING PRICE(S)	PRICE RELATIVE (S + 1/S)	LOG OF PRICE RELATIVE (X')	DIFFERENCE $(X'-\bar{X})^2$
01	20.00			
02	22.00	1.1000	0.0953	0.0035
03	27.00	1.2273	0.2048	0.0283
04	23.00	0.8519	−0.1603	0.0387
05	24.00	1.0435	0.0426	0.0001
06	28.00	1.1667	0.1542	0.0139
07	31.00	1.1071	0.1018	0.0043
08	30.00	0.9677	−0.0328	0.0048
09	27.00	0.9000	−0.1054	0.0201
10	33.00	1.2222	0.2007	0.0270
11	29.00	0.8788	−0.1292	0.0275
12	32.00	1.1034	0.0984	0.0038
13	31.00	0.9688	−0.0317	0.0047

Average return $(\bar{X}) = 0.0365$

$$\text{Monthly Variance} = \frac{\sum_{n=1}^{12} (x' - \bar{x})^2}{N - 1} = \frac{0.1766}{11.0000} = 0.0161$$

Monthly Standard Deviation $= \sqrt{0.0161} = 0.1269$

Annualized Variance $= 0.0161 \times 12 = 0.1932$

Annualized Standard Deviation $= \sqrt{0.1932} = 0.4395$

The stock variance is an important input variable for the convert-ible pricing model and other analytical models that assess risk. Some analysts make such predictions directly without using statistical mea-sures. The use of statistical measures allows for better comparison of opportunities without the interference of subjective factors. However, the investor must realize that stock variance is the most difficult vari-able to estimate. Stock models and convertible models assume that variance remains stationary, which may or may not be true. Although estimates are easily obtainable by many stock research services, con-siderable thought should be given to this input variable because past variance is an important guide to future volatility. Profitability de-pends on the accuracy of the estimates of input variables.

Expected Return on Investment: EROI

The convertible's expected return on investment (EROI) applies modern portfolio theory to convertible analysis. This measure estimates the underlying common stock's expected return through the application of the security market line. The projected stock price estimated by the security market line is assessed the highest probability of return.

$$Er = rf + b \ (Km - rf)$$

Where: Er = expected stock return
       rf = risk-free rate of return
       b   = stock's beta coefficient
       Km = stock market return

The stock price distribution is evaluated along with the corresponding probability weights for each stock price. The expected convertible security price and return are determined for each stock price along the stock distribution. The convertible returns are multiplied by the corresponding probability weighting. The sum of the convertible returns multiplied by the probability will determine the convertible's EROI.

$$EROI = \sum_{m=1}^{30} [Ws_1 \times Pcv_1] + [Ws_2 \times Pcv_2] + \ldots [Ws_m \times Pcv_m]$$

Where: Ws = Weighted stock price
Where: Pcv = Projected convertible price return

The convertible security's EROI is shown in figure 5.12. The horizontal axis represents the price range of the underlying common stock. The vertical axis represents the price range of the convertible security. The current stock and bond prices are indicated along with the security market line projected prices. The stock's price distribution is then overlaid to indicate the probability of returns. The convertible estimated price track is also overlaid for each stock price. For each price along the convertible price track, the corresponding area under the stock price distribution is determined. The sum of the expected convertible returns multiplied by the probability of return determines the convertible security's EROI.

FIGURE 5.12   Convertible's Expected Return

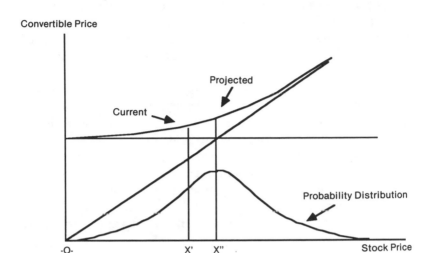

$$\sum_{n=1}^{30} [(Wr) \times (Pcvn)]$$

Where: Wr   = Weighted stock return distribution.
       Pcvn: = Projected convertible return for each possible stock price.

SUMMARY

We have considered both the fixed-income and equity characteristics of convertible securities. Each factor may be influenced by many variables—what remains is to put these factors together into a comprehensive model which properly evaluates the convertible security. It's apparent that the individual elements and how they are calculated are as important as the model.

APPENDIX: CONVERTIBLE SECURITIES INTEREST RATE SENSITIVITY

The effects of interest rate changes become complex when evaluating a convertible as a combination of bond value Sv(t) and equity or warrant value Wv(t). Increasing the risk-free rate or short-term interest rate will increase the warrant value of the convertible, holding all other variables constant.

The value of the convertible bond is also subject to changes in long-term bond yields. If long-term interest rates increase, then the debt value of the convertible will decrease, causing a decline in the convertible's value. The adjusted exercise price for the convertible will also decrease. Convertibles with smaller investment value premiums will be more responsive to changes in interest rates and less responsive to changes in stock prices. Thus, the duration of a convertible bond is strongly affected by the conversion and investment value premiums. In general, the larger the spread between conversion value and investment value, the lower the duration.

An upward shift in the yield curve would not under certain conditions, change the value of the convertible. For example, the short-term rate increases, thereby increasing the option portion of the convertible. But, the increase in the long-term rate would result in a loss on the bond portion of the convertible. It is possible to have the increase in the equity value offset any loss in the debt value; the net result being no change in the convertible value.

The duration (Dcv) of a convertible security can be explained as a function of the following:

$$Dcv = \frac{\partial \, Cv(t)}{\partial \, i} = f \left[\frac{\partial \, Sv(t)}{\partial \, i}, \frac{\partial \, K}{\partial \, Sv(t)}, \frac{\partial \, Wv(t)}{\partial \, K}, \frac{\partial \, Wv(t)}{\partial \, i} \right]$$

where $i =$ long-term interest rates

The following algorithms can be used to measure the duration of a convertible bond.

The dollar change in Sv(t) with respect to a percent change in interest rates:

$$\frac{\partial \, Sv(t)}{\partial \, i} = Sv(t) \, 1 + .01 \, \left((ti_t/(1+ym)^t)/Sv(t) \right) - Sv(t)$$

The dollar change in the adjusted exercise price with respect to the dollar change in Sv(t):

$$\frac{\partial K}{\partial Sv(t)} = (\ \partial Sv(t)/\partial i)/Cr(t)$$

The dollar change in the Wv(t) with respect to the dollar change in the adjusted exercise price:

$$\frac{\partial Wv(t)}{\partial K} = Cr(t) - e^{-rT} N(h - \sigma\sqrt{T})$$

The dollar change in Wv(t) with respect to a percent change in interest rates:

$$\frac{\partial Wv(t)}{\partial i} = Cr(t)\ TKe^{-rT} N(h - \sigma\sqrt{T})$$

The above equations determine the interest rate sensitivity of a convertible bond. Almost every variable is affected by the changing of interest rates, the debt being inversely related while the warrant portion is positively related. It can also be found that the duration of Sv(t) is equal to the duration of the adjusted exercise price. Also, the duration of a convertible cannot exceed the duration of Sv(t).

$$\text{Dur } Sv(t) = \text{Dur } K$$

and

$$\text{Dur } Cv(t) < = \text{Dur } Sv(t)$$

$Cv(t)$ = convertible value
$Sv(t)$ = straight bond value
i = long-term interest rate
k = exercise price (adjusted)
$Wv(t)$ = warrant value
t = time period (current)
Ym = straight bond value discount rate
$Cr(t)$ = number of shares the convertible is exchangeable into
T = time period remaining for convertibility
e = exponential functions
∂ = derivative notation
σ = stock's variance
N = univariate cumulative normal
h = upper limit of integration

6

Convertible Bond Pricing

DETERMINING FAIR MARKET VALUE

So far we have defined and discussed the various factors in a convertible security. How the factors interrelate in the marketplace determines the fair value or market price of a convertible security. Since the marketplace is generally an efficient mechanism for determining value, the convertible security's market price should tend toward its fair value. An astute investor should seek out convertibles trading below fair value and avoid those above their fair value price, thereby gaining an edge in the marketplace. Unfortunately, the determination of fair value is a complicated problem involving a number of assumptions.

In the fast-paced financial arena, some traders base their trading decisions on simple rules of thumb and ignore the more complicated fair value calculation. In convertible trading this typically takes the form of rules based simply on break-even analysis, or on a maximum number based on conversion premium. These guidelines are used to simplify a complex problem. A thorough analysis of a convertible security involves identifying key variables such as conversion premium and yield advantage. This chapter describes the evolution of the mathematical evaluation process and the underlying assumptions upon which fair value formulas are based. The discussion should provide some valuable insight as to how these variables dovetail to determine the market price of a convertible.

The valuation of convertible securities had not been pursued vigorously until recently. Benjamin Graham applied little mathematical analysis to convertible securities in his classic investment book, *The Intelligent Investor*[1]. His analysis was based on the underlying fundamentals of the issuing company and a subjective feeling as to whether conversion premium was high or low. His comments on convertibles, without the benefit of mathematical models in use today, indicate both his mastery of investing and the limitations of the technology of that era. Formulas today attempt to quantify what investment masters like Graham took years to assimilate.

The mathematical evaluation process used for convertible securities is paralleling the growth of modern portfolio theory. Some have attempted mathematical evaluation of convertible securities by analyzing the latent warrant embedded in the convertible security[2] or as a present value problem. Others have used the naive approach of drawing a French curve between the straight bond value, current market price and an assumed point where conversion price and market price would be equal. Four approaches are in use today: the stock picker, the current price track method, the historical price track method and the theoretical price formula. All except the stock picker seek to estimate the value of the convertible security for changes in the underlying stock price. Properly estimating the various prices at which the convertible may trade allows the investor to make important risk/reward estimates.

THE STOCK PICKER

Many convertible investors are stock pickers. They purchase a convertible in the hope that the underlying stock will increase in value. Investors who use fundamental analysis of the common stock as the primary reason to purchase the convertible will have to be extraordinarily successful in their stock selection. They may often find that they were correct on the stock, but the convertible did not follow. This method largely ignores the investment characteristics of the convertible and relies on the stock fundamental, often negating the basic advantage of convertible investing. Convertible investment managers using

---

[1]Benjamin Graham, *The Intelligent Investor* (New York: Harper, 1965), pp. 120–122.

[2]Edward O. Thorpe, *Beat the Market* (New York: Random House, 1967), pp. 141–161.

FIGURE 6.1   Risk/Reward Analysis, Westinghouse 9% of 8/15/2009

September 4, 1987

	Price	Current Yield
Common Stock Price	68.63	2.51%
Convertible Bond Price	225.00	4.00%

Profit /Loss Estimates over next 12 months					
Stock Change	−50%	−25%	0	+25%	+50%
Stock ROI%*	−47.5	−22.5	+2.5	+27.0	+53.0
Convert ROI%*	−41.0	−20.0	+4.0	+30.0	+54.0

* Includes income

NOTE: October 19, 1987

Stock price: 40.25	Drop since 9/04/87: −41.35%
Bond price: 140.25	Drop since 9/04/87: −37.67%

---

this method have a tendency not to sell convertibles as the underlying common stock advances.

One such manager held Westinghouse convertible bonds in his clients' accounts prior to the stock market crash of 1987. Figure 6.1 compares the risk/reward of the convertible bond and the common stock. Notice that in this case, the convertible had little advantage over the common stock.

Because the manager was hired to invest in convertibles, he might have maintained the convertible in the account even though it was inferior to the common stock. The Westinghouse convertible bond lost 100 points in the stock market crash of 1987, falling from 240 to 140 on October 4. The convertible provided no cushion on the downside and had the same risk/reward as the common stock.

Some advisory services recommend convertibles that have little risk/reward advantage over the underlying stock simply because they like the common stock. Investors basing their selection process on fundamentals alone will generally have higher-risk portfolios and more likely will negate any of the convertible's risk control advantages.

The question becomes: Should convertible investors ignore fundamentals and base their selection on the mathematics of the convertible security? Selecting convertibles by picking stocks and without regard to risk control attributes of the convertible security will eventually lead to high-risk portfolios and disappointing overall results over time. Performance probably will be erratic and will follow the roller coaster ride of the stock market.

Researching the fundamentals of the company is essential to successful convertible investing. Convertible investors who believe that diversification replaces fundamental analysis of individual securities are often disappointed when they rely only on leverage estimates. Convertible investors cannot perform an accurate mathematical analysis of the convertible security without analyzing the underlying common stock fundamentals. Ignoring those fundamentals will result in more defaults and overall poor performance. Therefore, investors must blend fundamental analysis with the proper analytical methods to determine fair value of the convertible security.

CURRENT PRICE TRACK—NAIVE APPROACH

The most simplistic method now in use to estimate the price track of a convertible security is called the "naive approach." It assumes all convertibles to be basically the same and has the least number of assumptions. It begins with the convertible price on the vertical axis and the stock price on the horizontal axis. The investment value becomes a minimum value below which the convertible price cannot fall. The conversion value becomes the diagonal line beginning at zero and determined by the conversion ratio as discussed in chapter 3. Earlier books on convertibles spent a great deal of time describing how to draw the price curve. It is based on the same minimum and maximum values and basic curve fitting. The minimum value is the investment value of the convertible. The maximum value is the point where conversion value and market price would converge. An assumption is made as to where this would occur (typically at 40 percent above par). With the current market price of the convertible security known, a curve is fitted through those three points as indicated in figure 6.2. The main problem becomes one of finding the correct curve-fitting technique once the three points are determined.

This method has the advantage of being quickly obtainable. All that is needed is graph paper and a French curve. Computer programs can be substituted for the cumbersome graph paper and French curve. These programs are curve-fitting mathematical formulas to draw a

FIGURE 6.2   Convertible Bond Price Track

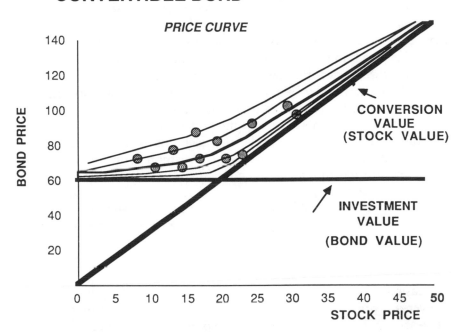

CONVERTIBLE BOND

smooth curve through the three points. The curve will probably approximate how the convertible trades for small price moves over relatively short periods of time.

The naive approach also has many disadvantages. To begin with, this method does not determine fair value. It assumes the current market price to be fair value and simply determines a track that the convertible *may* take if that assumption is correct. Every time the price of the stock or convertible changes, a new track could be drawn, making it difficult to determine which price track was correct. Also, this method does not adjust for convertibles that may be called. As we will see later, for many convertibles the actual price track is not a smooth curve between three points.

During rising markets, the estimates hold fairly well because convertibles will advance toward conversion value as the underlying stocks increase. There will be many occasions when investors will be disappointed because the convertible seems to lag the upside and not follow a smooth upward sloping curve. This occurs because under this method it is impossible to take into account other variables, such as if and when the bond is callable. There are many factors that will make the convertible price not follow the smooth curve and thus create errors. These errors may be masked in rising markets because they are resulting not in losses, but in forsaken gains.

A larger problem using this method occurs at the most critical juncture in the investment cycle: the declining phase. Investors purchase convertibles to provide a downside cushion in declining markets. If the investor has miscalculated how much the convertible's price will drop in response to a given price decrease in the underlying stock, then the reason the convertible was purchased becomes suspect.

This method can lead to severe estimate errors in declining markets. Market decreases are often accompanied by differences in market sentiment, causing the convertible price curve to shift. This method does not adjust for this, causing greater loss than had been originally forecasted. The margin for error is greatest during this phase because conversion premium is increasing as the underlying common stock is decreasing. The greater the conversion premium, the more accurate the convertible bond price track must be to avoid serious losses.

With all its shortcomings, this method at least attempted to predict the risk/reward of convertible securities and was better than making no estimate at all. It served investors well as a first step in understanding convertibles.

HISTORICAL PRICE TRACK—LOGARITHMIC REGRESSION

This method attempts to solve the main drawback of the naive approach by analyzing historical price relationships. Through the use of regression analysis, the relationship between common stock prices and convertible security prices is analyzed to determine the most accurate track based upon these historical relationships. Figure 6.3 indicates

---

FIGURE 6.3   Convertible Bond Price Track (Regression)

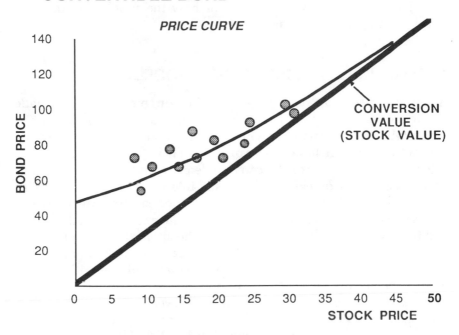

CONVERTIBLE BOND

PRICE CURVE

how a scattergram imposed on a track can indicate whether or not the convertible is priced on track.

Again, over small price moves and small time periods this method may be sufficient. It is easily accomplished by computing investment analysis and is widely used by convertible trading desks. This method seems to be a favorite among convertible market makers because over short periods of time they can make markets based on movements of the convertible along its regression line.

This method is definitely an improvement over the naive approach, but it still has some serious drawbacks. Any changes in interest rates would quickly move convertibles off their recent track, as will also happen when bonds become callable or when the underlying stock volatility changes. Changes in overall market sentiment often influence conversion premium levels, which could affect which price track the convertible would be trading on. Despite its shortcomings, this method is useful because it allows an investor to view the historical trading pattern of an unfamiliar convertible issue. Past trading patterns give the convertible investor a feel for how the supply and demand forces have interacted in the past.

THEORETICAL FORMULA-BASED MODELS

A significant step in determining fair value for convertibles was made by the application of the Black-Scholes option pricing model. Most of the drawbacks of the naive and historical methods are overcome by using formulas that include many variables. These formulas can quickly determine a fair value for the convertible price under various assumptions. They adapt quickly to changes in interest rates, stock volatility and whether the bond becomes callable. Since each fair value price is determined independently of the others, adjustments for call features and bond values can be predetermined. The application of option theory to many financial instruments has created a superior means by which to determine a fair value price of convertible securities and is further evidence of the versatility of option theory. Figure 6.4 indicates how the convertible price track would look over a wide range of prices for a callable bond. Notice the flat portion of the price track, caused by the fact that this particular convertible is callable. None of the other methods adequately adjusts for callable versus non-callable securities.

The examples above, figures 6.2 through 6.4, illustrate the evolution of convertible bond pricing. It is apparent that option theory provides a means to evaluate convertibles similar to listed options. The application of option theory to convertible pricing is compounded by the complexity of convertibles and by the intricacies of the Black-Scholes option pricing formula. For example, the call feature varies from issue to issue. Interest rate changes affect both the straight bond value assumptions and the latent warrant, as does stock volatility caused by changing fundamentals of the company. Before applying option theory to convertible pricing, a brief review of the Black-Scholes model is necessary.

FIGURE 6.4   Convertible Bond Theoretical Price Curve

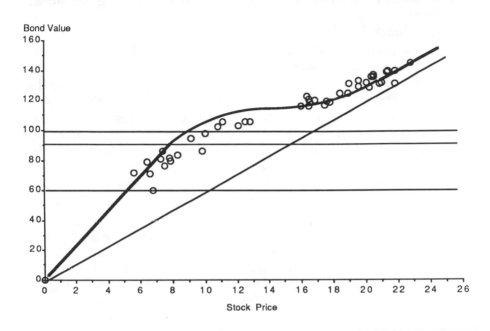

OVERVIEW OF THE BLACK-SCHOLES OPTION MODEL

The Black-Scholes option model, derived by Fischer Black and Myron Scholes in 1973, has been widely accepted by both the academic and investment community for the pricing of listed options. Many services provide theoretical option prices and hand-held calculators with instantaneous access to option prices. However, as Professor Bookstaber pointed out in *Option Pricing and Strategies in Investing*, "The number who use the formula exceeds the number who understand it."[3] The

---

[3]Richard M. Bookstaber, *Option Pricing and Strategies in Investing* (Mass: Addison-Wesley, 1985), p 40.

popularity of the Black-Scholes model is due in part to the ease in obtaining variables that are not subject to investors' preferences or attitudes toward risk. The only highly subjective variable is the stock's variance of returns.

The Black-Scholes option formula determines the value of an option for a given stock price and a given time to maturity. It does not depend on what the investor expects the stock to do. An investor who expected a particular stock to go down would not buy the stock or the call regardless of its price. The value of the formula is that it determines a fair value for the option without regard to investor preference. The simplest version of the option formula assumes that the short-term interest rate and the volatility of the stock do not change; that the stock pays no dividend, and that there are no transaction costs. There are five variables needed in the formula: (1) the stock price, (2) the time to maturity, (3) the exercise price, (4) the interest rate and (5) the volatility of the stock.

Once the fair value price is determined, assuming that the formula is giving the correct value, then if the *market price* of the option is below that value, the buyer would have an advantage; if it is above the *fair value price*, the seller would have the advantage. The seller's gains are the buyer's losses and the seller's losses are the buyer's gains.

This model is based on the neutral option hedge argument and states that individual stock risk (unsystematic risk) can be completely eliminated through the use of option hedging. A neutral hedge is one that is low in risk for small moves in the stock price. Any change in stock price would cause an instantaneous offset in the option position. The model determines the hedge ratio, which is the ratio of stock to options needed for a neutral hedge. It is based on the input variables for a particular security, and the value of the long position need not equal the value of the short position. The gains and losses of the long position will offset the gains and losses of the short position. Since the risk-free interest rate remains constant over the short term, the fair value for the option can be determined.

The mathematics used in the Black-Scholes model is complicated, but it is also logical. The model calculates the present value of the stock price at expiration of the option, multiplied by the probability that the stock price will exceed the exercise price. From this we subtract the present value of the payment of the exercise price, multiplied by the probability of payment. The formula is shown in the appendix to this chapter.

There are a number of shortcomings with the Black-Scholes model which are apparent when reviewing the underlying assumptions. For example, it assumes that the option can be exercised only at maturity and ignores transaction costs. It assumes that stocks pay no dividends and that there is a single risk-free interest rate. It also assumes a lognormal distribution of stock prices so that calculations could be made easily within the formula.[4] However, studies have indicated that the actual distribution of stock price changes do not necessarily follow a lognormal curve. Still, the main benefit of the Black-Scholes model is that it has five variables, of which four are known. Therefore, from a practical viewpoint, it is relatively easy for investors to apply in determining the fair value of options.

The academic and investment communities have attempted to match option pricing theory formulas with marketplace realities. Serious studies have been undertaken to adjust the formula for more realistic price distributions and to explain differences between fair value computations and observed market anomalies. Other academic studies have used the Black-Scholes model to price various financial instruments. Therefore, the Black-Scholes model is the starting point for the development of a fair price model for convertible securities.

Applying the Black-Scholes model to option pricing involves inputing the current stock price, the exercise price of the option, the time to expiration and an estimate of the underlying common stock variance. Floor traders on the Chicago Board Options Exchange have hand-held calculators with the formula so that trades can be made quickly on the basis of over- and undervaluation. In addition, most reviews of actual option pricing indicate wide acceptance of the model.

The application of Black-Scholes to convertibles is more difficult because of the complex nature of the convertible security. The exercise price can vary depending upon conditions. The time to expiration of the conversion feature also can vary depending on whether the bond is callable or non-callable. A model must adjust for these factors and others to determine accurate fair value prices for convertibles in all cases. The following pages discuss the adjustments that need to be made and the logic behind those adjustments.

---

[4]Gary Gastineau, *The Stock Options Manual* (New York: McGraw-Hill, 1979) pp. 249–251.

CONVERTIBLE FAIR PRICE MODEL

Through the application of option pricing theory, this model for theoretical pricing of convertible securities considers all factors and is not dependent on investors' subjective attitudes. It encompasses both callable and non-callable bonds, synthetic convertibles and warrants. This section discusses the model as an extension of the basic convertible factors outlined in previous chapters.

   This evaluation process is complicated by the fact that a convertible security actually incorporates a "dual option." The bondholder has the option to convert to the underlying common stock of the issuing firm with certain restraints, and the issuing company has the option to call the bonds for redemption within certain restraints. Both options must be clearly identified and quantified within the model.

   In each convertible security there is an *investment value*, Sv(t), and an option or *warrant portion*, Wv(t). The warrant is embedded in the security and in most cases is not detachable. Each portion of the security is evaluated separately and then combined to determine the theoretical value of the convertible security, Cv(t).

Thus: Theoretical   Investment   Warrant
          Convertible Value   =   Value   +   Value

             Cv(t)   =   Sv(t)   +   Wv(t)

   Where t = current time period and Cv(t) and Sv(t) is greater than zero

   To determine the fair value price of a convertible the formula must be modified to reflect the individual investment characteristics of a particular convertible issue. In the next section we discuss the basis that the convertible investor must use in modifying the formula to determine the theoretical fair value. The specific mathematical adjustments to the formula are not given, but the appendix to this chapter provides a version to determine the fair value of a convertible security.

CONVERTIBLE SECURITY'S INVESTMENT VALUE (Sv(t))

At first glance, the straight fixed-income portion, Sv(t), of the convertible security is a relatively straightforward calculation based on the yield-to-maturity calculation discussed in chapter 3. That calculation is accurate for non-callable securities and for those with a low probability of being called. However, upon closer examination, some adjustments need to be made to reflect the fixed-income value and to determine a theoretical convertible value that would apply in all cases. Depending on whether the security is callable or non-callable, as well as its coupon rate relative to current rates and other factors, a determination must be made as to the probability of its being called. A convertible security that is likely to be called tends to trade on a yield-to-first-call basis rather than a yield to maturity. The investor must then make that determination and adjust the investment value accordingly.

ADJUSTMENT FOR HIGH PROBABILITY OF CALL

The investment value of the convertible is sensitive to the probability of being called for redemption.

For example, during periods of declining interest rates, many convertible bonds would be considered to have a high probability of call. This adjustment is particularly important in determining fair value prices during those periods. Companies will call bonds to refinance their debt at the then current lower interest rate. Under these conditions, the convertible bonds are very likely to be called at their next call date. Thus, the bonds trade as short-term paper maturing at the first call date, and the duration of the bond is significantly reduced. This becomes apparent when a bond is subject to call and carries a significantly higher coupon rate than a similar bond in the new issue market. Since most bond indentures require 30-day notice of call, the minimum value becomes its present value, plus a 30-day option on the underlying stock.

ADJUSTMENT FOR FORCED CONVERSION

Convertible securities are often called prior to the interest payment date. This is usually done to force conversion because the conversion value at the time is well above that of its call price. By forcing conversion at that point, the company saves the six-month interest payment. The bondholder is forced to convert to the underlying stock and forgoes the interest that has accrued from the previous payment date. In most cases, there is no loss in value because the marketplace anticipates most calls, so the bonds have been trading at a discount from conversion value. That discount is typically the amount of accrued interest due at the time. Unless this is taken into account in a pricing model, the convertibles trading at slight discounts from conversion value will seem to be mathematically undervalued as compared to non-callable bonds.

In developing a convertible pricing model, boundary positions must be established that hold true for all convertibles under normal conditions. Special boundary conditions must also be established that distinguish between callable and non-callable convertibles.

BOUNDARY CONDITIONS

There are a number of minimum and maximum values for the convertible security that must be included as boundary conditions for the formula. These conditions are discussed below.

The market value cannot fall below conversion value because that would present a no-risk profit opportunity that the floor specialists or arbitragers would quickly seize upon. This was discussed in general terms in chapter 2. They would only have to short stock in the amount equal to the conversion ratio of the bond, then purchase the bond and convert it to stock. Transaction costs are minimal for professional arbitragers at broker dealers.

For this strategy to work, market value must be equal to or greater than conversion value, and the convertible price must exceed the investment value. If this condition is not met, bond market traders will avail themselves of this potential arbitrage profit and the excess demand for the convertible will push the bond back to equilibrium. Although an arbitrage opportunity may exist whereby a trader would short a straight bond against a convertible bond of the same coupon, quality and maturity date, this is less likely to occur. Nevertheless, fixed-income and convertible traders are quick to take advantage of convertible bonds that are trading below the market's perception of their straight bond value.

The result is the second arbitrage condition, which states that the convertible price must always be greater than its straight bond value. This holds true no matter how unlikely it is that the stock price will reach its conversion price. For most purposes, investors should consider that the convertible price will always be greater than or equal to investment value.

The remainder of the boundary conditions result from the call provisions of the bond or the investor's determination of the probability of call. The bondholder, in the interest of maximizing profits for a bond that has been called, will always choose the greater of conversion value or the call price.

ADJUSTING FOR CALLABLE BONDS

Bonds that are currently callable but seem unlikely to be called due to the current interest rate level and the coupon rate on the bond must be evaluated differently by investors. Although call protection remains, if the bonds are not likely to be called, then the convertibility option should command some time premium.

The first step in evaluating bonds with conversion values above or very near the call price is to determine at what level the issuing corporation will call the bonds. Although the optimal call strategy would be for the firm to call the bonds when the conversion value equals the call price, this is rarely the case. Studies have determined that firms typically call convertibles when the conversion value exceeds the call price by an average of 43.9 percent.[5] Firms do not call at the theoretically optimal point (when the conversion value reaches its call price) because slight market fluctuations in the underlying common stock could cause a redemption of the bond at the call price, rather than forcing conversion. Companies typically call bonds to force conversion and usually wait until the conversion value is well above their call price. For example, in September 1987, IBM called the IBM Eurobond, convertible into Intel common stock. Although the conversion value was well above the redemption price of the bond at the time of the announcement, by the final redemption date some 30 days later, it was to the investor's advantage to redeem rather than convert. This was caused by the stock market crash of 1987, which precipitated a dramatic decline in Intel common stock over that 30-day period.

Considering these actual call policies of convertible issuers, the expected time remaining on the warrant portion of the convertible must be estimated.

---

[5]Jonathan E. Ingersoll, "An Examination of Corporate Call Policies on Convertible Securities," *Journal of Finance* 2 (May 1977): 289–321.

One should carefully examine the company's or industry's past call patterns as well as its financial ability to call the bonds. In addition, the bond indenture should be checked for provisions that could initiate a call. For example, the bond may not have been callable until a specified date or unless the common stock is at or above 150 percent of the conversion price for 30 days. This is commonly called the 150 percent provisional call. This may be an indication of the target price the company set before it would force conversion even though the call date has passed. If this information is not available, the average of 43 percent above the call price may be used as an estimate.

Time to Expiration

The final step is to estimate the change that is necessary for the underlying stock to move from current stock price to an estimated stock price in the future. This is an extremely important step since it determines the range of stock prices used in the risk/reward analysis. Almost all convertible advisory services use an arbitrary percentage move in the common stock to determine leverage estimates. Utilizing this analysis, the implied time premium and the conversion premium at that point can be determined more accurately.

Consideration of the time premium remaining on the convertible bond assumes that the buyer and seller of the bond reach an equilibrium position in order to facilitate a trade. In this process, the buyer attempts to minimize the value of the bond and the seller attempts to maximize the value of the bond. Specifically, the formula considers the "time premium" for a callable bond with a low probability of call. The buyer of a convertible bond should be willing to pay the premium for the time that remains or less because this represents a fair evaluation for the value of the implied warrant based on the stock's historical volatility. Any price higher than that would be to the seller's advantage.

CONVERSION FEATURE EVALUATION ($W_V(t)$)

It should be clear that the underlying stock volatility influences both the investment value portion and the warrant component of the convertible security. The fair value of a convertible must consider how the various factors interact with one another under many different circumstances.

The conversion feature or warrant portion of the convertible bond is complicated by a number of conditions. There are two variables that need to be input to the Black-Scholes option formula to use the model for evaluating the conversion portion of our model: the time to expiration and the exercise price. The time premium that remains on the conversion feature must be carefully considered. If it is known that the convertible security will be called on a specific date, the input variable would simply be the time period. However, convertibles may or may not be called for a number of reasons. Also, the exercise price varies with changes in interest rates that affect the straight bond value. The adjustments to the convertible fair price model for these various conditions are discussed below.

Estimating Conversion Time Premium

The longer the time available in which to convert the convertible security to common stock, the more valuable the implied warrant of the convertible would be to the investor. Many convertible securities have long maturities, implying that there are opportunities to convert over a long period of time. However, most convertibles can be called by the issuer years prior to the maturity date of the bond. The time period at which the warrant ceases to be exercisable becomes an important consideration and affects the value of the convertible security. The simplest case would be a non-callable bond. In that case, the maturity date of the bond coincides with the time period when the convertibility expires. For callable bonds, the investor must estimate the minimum time that the convertible bond will likely be outstanding and adjust the time to expiration. That becomes the worst-case scenario and is based on the assumption that the issuer will call the bond at a time that is most beneficial to the company. The factors to consider in estimating this time are: (1.) the date that the security becomes callable and, (2.) if callable, the probability that the bond will be callable based on its stock price.

This time period then becomes an input factor to determine the warrant portion value.

Determining Exercise Price

In the process of pricing a convertible bond as a straight non-convertible debt instrument with a warrant attached, an adjustment must be made to the conversion price or exercise price of the warrant portion. The convertible bondholder must give up the bond portion in order to exercise the convertibility feature. Therefore, the exercise price continually changes as the value of the straight bond portion changes. This becomes apparent in situations where the warrant is actually detachable from the bond. These types of convertibles (called *units*) are issued much like typical convertible bonds, but they can be traded separately soon after being offered. The warrant retains a specific exercise price that does not change. However, the bond portion, which now trades independently of the warrant, can be used at par value in lieu of cash when exercising the warrant. Obviously, if the straight bond is trading at a discount from par due to the current interest rate structure, it could be purchased and submitted to the company along with the warrant to obtain the stock. The exercise price of the warrant is effectively reduced by the amount of discount on the bond, and as the straight bond value changes, the effective exercise price of the warrant also changes. Therefore, the formula used must take these changes into consideration.

This adjustment to the warrant exercise price should be made in evaluating warrants where usable bonds apply. For example, Tiger International has a warrant outstanding with an exercise price of $12.50 per share. Since the straight bond can be used in lieu of cash upon the exercise of the warrant, the effective exercise price is reduced by any discount from par for which the bond can be purchased. In this case, with the bond trading at 85 (November 1987), the exercise price is reduced by 15 percent to $10.63. This becomes the *adjusted exercise price*.

It is obvious, then, that our model can evaluate the theoretical price of warrants by simply removing the fixed-income portion of our formula.

It's apparent that the exercise price of the convertible is now inversely related to interest rates and is subject to further adjustments due to the creditworthiness of the issuing company and the call probability of the bond.

Adjusting for Dividends

The assumption that the stock pays no dividend is a serious drawback of the Black-Scholes formula when applied to convertible securities. Convertibles that have little or no yield advantage over the underlying common stock dividend will command little or no conversion premium. Conversely, when the yield advantage is high, investors expect to pay a higher conversion premium. This is the essence of the commonly used break-even analysis calculation for evaluating convertibles. Therefore, the amount of the underlying stock dividend cannot be ignored, and an adjustment for dividends is necessary in determining the theoretical fair value price.

The dividend adjustment to the Black-Scholes model is due to the fact that the stock price will decline on the ex-dividend date by the amount of the dividend. For ease of calculation, the dividend adjustment is assumed to be at a continuous rate. The adjustment is accomplished by reducing the stock price by the present value of the dividend payout and reducing the risk-free yield by the amount of the dividend to reestablish a no-risk hedge.

Several important variables have been determined thus far:

- the straight bond value with its adjustments for callable and non-callable bonds
- the time to expiration with its adjustment for callable bonds
- the exercise price and its relationship to interest rates
- the adjustment to the Black-Scholes model for the underlying common stock dividend

THE CALAMOS FAIR PRICE MODEL FORMULA

In this chapter we have discussed how option theory can be applied to the pricing of convertible securities. We explored the many factors that must be taken into account to arrive at the theoretical fair price of a convertible security. The appendix to the chapter explains the mathematical derivation of such an application.

The Calamos fair price model (CFP) has considered many variables to determine the fair price of a convertible security and is, in our opinion, an accurate determination of the fair value price. Other analysts may make different assumptions as to when bonds may be called, the underlying stock's price distribution and other important factors that are critical to the analysis. Our purpose here is to show that option theory can provide the basis for determining the fair value price of a convertible security. Although it is a complex problem, we are confident that the CFP model considers the many variables and accounts for their influence to the fair value price. Whether investors accept our model or derive their own similar model, it is clear that this is the most accurate means currently available to determine fair value. In the remainder of the book the CFP model will be used as the method for determining the fair price of a convertible.

APPENDIX: A CONVERTIBLE PRICING MODEL

The convertible price model used is derived from the Black-Scholes model and will be explained in its simplest form. The convertible fair price model of a convertible security is comprised of part latent warrant and part straight bond, with each component priced separately. The model combines the two parts to determine the fair price of the convertible security.

The convertible pricing model is subject to many more variables than the option pricing model. It also includes many variables that are dependent upon estimates (i.e., time to expiration, call probability and bond discount factor). For explanatory purposes we will assume we know all variables with certainty. The value of XYZ Company's convertible bond 7.00 percent of 11/15/2004 can be determined given the following values:

(1) Stock Price =	$30.00
(2) Conversion Price =	$25.00
(3) Stock Volatility =	35.00%
(4) Risk-free Rate (two-year) =	8.50%
(5) Time to Known Expiration =	2.00 years
(6) Call Features of Bond =	2.00 yrs. of Absolute Call Protection
(7) Bond Discount Factor =	8.50%
(8) Debt Spread =	4.00%
(9) Adjusted Conversion Price =	$24.30
(10) Bond Coupon Rate =	7.00%
(11) Stock Dividend Yield =	0.0 %
(12) Bond Call Price =	$1,000.00
(13) Conversion Ratio =	40.00 shares
(14) Call in two years is known to be certain	
(15) Market Value Convertible =	130.00

Straight Bond Value Sv(t):

$$\sum_{t=i}^{n} \frac{C}{(1+Ym)^n} + \frac{P}{(1+Ym)^n} = \text{Straight Bond Value}$$

$$\sum_{t=i}^{2} \frac{70}{(1.085)^2} + \frac{100}{(1.085)^2} = 972.9$$

Black-Scholes Warrant Value:

$$d_1 = \frac{1n\frac{1}{2} + \left(r + \left(\frac{s}{k}\right)\sigma 2\right)T}{\sqrt{T}}$$

$$d1 = \frac{1n(1/2) + (.085 + \frac{30}{24.3} \times 0.123)(2)}{0.35\ \sqrt{2.0}} = -0.443$$

$$(N)\ d1 = 0.4801$$

$$d_2 = d1 - \sigma\sqrt{t}$$

$$d2 = -0.443 - .495 = -0.938 \qquad\qquad (N)\ d2 = 0.1711$$

Warrant Value = Wv(t) = SN(d1) – Ke^{-rT} N(d^2)
30(.4801) – 24.3(.844) (.1711) = 10.89.
Convertible's Equity Portion = Wv(t) × Cr(t)
(10.89)(40.00) = $435.60.
Theoretical Convertible Value =
Sv(t) + Wv(t) = Cv(t)
$972.90 + $435.60 = $1,408.50

Over/Under Valuation:

The theoretical convertible value is then compared to the current market value to determine under/over valuation.

$$\frac{\text{Actual} - Cv(t)}{Cv(t)} = \text{Over/Under}$$

$$\frac{137.0 - 140.85}{140.85} \times 100 = -2.73\%$$

The application of the option theory to a security as complex as a convertible requires many estimates. To determine the fair value of an option there are six variables, all of which are known except one, volatility. For convertibles there are seven variables of which five must be estimated. Because analysts may arrive at different conclusions as to the value of the estimates, the convertible market will most likely continue to exhibit pockets of inefficiencies.

7

Applying the Calamos Convertible Fair Price Model

Developing a theoretical formula is an important first step in investment analysis, but financial journals are littered with formulas that are not of practical use. To be of value to investors, a formula must meet the test of real world investing, and it must produce results that are accurate and profitable. The investor must evaluate the conditions under which the formula was derived and must then accept its underlying assumptions. If the assumptions do not apply, they must be revised in order to produce meaningful results.

The application of the Calamos fair price (CFP) model to the pricing of convertible securities introduces a series of changes in the variables that are, in part, subject to investors' best estimates. How different investors arrive at these estimates can determine how accurately the model portrays reality. Experience in the marketplace is important in adjusting the model. For example, the probability of call not only affects the adjusted exercise price, but also the term to expiration of the option portion of the convertible. These variables would be static under normal option pricing conditions. The exercise price also becomes sensitive to changes in interest rates and the credit of the issuing companies' debt securities. For these reasons and others, the convertible market will most likely always display a degree of inefficiency. This is good news for the investor who is able to seek out those opportunities.

It is also important to distinguish between short-term inefficiencies that traders or abitragers may be able to exploit and their meaning to the long-term investor in the convertible market. The efficient mechanism of the marketplace contributes to the long-term trading process by pricing convertibles at or near their fair value. Swaps from one convertible to another may be accomplished more readily in an efficient marketplace. Investors who can consistently exploit the undervaluation of the convertible market should gain a significant advantage in relative performance.

In utilizing the formula, a number of inputs are required: the stock price, the exercise price, the time to maturity, the interest rate and the volatility of the stock. Of these, only the stock price and the interest rate are easily obtainable. By investigating the sensitivity of these variables to our formula, the investor will gain a greater understanding of the model's application.

In addition to understanding how the model reacts to changes in the variables, investors will be able to determine how different factors will affect convertibles in general. Here we review the effect of factors such as changing interest rates, an increase in stock dividends and the difference between callable and non-callable bonds. The real effect of these changes and how convertibles react to them often confuses investors, so we are simultaneously testing our model against how we intuitively feel the price of a convertible would react to such changes while helping the reader understand how those changes will influence the price of convertibles.

INVESTIGATING THE SENSITIVITY OF THE VARIABLES

Combining the investment value and the implied warrant to determine a fair value convertible price will cause the variables to react quite differently than when calculated by the Black-Scholes model. The interactions between the variables, using the CFP formula, gives the net effect of the change in the convertible price. Throughout this analysis, all other variables remain constant so that the effect of the single variable can be illustrated.

Volatility

Changes in the volatility of the underlying stock become a complex matter in evaluating a convertible. Under normal option pricing condi-

**FIGURE 7.1   Convertible Bond Sensitivity Analysis
Relative to Underlying Stock Volatility**

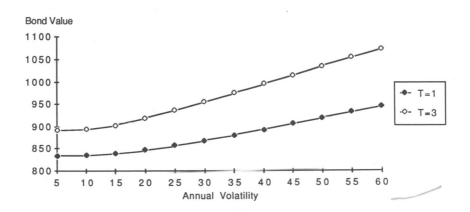

Assumptions:
- T – Time of absolute call in years
- Stock price = 20
- Conversion ratio = 40
- Investment value = 700
- Risk-free rate = 6%
- Dividend yield = 1%

tions, increasing volatility would increase the value of an option; but the bond portion of a convertible security would be expected to decrease if the stock's volatility increases because of the increase in the firm's risk, which may affect estimated earnings, financial ratios, interest coverage analysis and other measures of the firm's financial stability. If the increase in volatility causes the firm's beta, or risk factor, to increase, then equity and debt holders will probably expect a higher return to compensate for the higher risk factor. The effect of an increase in the stock's volatility on the convertible bond is illustrated in figure 7.1.

As volatility increases, so does the value of a convertible bond, holding all other variables constant. Figure 7.1 also shows the effect of time remaining before which the bond may be called. If the time of absolute call increases from one year to three years, the impact of the change increases. Notice the increasing value of the convertible bond as volatility increases and that the longer the time to absolute call, the greater the increase in the convertible bond price.[1]

Figure 7.1 ignores the impact of the change in the debt value of the convertible bond due to changes in the underlying stock's volatility. This could be measured by applying a Merton's debt valuation model that prices the debt of a firm as a function of the value of the firm, maturity value of the debt, time to maturity of the debt, risk-free rate of return and the volatility of the equity.[2]

The application of Merton's model[3] implies that as the volatility of the firm increases the value of the debt will decrease in order to produce a higher return to bondholders. The results of increasing volatility, while the equity of a firm is decreasing, can lead convertible investors into a trap. The convertible holder who has evaluated the increase in volatility from the equity side of the convertible will ignore the decreasing debt value and greatly underestimate the downside risk of the convertible. This is why some convertible securities decline in value as much as their common stock counterparts. Investors who evaluate convertibles on the basis that the bond value is constant are, to their chagrin, usually surprised to see their convertible bond price fall below their poorly estimated bond value. This is particularly common with convertibles issued by secondary or low capitalization companies. Even high capitalization companies are not immune to this phenomenon.

---

[1]This relationship can be explained by the following equation:

$$\frac{\$ \text{ change in Cv(t)}}{1\% \text{ change in } \sigma} = \frac{\partial \, Cv(t)}{\partial \, \sigma} = Cr(t) \; S \; \sqrt{T} \; N'(h)$$

Where
$$N'(h) = 1/\sqrt{2\pi} \; e^{\frac{-h^2}{2}}$$

and
$$h = \log(S/Ke^{-rT})/\sigma\sqrt{T} + 1/2\sigma\sqrt{T}$$

[2]$D = f(V, T, B, r, o)$, Merton.

[3]R.C. Merton, "On the Pricing of Corporate Debt: The Risk Structure of Interest Rates," *Journal of Finance* 29 (May 1974): 449–470.

FIGURE 7.2   Convertible Bond Sensitivity to Short-Term Interest Rates

---

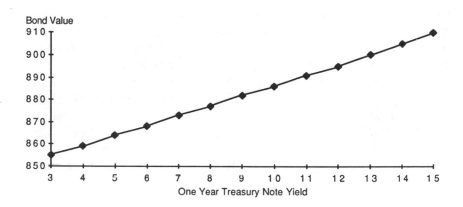

Assumptions:
- Stock price = 20
- Conversion ratio = 40
- Investment value = 700
- Risk-free rate = 6%
- Dividend yield = 1%
- Annual standard deviation = 30%

Union Carbide's Bhopal disaster in 1986 caused the volatility of the stock to increase substantially due to the financial liability the company could have incurred from the accident. The convertible bond value and its accompanying straight bond value also decreased substantially. Most cases where this occurs are not signalled by such dramatic events. Accurately estimating the stock's future volatility becomes extremely important in determining the convertible bond's value. Historical volatility and fundamental data of the company become important input in estimating future volatility.

Convertible Interest Rate Sensitivity

The effects of changes in interest rates on convertible securities can be seen using the CFP. If the short-term, risk-free rate is increasing, the equity value of the convertible should also increase, assuming all other variables are held constant. It is unlikely that short-term rates would change without a corresponding change in long-term rates, however, this example illustrates the influence of changes in short-term rates alone. This is demonstrated graphically in figure 7.2.

A convertible bond trading at $872 with one-year Treasuries at seven percent, would increase to $890 if one-year Treasuries were to increase four percent to an annual rate of 11 percent. This is consistent with how stock options react to changes in short-term interest rates. The option premium increases in value as short-term rates rise. The embedded warrant in the convertible also increases with rising short-term interest rates.

Convertible Sensitivity to Long-Term Interest Rates

The value of the convertible bond is also subject to changes in long-term bond yields. The effect of changes in long-term interest rates on bond value was discussed in chapter 2. If long-term interest rates increase, then the debt value of the convertible will decrease, causing a decline in the value of the convertible. The adjusted exercise price for the convertible will also decrease, as explained in chapter 6. Figure 7.3 indicates the net effect of changes in the convertible bond price and straight bond values with changes in long-term interest rates. This is the measure of duration for a convertible bond. Figure 6.4 measured the duration for a convertible bond with a large premium over investment value. It was found that the larger the premium over investment value, the less likely it is that the convertible bond will be sensitive to changes in long-term interest rates. Figure 7.3 indicates that the long-term straight bond is much more sensitive to interest rates than a bond trading high above its investment value. Duration analysis of a convertible bond becomes an excellent method with which to determine its sensitivity to changes in interest rates.

In general, the higher the investment premium, the less susceptible the convertible is to changing interest rates. The dominant influence becomes the stock price rather than its bond attributes. If both long-term and short-term interest rates increase, there may be no change in

**FIGURE 7.3   Convertible Bond Duration (Interest Rate Sensitivity)
7% – 20 years**

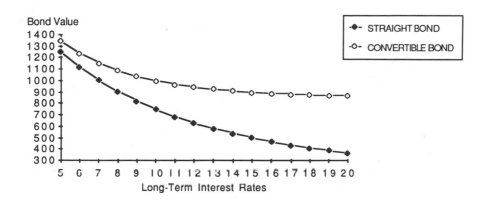

Assumptions:

- 20% Conversion premium with rate at 7% (low conversion
  premium)
- Stock price = 20
- Conversion ratio = 40
- Risk-free rate = 6%
- Dividend yield = 1%
- Annual standard deviation = 30%

the convertible price. For example, when short-term rates increase, the option portion of the convertible increases. But the increase in the long-term rate results in a decrease in the bond portion of the convertible. An increase in the equity value can offset any loss in the debt value, with the net result being no change in the convertible value.

Figure 7.4 indicates how interest rates affect a convertible bond with a high conversion premium and low investment premium. Unlike the previous example, the convertible bond and the straight bond are affected nearly the same. Convertible bonds that are trading close to their investment value become more sensitive to changes in long-term interest rates.

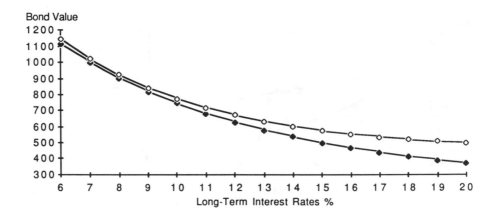

**FIGURE 7.4   Convertible Bond Duration
High Conversion Premium**

Assumptions:

- 150% Conversion premium at 7
- Stock price = 10
- Conversion ratio = 40
- Risk-free = 6%
- Dividend yield = 1%
- Annual standard deviation = 30%

Nearly every variable is affected by changing interest rates; the investment value is inversely related, while the warrant portion is positively related.

Convertible Sensitivity to Stock Dividend Yield

The convertible bond value will also be inversely related to the underlying stock's dividend yield. The effect is due primarily to the decrease in the warrant value. Figure 7.5 illustrates the sensitivity of a convertible to changes in the stock's dividend yield. Note that as the dividends increase the conversion premium loses value, all other factors remaining constant. The CFP model accounts for this by reducing the warrant value of the convertible.

**FIGURE 7.5   Convertible Bond Price Sensitivity to Stock
Dividend Yield**

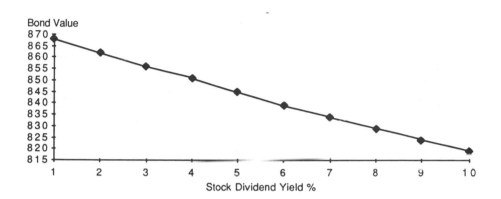

Assumptions:
- Stock price = 20
- Conversion ratio = 40
- Investment value = 700
- Risk-free rate = 6%
- Dividend yield = 1%
- Annual standard deviation = 30%

Convertible Sensitivity to Time to Expiration

The more time an investor has to exercise the convertibility feature, the more premium an investor should expect a convertible to command. Like stock options, a longer-term convertible option is much more valuable than a short-term option. The amount of time remaining to expiration is affected by the maturity date of the bond or the amount of the call protection. The investor must assume that the company may call the convertible at the earliest possible time and pay only for the value of premium to the first call. Figure 7.6 indicates that as the years of absolute call protection decreases, the convertible bond price will also decrease. It's interesting to note that under the same assumption, the straight bond value also increases to its call price. Again, the CFP model matches what convertible holders would expect to occur.

FIGURE 7.6   Convertible Bond Time Premium Decay

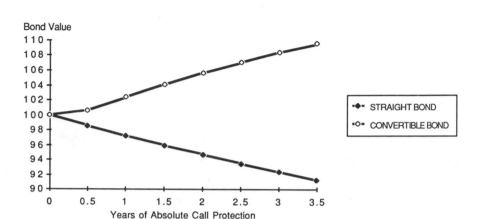

Assumptions:
- Stock price = 20
- Conversion ratio = 40
- Investment value = 700
- Risk-free rate = 6%
- Dividend yield = 1%
- Annual standard deviation = 30%

Convertible Sensitivity to Common Stock Price Changes

Finally, with all other variables considered, the common stock price is input into the formula and a theoretical convertible bond price results. The model now can estimate convertible bond prices for various changes in the common stock price. The resulting changes in the convertible bond price can be utilized to develop the expected price track of the convertible security. An increase in the stock price, holding all other variables constant, will result in an increase in the convertible price.

SUMMARY

Throughout this chapter we have tested the CFP model by holding all except one variable constant. As we have seen, the model accounts for the variables and matches what experienced convertible investors would expect to occur, given changes in the many variables. Any model that attempts to encompass all situations must be scrutinized for subtle errors.

Many analysts feel that deep-in-the-money options tend to be underpriced relative to their true value, whereas out-of-the-money options are usually overpriced relative to their true value. Since the CFP model applies the Black-Scholes formula, the same errors may occur. Yet, as we test and work with the CFP model, its usefulness in evaluating a convertible security becomes apparent. As we learn more about the intricacies of these complex securities, the model also changes.

What is clear is that the CFP model fills a void in convertible evaluation. It determines more accurately than past models the fair value price of a convertible security. Its application to what-if scenarios replaces the guesswork of the past. Investors can determine how changes in interest rates, dividends, volatility and other factors will influence their convertible portfolios.

The most direct benefit of the CFP model is that it can be used to estimate the price track and, thereby, derive the important risk/reward analysis of the convertible security.

8

Estimating Risk and Reward of Convertibles

EVALUATION PROCESS

In prior chapters we saw how the convertible's price track can be estimated using option theory. In this chapter, we compare how convertible leverage has been used in the past and how our application of the CFP model can be used to improve on the analysis. Accurately estimating that price track is important because this process culminates in the risk/reward analysis and shows the potential profit and loss of a position. If the price track is incorrect, the risk/reward that follows will also be incorrect. The investor should also be concerned with whether the convertible security is mathematically under- or overvalued because over time it should tend toward its fair value price track.

The following process ascertains whether a convertible security has favorable leverage. Since the convertible is being compared directly to its underlying common stock, the range over which stock prices may move becomes an integral part of the profit and loss estimate. Generally, a relatively large move is required to determine a meaningful risk/reward relationship.

The traditional method used by many popular convertible advisory services assumes large, arbitrary movement in the underlying stock and then estimates the corresponding convertible security price. The comparison among many different issues under this method is of-

---

FIGURE 8.1   Risk/Reward Analysis: Traditional Method

XYZ COMPANY Risk/Reward Analysis

Stock Change	−50%	−25%	−0−	+25%	+50%
Stock Price	8.50	12.75	17.00	21.25	25.50
Convertible Price	93.50	97.90	110.00	125.40	143.00
Convertible % Move	−15.00	−11.00	−0−	+14.00	+30.00

NOTE: Based on 12-month holding period.

---

ten meaningless because each common stock has its own particular range of movement. We will use this method as a frame of reference to show how it can be improved upon.

RISK/REWARD ANALYSIS: TRADITIONAL METHOD

Under the traditional method, the common stock is assumed to advance or decline by 50 percent; then the corresponding convertible security price is estimated. The risk/reward and the advantage the convertible enjoys over the underlying common stock are then determined to complete the evaluation. Figure 8.1 shows a typical risk/reward analysis for a utility company whose stock has exhibited low volatility.

Several problems arise in using this method. First, as discussed in the previous chapter, the price track that determines the convertible prices should take into account all variables. Secondly, the arbitrary price moves have no relationship to the most probable movement of the underlying common stock. It becomes extremely difficult to compare the relative attractiveness of convertible securities using this method. For example, utility stocks' variance, as well as their betas, are typically lower than those of the average common stock. Applying the risk/reward analysis to such a security could make it appear more attractive than other alternatives.

Figure 8.1 compares the risk/reward of XYZ to that of its convertible security. An investor using this information would probably de-

FIGURE 8.2   Calamos Convertible Evaluation Service

Convertible Security Worksheet

Company: XYZ COMPANY

Sector: Capital Gds-Techn
Industry: (14) F-COMPUTER & PERIPHE

	Symbol	Market	Curr Yld
Common Stock	XYZ	33.000	2.12
Convertible	XYZ-R	94.000	7.97

Common Stock

Beta: 1.45	Fund. Rating: B	Debt/Equity: 0.32
Stnd Risk: 43.71	Opin Rank: 2,	Tech Rank: 3
Cap (mill $): 660.00	Stock Div: 0.70	RX Agency: Internal

Convertible   Security

Desc: 7.500-06/15/2010	Pymts: JUN-DEC-15	Call Feature: 12/90 *150
Risk Level: AGG	Inv. Val YTM: 12.90	Credit Rating: BBB
Issue Size (mill $): 175.00	CCES Grade: 10	Conv. Ratio: 24.0000
Next Call Price: 105.075	Underwriter: Drexel	Bnd Hld Rts: None

Convertible   Analysis

Conversion Value	Conversion Premium	Investment Value	Invest Value Premium
79.20	18.68%	60.88	54.38%

BARA	Yield to Maturity	Fair Value Over/Under	Interest Rate Sensitivity
1.35	8.00%	-0.56%	4.47

EROI	Upside Beta	Downside Beta	Break Even
17.44%	1.04	0.63	3.19

cide to buy. However, a more complete analysis will demonstrate why this would be an incorrect choice. We will develop a worksheet that takes into account the multitude of factors that should be considered before investing in a convertible security.

CALAMOS CONVERTIBLE EVALUATION WORKSHEET

Company and Common Stock Information

Figure 8.2 indicates the beginning of the process by considering both the fundamentals of the company and some statistical risk measures. The common stock section takes both *beta* and *total risk* factors into account. The rating of the common stock is considered along with the capitalization and the important debt-equity ratio. The analyst can add both the fundamental opinion of the stock and technical price action. Both are subjective factors.

The convertible security section gives details of the particular convertible. These include the coupon, maturity date, interest payment dates, call terms, issue size, rating and conversion ratio. The investment value yield is determined by the analyst's evaluation, as discussed in chapter 4, and corresponds to the Calamos convertible evaluation grade. These grades allow the analyst to fine tune the investment value yield and override the security bond rating. Investment value grades vary from 1 to 20. Depending on the investment value grade and the underlying risk factors of the common stock, the risk level of the convertible is determined. The current market prices of both the common stock and the convertible, with their corresponding yields, are also given. The following describes the individual items included in the worksheet analysis.

Sector

Indicates the economic/industry sector to which the company belongs. An analysis of the economy and financial markets is helpful in deciding which sector may perform best given the investor's forecast of economic conditions.

The main sector includes:

- credit cyclicals
- financial
- consumer growth staples
- consumer defensive staples
- consumer cyclicals
- capital goods—technology

- capital goods—industrial
- energy
- basic industrial
- transportation
- utilities

Industry Group

Refers to the industry group to which this particular convertible's issuing company belongs. After selecting the economic sectors most likely to perform best, a further analysis should be undertaken to decide which industry group(s) within each sector are likely to perform best. Industry diversification is an important consideration.

Many research organizations provide a breakdown of industry groups.

SIC codes list 46 industry groups from aerospace to utilities.

Beta

The beta coefficient presented here is the underlying common stock beta. It measures the stock's historical systematic risk or the portion of a stock's volatility that can be explained by the volatility of broad stock market movements. A weighted portfolio beta is utilized in evaluating a portfolio's total systematic risk exposure. Carefully selected convertibles may reduce the company's systematic risk in declining phases of the market while allowing for a significant portion of the company's systematic risk in rising phases of the market.

Merrill Lynch, Value Line, Standard & Poor's and other research departments publish beta coefficients. It is best to be consistent as to which beta measure you use in your research because betas are regressed against various indices and over different time frames.

Standard Risk

The stock's volatility (total risk) measures the standard deviation of the stock returns over a specified time period. It is based on the stock's historical volatility of returns and is utilized as an estimate for the expected future stock distribution of returns and total risk. This becomes the relevant risk measure for a non-diversified portfolio.

The standard deviation may be calculated from as little as the past 30 days' stock returns to as long as the previous five years' weekly returns. The most meaningful time frame probably falls somewhere in between. Companies that have been reorganized or have been involved in merger activities will have to be scrutinized very closely before implementing past volatility measures into the analysis.

Value Line provides this risk measure for 1,700 stocks on a relative basis. They calculate it using five years of weekly price changes comparing each stock's volatility with the other 1,699 in their universe. Value Line's relative volatility values range from approximately 50 to 230. The stocks that exhibit average volatility are assessed a value of 100, while stocks that are 50 percent more volatile than the average are assessed a value of 150.

Financial Rating

This measure provided by the Standard & Poor's stock guide is helpful in establishing a stock's risk class. Specifically, it indicates the company's consistency of dividend payments and stability in earnings. A + is the highest rating and is reserved for companies that have shown a history of paying dividends and stable earnings. The stock ratings range from A + to D.

Debt/Equity Ratio

The debt-to-equity ratio is an indication of the firm's leverage. Although the beta coefficient to some degree is a measure of the company's leverage, it is usually calculated over a long time and may not be a clear indication of the company's sensitivity to changing market conditions. Firms with higher debt-to-equity ratios are generally more sensitive to changing market environments than firms with lower debt-to-equity ratios.

It is important to compare the debt-to-equity ratio with the average within the company's industry group.

Capitalization

Capitalization is a measure of the firm's equity market value. It is calculated by multiplying the total common shares outstanding by the market price of the common stock.

CONVERTIBLE SECURITY INFORMATION

Description

Provides the convertible's coupon rate, maturity date of the bond and other pertinent information.

Payments

Indicates the dates the bond pays interest, typically semiannually for domestic bonds and annual payments for Eurodollar issues.

Call Features

The call features of the convertible security are extremely important. The convertible's provisional or absolute call protection and the date of loss of call protection are noted here. This information can be obtained from various research sources.

Risk Level

This is an indication of the broad overall risk level of the convertible, including both equity and bond risk measures. It is a means to distinguish between the various opportunities available on the basis of relative risk. Three levels of risk are recommended: low, medium, aggressive.

Investment Value Yield

The investment value yield is the estimated yield to maturity utilized to calculate the straight bond portion of the convertible. This can be determined by evaluating any straight debt the company may have outstanding or similar quality debt in the marketplace. This was discussed in detail in chapter 5.

Conversion Ratio

The conversion ratio determines the number of shares of common stock into which each convertible can be exchanged. The conversion ratio is determined upon original issuance of the security and is provided for in the indenture.

Issue Size

Indicates the size of the convertible issue in million of dollars for bonds and millions of shares for preferreds. Issue size can be helpful in determining the liquidity of an issue.

Credit Rating

The convertible provides an indication of the creditworthiness for the security. The ratings range from the highest AAA + to the lowest D. This may be a good place to begin the credit analysis.

CCES Grade

The CCES grade is the grade classifying the convertible risk. A grade of 1 is the highest quality, and the lowest grades are assigned a 20. This allows for a wider classification of grades than obtained through the rating services.

Next Call Price

Determined at or prior to issuance, this is the price at which the issuer may redeem the bond or preferred stock prior to maturity. The call price is usually above the par value of the security in order to compensate the holder for the loss of income prior to maturity. The first dates when an issuer may call bonds are specified in the prospectus that has a call provision in its indenture.

Underwriter

The lead underwriter for the security. This is useful because the lead underwriter often can provide information on the security and company.

Bondholders Rights

The protection against the elimination of conversion rights because of takeovers should be reviewed by investors. Convertibles without adequate protection are less valuable than those with protection. Avoid new issues lacking protective clauses in the trust indenture against takeovers, be they friendly or hostile.

CONVERTIBLE ANALYSIS

Conversion Value

This can be determined by multiplying the common stock price by the conversion ratio. The conversion value is the equity value of the convertible security.

Conversion Premium

As explained in chapter 5, this is a measure determining the convertible's additional premium above the equity value of the security.

Investment Value

This is the convertible security's straight bond value as discussed in chapter 5. It becomes significant in determining the downside risk of the convertible.

Investment Premium

This is a measure of how much additional premium above the straight bond value the convertible commands. In essence, it is the difference between the market value and the investment value as a percentage of the convertible's investment value.

Balanced Approach Relative Advantage (BARA)

The balanced approach's advantage is a measure of the convertible's attractiveness relative to a combination of bonds and stocks. The balanced approach in portfolio construction involves a combination of common stocks and bonds (usually 50 percent of each) to provide growth from the equity markets with stability and income from the bond markets.

The highly volatile interest rate environment of the late 1970s and 1980s brought about a change in the balanced approach investing that included Treasury securities as an important stabilizing vehicle. Convertible securities can be compared to the balanced approach and for investment purposes would preferably offer an advantage to it. The following algorithm indicates the relative advantage offered by the convertible.

$$\frac{\dfrac{CV_G + Y}{(0.5)(ST_G + DY) + (0.5)YTM} + \dfrac{(0.5)(ST_L + DY) + (0.5)YTM}{CV_L + Y}}{2.0} = BARA$$

Where:

CV_G = Convertible Percent Gain
CV_L = Convertible Percent Loss
ST_G = Stock Percent Gain
ST_L = Stock Percent Loss
Y   = Convertible Yield
DY   = Dividend Yield
YTM = Investment Value

Over/Under Valuation

Indicates the percentage value that the convertible is mispriced. Positive numbers indicate the convertible is currently overpriced, while negative numbers indicate the convertible is currently underpriced. This is determined by the CFP model discussed in chapter 6.

Interest Rate Sensitivity

This is a measure of the convertible security's sensitivity to changes in interest rate(s) as discussed in chapter 5.

EROI (Expected Return on Investment)

This is a measure of the convertible security's expected return. The details of the calculation are discussed in chapter 5. Generally, convertible securities with EROIs below your long-term benchmark returns should be avoided.

FIGURE 8.3   Risk/Reward Analysis

Risk / Reward Analysis Estimated stock move Percent Change 1 In	12 mo. -35.3%	6 mo. -26.5%	CURRENT	6 mo. + 36.2%	12 mo. + 54.8%
Stock Price	21.313	24.224	33.000	44.953	51.094
CFP Convertible Track	79.390	82.220	94.530	124.860	131.200
Convertible Percent Change	−15.543	−12.532	0.564	32.830	39.574
Conv. Total Return %	−7.564	−8.542	8.543	36.819	47.533

Upside Beta and Downside Beta

This measure indicates the convertible's price sensitivity to changes in the overall stock market (not including the income portion of the convertible). Upside and downside betas are outlined in chapter 5.

Break-even

The break-even determines the time necessary for the convertible's yield advantage to make up the conversion premium paid. This is also discussed in chapter 5.

Risk/Reward Analysis

With these factors in mind, the analyst has determined that this convertible has an attractive yield relative to both the stock and the bond market. The risk factors of both the common stock and the convertible have also been considered. The next step is to consider the advantage the convertible has over its common stock. This is determined by the risk/reward analysis shown in figure 8.3.

Notice how the price range in this analysis differs from the arbitrary movement in stock prices under the traditional method. It is recommended that investors use a range of stock prices that suits the volatility of the security under consideration. This is a major change in how convertible leverage estimates have been made in the past and enhances the investor's ability to select convertibles.

Estimating Stock Price Range

To estimate the most likely price range the common stock may follow in the future, the investor should consider the underlying common stock's past volatility. Volatility of the stock is measured by its standard deviation and is widely applied in modern portfolio theory. The standard deviation is a statistical measure of the degree to which an individual stock in a probability distribution tends to vary from the mean of the distribution. The greater the degree of dispersion, the greater the risk. Since it includes both general market risk (systematic risk) and individual company risk, it is an excellent measure of total risk and can give the investor the means to estimate the probable range of stock prices for the risk/reward analysis. Fortunately, there are many services that provide these statistical measures.

The variance is based on the historical trading pattern of the stock. It is used as an estimate of future volatility. The investor can and should make a judgment as to whether that past volatility is an accurate guide to the future. In our example here, we present a lognormal distribution based on the underlying stock volatility factor at a one standard deviation move for both six and 12 months.

Now that the price range has been determined, the actual stock and convertible price and their percent changes are shown. Notice how the range of stock price is a more clear reflection of the potential of the underlying stock. The analysis provides investors with an estimate of future performance as well as downside risk, based on the stock's underlying trading habits. Should the investor decide the recent events might increase the stock's future volatility, the model can quickly incorporate this subjective judgment into the decision-making process by estimating the effect of the increased volatility on the convertible price.

The current yield can also be incorporated to analyze the convertible security on a total return basis. Total return is an important consideration to convertible investing because a large portion of its return is from the coupon or dividend received from the convertible. Investors often shun convertibles that have little or no yield advantage. The break-even analysis' main drawback is that it ignores total return in favor of relative return.

The consideration of total return, as indicated above, puts the yield factor in a proper perspective. Investors who continually use yield advantage as the major determinant in selecting a convertible will find that they unwittingly constructed a high-risk portfolio whose underlying common stocks pay few dividends but do represent a cross-section of the market. Their selection process has narrowed their universe to the more risky segments of the financial markets.

The total return in our example shows that this convertible demonstrates a favorable risk/reward relationship over the common stock. Its upside potential is a 47.6 percent return for a 54.8 percent move in the common stock. The convertible retains 87 percent of the upside potential of the common stock. On the other hand, if the stock were to decline 35.3 percent, the convertible would show a decrease of only –7.6 percent. Obviously, the convertible preserves capital on the downside while retaining the upside potential of the common stock. In addition, its current yield of 8.5 percent is an attractive sideways yield.

It's important to keep in mind the underlying assumptions the worksheet is based upon. The investment value is based on interest rates remaining stable throughout the period under consideration. However, since we have determined the interest rate sensitivity, the investor can estimate how any change in interest rates would influence the convertible. Also, the worksheet assumes a holding period of either six or 12 months. An important component of the total return is the interest received over that period of time. If the stock moves dramatically in shorter periods of time, then the estimates of return may not hold. The advantage of the worksheet is that it considers all factors and provides the *most probable* risk/reward relationship of a particular convertible in light of uncertain markets. Figure 8.4 shows the completed worksheet.

The worksheet, when applied to the example using the traditional method, shows the value of a more complete evaluation. Figure 8.5 indicates a more likely risk/reward analysis for the convertible under consideration. Because it uses a more probable price range for the stock, it reaches the opposite investment conclusion. XYZ Company, in this case, was a low volatility stock. Experienced investors do not need statistical analysis to know that this particular convertible's price range is grossly inaccurate. But every stock has its own price range based on its total risk. If the traditional method can present an investment trap when comparing a utility stock to an industrial stock, won't it also present a trap when comparing one industrial stock to another with more subtle changes? The value of the convertible risk/reward analysis is that it can account for even the most subtle changes in risk factors.

FIGURE 8.4   Convertible Security Worksheet

Convertible Security Worksheet

Company: XYZ COMPANY   Sector: Capital Gds-Techn
                                              Industry: (14) F-COMPUTER & PERIPHE

	Symbol	Market	Curr Yld
Common Stock	XYZ	33.000	2.12
Convertible	XYZ-R	94.000	7.97

Common   Stock

Beta: 1.45	Fund. Rating: B	Debt/Equity: 0.32
Stnd Risk: 43.71	Opin Rank: 2	Tech Rank: 3
Cap (mill $): 660.00	Stock Div: 0.70	RX Agency: Internal

Convertible   Security

Desc: 7.500-06/15/2010	Pymts: JUN-DEC-15	Call Feature: 12/90 *150
Risk Level: AGG	Inv. Val YTM: 12.90	Credit Rating: BBB
Issue Size (mill $): 175.00	CCES Grade: 10	Conv. Ratio: 24.0000
Next Call Price: 105.075	Underwriter: Drexel	Bnd Hld Rts: None

Convertible   Analysis

Conversion Value	Conversion Premium	Investment Value	Invest Value Premium
79.20	18.68%	60.88	54.38%

BARA	Yield to Maturity	Fair Value Over/Under	Interest Rate Sensitivity
1.35	8.00%	-0.56%	4.47

EROI	Upside Beta	Downside Beta	Break Even
17.44%	1.04	0.63	3.19

Risk / Reward   Analysis

	12 mo.	6 mo.		6 mo.	12 mo.
Percent Change 1 In	-35.3 %	-26.5 %	CURRENT	+36.2 %	+54.8 %
Stock Price	21.313	24.224	33.000	44.953	51.094
CFP Convertible Track	79.390	82.220	94.530	124.860	131.200
Convertible Percent Change	-15.543	-12.532	0.564	32.830	39.574
Conv. Total Return %	-7.564	-8.542	8.543	36.819	47.553

SOURCE: Calamos Asset Management, Inc. 1987.

FIGURE 8.5   **Comparison of Risk/Reward Analysis Methods**
Traditional vs. Volatility Adjusted

Traditional Method

Stock Change	-50%	-25%	-0-	+25%	+50%
Stock Price	8.50	12.75	17.00	21.25	25.50
Convertible Price	93.50	97.90	110.00	125.40	143.00
Convertible % Move	-15.00	-11.00	-0-	+14.00	+30.00

Volatility Adjusted Method

Standard Deviation	-17.6%	-12.7%	-0-	+14.7%	+21.4%
Stock Price	14.00	14.84	17.00	19.50	20.64
Convertible Price	100.10	104.50	110.00	115.50	121.00
Convertible % Move	-9.00	-5.00	-0-	+ 5.00	+10.00

NOTE: Does not include income.
NOTE: Based on 12-month holding period.

SOURCE: Calamos Convertible Evaluation Service.

APPLICATION TO THE NEW ISSUE MARKET

The CFP model allows for easy analysis of new convertible securities. Its flexibility enables the investor to evaluate risk factors of the issuing company in order to determine whether the convertible is fairly priced. This evaluation may also benefit the issuer. More convertibles could be issued at higher conversion premiums and higher coupons if investors felt the trade-off was equitable. In the past, this type of convertible has always been difficult for investors and issuers to evaluate. The CFP model can show how the trade-off between higher coupon and conversion premium affects the fair value. As long as the convertible was issued at a fair value price, new issue buyers would be adequately compensated for the difference between conversion premium and yield.

The Calamos convertible evaluation worksheet can be applied to the new issue market. Figure 8.6 shows an analysis of the General Instrument convertible bond issued on May 28, 1987. The preliminary term of the offering indicated that this convertible was priced below its fair value price as determined by the model. The subsequent trading after the offering confirms the advantage of using the model to determine whether to buy a new issue. Immediately after the offering, the common stock price dropped from 33.27 to 32. The convertible bond price actually increased to 103 from 100 as it tended toward its fair price value. Reviewing the new issue market can give investors a means to evaluate the level of conversion premium over time.

CONVERTIBLE OFFERINGS AND THEORETICAL FAIR PRICE VALUES

An often-debated question among convertible investors is whether the new offerings of convertibles are fairly priced. There are subjective fundamental factors that enter into the decision process that will affect the supply and demand for convertibles. Future prospects of the company, the industry group and other fundamental elements, along with persuasive security salespeople, all play an important role in the pricing of new offerings. Our studies indicate that general market sentiment also is a critical item causing convertible new offerings to be underpriced sometimes and overpriced at other times.

Using the CFP model to price the new issues, an average under/over valuation was calculated and plotted in figure 8.7. The stock market is also shown and indicates a close correlation to the under/over pricing of convertibles. Notice that in early 1987 with the stock market advancing how convertible new offerings continually both became more and more overvalued and an increasing number of issues were brought to the market. The stock market correction during the last half of the year resulted in fewer issues, but at prices which were more in line with our estimates of fair value. Theoretical fair price values should carry significant weight in the convertible investors' purchase decision of new issues.

The application of CFP from individual securities to a portfolio of convertibles becomes a relatively easy transition. In the next chapter the CFP model is used to evaluate a convertible portfolio.

FIGURE 8.6   Convertible Security Worksheet

Company: GENERAL INSTRUMENT

Sector: Capital Gds-Techn
Industry: (58) F-ELECTRONICS

	Symbol	Market	Curr Yld
Common Stock	GRL	33.250	0.75
Convertible	GRL-RB	100.000	7.25

Common   Stock

Beta: 1.35	Fund. Rating: B	Debt/Equity: 0.19
Stnd Risk: 42.09	Opin Rank: 3	Tech Rank: 3
Cap (mill $): 1,108.95	Stock Div: 0.25	RX Agency: Internal

Convertible   Security

Desc: 7.250-06/15/2012	Pymts: JUN-DEC-01	Call Feature: 06/90 ABS
Risk Level: AGG	Inv. Val YTM: 10.80	Credit Rating: BBB
Issue Size (mill $): 175.00	CCES Grade: 7	Conv. Ratio: 24.6520
Next Call Price: 105.075	Underwriter: SB,MER	Bnd Hld Rts: None

Convertible   Analysis

Conversion Value	Conversion Premium	Investment Value	Invest Value Premium
81.96	21.99%	69.64	43.57%

BARA	Yield to Maturity	Fair Value Over/Under	Interest Rate Sensitivity
5.32	7.25%	-4.11%	6.17

EROI	Upside Beta	Downside Beta	Break Even
19.04%	0.94	0.33	3.38

Risk / Reward   Analysis

	12 mo.	6 mo.		6 mo.	12 mo.
Estimated stock move					
Percent Change 1 In	-34.3 %	-25.6 %	CURRENT	+34.7 %	+52.3 %
Stock Price	21.825	24.689	33.250	44.778	50.654
CFP Convertible Track	91.520	92.980	104.110	125.970	136.570
Convertible Percent Change	-8.480	-7.020	4.110	25.970	36.570
Conv. Total Return %	-1.230	-3.395	11.360	29.595	43.820

Remarks: New Issue

SOURCE: Calamos Asset Management, Inc., 1987.

FIGURE 8.7 Convertible Securities New Issues,
January 1, 1985, through June 30, 1987

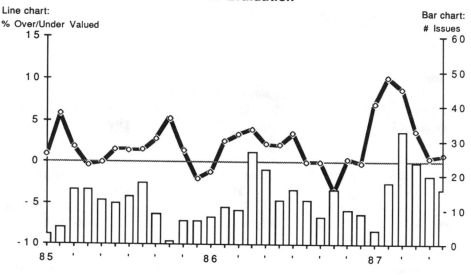

Convertible Securities New Issue Market
Fair Price Evaluation

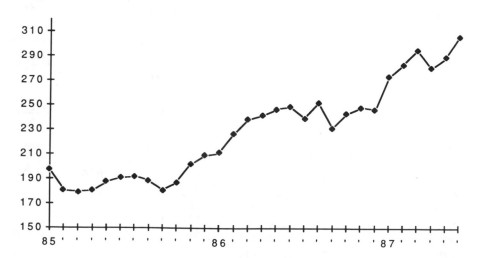

SOURCE: S&P 500 data courtesy of Standard & Poor's Corp.

9

Portfolio Management

The application of the CFP model to a portfolio of convertible securities allows for easy risk/reward comparison. Figure 9.1 indicates a typical convertible screen of convertible opportunities evaluated in this fashion. The convertible portfolio summary, the CPS screen, is notable because each security's individual potential is then related to the market. Gone is the arbitrary stock movement used to determine the relative risk/reward advantage. Each security can now be compared to each other on the same basis. Also, comparison to the market is accomplished, as well as a statistical evaluation of risk. This analysis provides an important tool for estimating total market risk of the portfolio.

The CPS screen is made up of four segments: the fundamentals, statistical information, the risk/reward analysis and portfolio averages (see fig. 9.1). This information is taken from the more detailed worksheet discussed in chapter 8.

FUNDAMENTAL INFORMATION

This basic information is provided by such well-known sources as Standard & Poor's or Moody's. It includes such common information as stock symbol, ratings and current price information of the securities involved. Since equity participation is an important aspect of convert-

FIGURE 9.1   Calamos Asset Management—Portfolio Analysis Summary of Convertible Securities

SYMBOL / COMPANY NAME		CONV. CPN%	STOCK PRICE	CONV. PRICE	CONV. PREM.	INVEST PREM.	BLAR ADV	DUR FLR	LEVERAGE 12Mo.	LEVERAGE 6Mo.	W/INCOME 6Mo.	W/INCOME 12Mo.	CONV. YLD	STOCK YLD	S&P CONV	S&P STOCK	CCES GR	BETA	STND RISK
B-Bank	79																		
BKB Bank of Boston		7.75	21.63	109.00	18.01	37.94	1.11	9.70	-5.50	-5.80	14.60	23.30	7.11	4.62	AA-	A+	4	1.20	29.80
******** Financial (15.4%) *********																			
B-Industrial Services	9																		
B-Insurance (Prop Casualty)	16																		
BFI-RA Browning-Ferris		6.25	25.00	91.00	49.24	42.41	1.05	10.00	-6.60	-6.30	14.20	22.40	6.86	1.60	A	A+	5	1.25	39.73
CB-EUR Chubb Corp.		5.50	61.25	90.50	26.03	8.41	1.30	4.70	-0.80	-1.80	14.30	22.10	6.07	3.06	AA	B+	3	1.10	33.44
B-Insurance (Diversified)	36																		
CIPRC Cigna Corp.		4.10	51.50	49.75	31.79	26.19	1.10	11.00	-0.60	-2.30	12.30	20.00	8.24	5.43	A	B	5	1.05	28.14
******** Consumer Staples (11.5%) *********																			
D-Distilling/Tobacco	15																		
AMB-EUR American Brands		7.75	41.88	100.00	35.38	20.90	1.17	8.30	-2.00	-3.30	14.00	22.60	7.75	4.96	A+	A	4	0.90	36.75
D-Food Process	48																		
STAPR Staley Cont.		3.50	19.38	41.00	48.04	34.71	1.03	10.60	-2.80	-4.00	13.30	21.70	8.53	4.12	BBB-	B-	8	1.10	36.42
D-Furniture/Home Furnishings	27																		
LEG-RA Leggett & Platt		6.50	23.75	84.00	32.63	27.74	1.09	9.00	-2.20	-3.40	12.40	20.20	7.73	2.35	BBB	A-	7	0.95	31.45
E-Auto Parts-OEM	80																		
DCN-RD Dana Corp.		5.87	34.50	84.00	22.78	38.06	0.99	9.30	-5.40	-5.70	13.10	21.30	6.99	4.17	A-	B	7	1.10	31.45
E-Recreation	23																		
WCIPRA Warner Communicati		3.62	26.00	54.75	26.32	66.13	1.14	10.90	-12.10	-10.20	19.00	29.20	6.62	1.53	BBB	B-	7	1.10	41.39
E-Retail Store	67																		
PST-RC Petrie Stores		8.00	20.88	105.50	11.79	45.89	1.23	8.90	-8.10	-7.80	18.20	28.80	7.58	3.35	BBB-	B+	8	1.05	33.11
******** Capital Gds-Techn (23.1%) *********																			

Sector / Ticker	Company																		
F-Comp. & Peripherals 10																			
UISPRA	Burroughs Pref. (Un	3.75	32.88	59.75	8.75	75.26	1.-1	10.80	-10.50	-9.2C	16.20	25.50	6.27	2.79	BBB	B+	7	1.10	28.14
CYR-RA	Cray Research	6.12	69.13	99.75	21.20	66.12	1.34	9.60	-13.50	-10.90	22.90	34.30	6.14	0.00	BBB	B+	7	1.35	43.04
IBM-RC	IBM	7.87	121.63	104.00	31.38	21.70	0.71	9.00	-1.10	-3.40	5.30	11.30	7.57	3.61	AAA	A+	1	1.00	21.52
PRM-RA	Prime Computer	5.75	15.00	74.50	37.82	37.97	1.18	9.50	-7.50	-7.30	17.20	27.20	7.71	0.00	BB+	B	8	1.20	46.35
F-Computer Software & Services 5																			
AUD-RA	Automatic Data Proc	6.50	41.75	117.00	16.93	71.54	1.19	10.00	-10.30	-8.50	13.80	25.60	5.55	1.05	A+	A+	4	1.30	31.45
F-Electronics 58																			
GRL-RB	General Instrument	7.25	25.63	92.00	45.60	33.68	1.16	9.40	-5.60	-6.00	15.70	25.00	7.88	0.97	BBB	B	7	1.30	44.70
******** Capital Goods (11.5%) ********																			
G-Machinery 25																			
CUMPR	Cummins Engine	3.50	48.13	42.75	36.86	40.46	1.07	10.60	-2.30	-3.30	13.50	21.60	8.18	4.57	BBB-	B-	8	0.95	29.80
OG-EUR	Ogden Corp.	6.00	25.63	83.50	29.91	27.29	1.05	8.60	-3.50	-4.30	13.60	21.80	7.18	3.90	BBB	B+	7	0.90	33.44
G-Precision Equipment 60																			
EK-EUR	Eastman Kodak	6.37	49.38	110.00	12.86	44.04	1.04	8.50	-3.10	-3.50	10.70	16.90	5.79	3.64	AAA	A-	2	0.85	18.21
******** Basic Industries (23.1%) ********																			
I-Aluminum 1																			
AA-EURO	Alcoa	6.25	44.63	94.00	30.58	39.61	1.00	8.50	-5.30	-5.50	12.80	20.50	6.64	2.68	BBB	B-	7	1.15	31.78
I-Copper 3																			
PDPRB	Phelps Dodge	3.00	39.00	54.63	9.26	133.08	1.24	10.10	-21.10	-16.40	26.50	38.20	5.49	0.00	BB-	B-	10	1.30	41.39
I-Metals Fabr 19																			
TKR	Timken (Tennax)	8.37	54.75	108.00	18.35	37.40	1.33	9.10	-1.50	-2.50	14.00	21.90	7.75	1.82	BBB	B-	7	0.75	23.17
I-Metals & Mi (General) 8																			
FTXPR	Freeport-McMoran	1.87	20.88	23.50	25.05	50.40	1.1C	12.10	-8.10	-7.90	16.80	26.90	7.97	2.87	BB-	B	9	1.10	38.07
I-Paper & Forest Products 22																			
PCH	Potlatch	5.75	26.38	77.00	32.26	36.36	1.01	9.80	-3.60	-4.40	12.40	20.30	7.46	3.48	BBB	B	7	1.15	31.45
I-Steel/ Integrated 17																			
XPRE	USX Corp. Pref. E	3.50	28.38	47.88	28.68	57.32	0.97	10.60	-6.60	-6.50	13.80	22.30	7.31	4.22	BB-	B-	8	0.95	31.45
******** Conglomerates (3.8%) ********																			
L-Multiform 68																			
EMH-EUR	Emhart Corp.	6.75	18.75	92.00	30.02	24.36	1.03	8.50	-0.60	-2.10	10.80	17.70	7.33	4.26	A-	B+	5	0.90	25.16
PORTFOLIO AVERAGES:					27.60	44.04	1.11	9.54	-5.83	-5.91	14.79	23.46	7.14	2.89		0.55		1.08	33.11

ible investing, both stock ratings and convertible security ratings are shown.

One would think that it would be relatively simple to obtain current price information, but obtaining accurate prices of convertible securities continues to be a problem in the industry. Although most convertible bonds are listed on the major exchanges, they frequently trade away from the exchanges. The New York Stock Exchange has the nine-bond trading rule that allows member firms to trade away from the exchange for orders of more than nine bonds. Therefore, most bond trades are done away from the exchange in a very active dealer network. The exchange prices, for the most part, reflect the prices that bonds trade at in the over-the-counter market.

Another problem with pricing of convertibles stems from the fact that convertible trading is more infrequent than stock trading. If prices are based on last sale for the convertible, errors can occur. If the stock has changed dramatically, the last sale of the convertible was based on a stock price that is no longer appropriate. This presents a problem in active markets. A well-known convertible service has actually unknowingly made purchase and sale recommendations for convertibles on erroneous, unobtainable prices.

Stock and bond ratings are another important item to consider. Ratings of the securities by agencies is important because of the input needed to determine the investment value.

STATISTICAL INFORMATION

The statistical information provides relevant risk measures for beta and for total risk. The average weighted betas and average standard risk factors are important considerations in determining the overall risk of the portfolio. The beta given in figure 9.1 indicates the underlying common stock's beta and not that of the convertible. The convertible's beta in most cases will be much lower than that of the common stock.

RISK/REWARD ANALYSIS

The risk/reward section completes the analysis by indicating the leverage of each individual security within the portfolio. With each individual position's risk/reward defined, the total risk/reward of the portfolio can now be calculated.

PORTFOLIO AVERAGES

Figure 9.1 indicates the average for the portfolio. In a sense the portfolio can now be viewed similarly to one individual convertible. The average conversion premium of this portfolio is 27.6 percent with a premium over investment value of 44.04 percent. The current yield of the portfolio is 7.14 percent, providing a significant yield advantage of 4.25 percent over the underlying common stock dividend yield. Notice that the underlying stocks represented in this portfolio have an average beta that is slightly higher than the typical stock and a standard risk of 33.11 percent, which is in line with market averages. The important risk/reward characteristics show that the portfolio should have advanced 23.46 percent for a 33.11 percent advance in the market over a 12-month period. Whereas, if the market were to decline by 33.11 percent the portfolio would decrease by only 5.83 percent. The portfolio has 70 percent of the market potential on the upside, but a significant decrease in risk on the downside. Figure 9.1 assumes interest rates will be constant throughout that period and the convertible's risk/reward includes bond interest.

The CPS summary is an important tool for monitoring the convertible portfolio. As prices change, so does the risk/reward of the portfolio. Important buy/sell decisions can be made to maintain the desired risk/reward relationship in the portfolio. The investor can also apply what-if scenarios to determine the effect on the portfolio. For example, if the investor has a strong opinion as to the trend of interest rates, he or she can determine its effect on the portfolio and take action to minimize its influence.

The easy application of sound principles of portfolio management is the main benefit of the CPS summary. Portfolios can be quickly monitored for proper diversification with regard to the number of positions and the breakdown among industries. Total risk and the portfolio beta can be easily determined and controlled.

Although it is difficult to prepare the CPS without the support of computer software, it is a necessary tool to effectively manage convertible portfolios in volatile market environments.

PART
III

Convertible Strategies

10

Convertible Bond Strategies

Convertible bonds are attracting more interest now among institutional and individual investors than ever before. Over 25 mutual funds using convertible securities exclusively have been brought to the market in recent years. Many pension funds currently earmark a percentage of their assets for convertible strategies. Fueling this interest has been the new issue market, with back-to-back record years in 1985 and 1986. The combination of high yields and excellent performance throughout the 1970s and 1980s has generated enthusiasm for these issues among many individual investors. With all the excitement about the convertible market, it is well to remember that the old adage, "It's a market of stocks, not a stock market," applies equally to the convertible market.

Lumping convertibles together without regard to their differences in risk and other factors could substantially limit the benefit of a convertible program. A solution to this problem is to focus on the various sectors of the convertible market. Since companies are categorized by financial analysts as either high capitalization or low capitalization stocks, this provides a convenient method of distinguishing between convertible issues. The blue-chip, or high cap, market often performs very differently from the low cap, or secondary, market. This same distinction applies to convertible bonds. Two broad sectors of the convertible market are low-risk convertibles, those of investment-grade quality, rated BBB or better by Standard & Poor's, and aggressive convertibles, those not rated or rated below investment grade. Since the convertible market reflects what is happening in the stock and bond markets, it is better to look at these sectors of the market rather than at broad generalizations about the total market. Keeping these sectors in mind, investors can define a convertible program that meets both their investment objectives and their individual tolerance for risk. Only then can risk and reward be properly matched.

Whether the convertible is high cap or low cap, the evaluation process should take both of its parts into consideration. The convertible bond income characteristics include the coupon rate, maturity date, call features and investment quality. The equity side includes the analyst's opinion as to the future prospects of the company, the risk measures of the common stock and how much equity participation the convertible bond represents. As suggested in previous chapters, the fair price evaluation should be completed to gain the maximum advantage.

LOW-RISK EQUITY ALTERNATIVE

Several strategies can be employed using convertible securities. Each has its own investment objective and risk/reward relationship. The most straightforward strategy is to use convertibles as a low-risk alternative to the stock market. Convertibles selected on this basis have a balance between the upside potential of the stock and the downside safety provided by the bond's income characteristics. The sample portfolio shown in chapter 9 has such balance. Convertibles are selected on the basis of their risk/reward analysis, with two-thirds of the upside potential of the common stock and one-third of the downside risk.

Convertibles selected on this basis are sold when that risk/reward ratio changes dramatically. As the common stock increases, so does the convertible. However, as the convertible increases in price, the risk/reward profile changes, reducing the advantage the convertible enjoyed near par. When the risk/reward of the convertible is no longer favorable, the convertible should be sold and replaced with one that has a favorable risk/reward relationship. This protects the profit taken in rising markets while continually upgrading the portfolio's risk/reward ratio.

Portfolio adjustments must also be made in declining markets. As a common stock declines in value, the convertible's income attributes work to preserve value. However, the risk/reward relationship is no longer favorable even though the convertible has accomplished its purpose. Swaps need to be made to upgrade that relationship.

The timing of these changes is based on the individual's tolerance for risk. The continual monitoring of positions, as described in previous chapters, is necessary when making those decisions.

AGGRESSIVE CONVERTIBLES

"Aggressive convertibles" is a more reassuring term than "high-risk convertibles." In fact, these convertibles are generally on smaller companies or companies whose underlying stocks are much more volatile than those of seasoned companies. Many investors feel that this sector of the financial market and over-the-counter stocks present good opportunities, and with good reason. Many academic studies have shown that small company stocks have outperformed those of larger companies over many years. Unfortunately, this was not the case in the bull market of the eighties. Small company stocks disappointed many investors who were relying on that trend to continue.

Investing in these smaller companies has always been a risky proposition. Using their convertibles provides an excellent means to reduce risk and participate in the low cap sector of the market. Generally, the current yields are very attractive, sometimes averaging as much as 500 basis points greater than the investment-grade issues.

Aggressive convertibles offer investors less risk than their underlying common stock, although the companies they represent are generally more risky. As a subset of the low cap sector, the convertibles on these companies represent firms that have substantial long-term debt. This additional risk can be reduced with thorough fundamental and credit analysis, a process not easily accomplished with small companies. Investors should be aware that this group exhibits spikes, either up or down; therefore, measures of stock risk, such as beta, are not as helpful. The preferred measure is stock variance (standard risk), which measures its total risk. It is an important ingredient in estimating the price range of the convertible in risk/reward analysis.

Figure 10.1 shows such a sampling of aggressive convertibles. The characteristics of this portfolio are indicated in the portfolio averages. The average conversion premium is 19.94 percent with an 81.69 percent premium over investment value. The portfolio indicates an attractive current yield of 7.38 percent, as well as a significant yield advantage over the low dividend paying underlying common stocks.

FIGURE 10.1 Calamos Asset Management—Portfolio Analysis Summary of Aggressive Convertibles

SYMBOL	COMPANY NAME	CONV. CPN%	STOCK PRICE	CONV. PRICE	CONVN PREM.	INVEST. PREM.	BLAR ADV.	DUR FLR	LEVERAGE 12Mo.	LEVERAGE 6Mo.	W/INCOME 6Mo.	W/INCOME 12Mo.	CONV. YLD	STOCK YLD	S&P CONV.	S&P STOCK	CCES GR	BETA	STND RISK
A—Savings & Loan 92						********* Credit Cyclicals (5.3%) *********													
GLN-EUR	Glenfed, Inc.	7.75	24.50	102.50	18.18	36.91	1.17	7.6	-7.8	-7.7	18.5	29.3	7.56	4.08	NR	NR	7	1.40	38.85
B—Insurance/Life 59						********* Financial (5.3%) *********													
ALWCG	A.L. Williams Corp	7.25	18.25	84.00	31.17	45.78	1.20	7.8	-9.9	-9.4	20.8	32.8	8.63	0.00	NR	NR	10	0.90	50.19
C—Publishing 33						********* Cons Grwth Stapl (10.5%) *********													
NEC-RA	National Education	6.50	22.00	101.00	14.77	79.00	1.22	8.8	-15.8	-13.0	22.1	33.9	6.43	0.00	BB+	B+	8	1.15	42.09
C—Retail/Special Lines 72																			
PCLB	Price Company	5.50	39.75	93.60	19.22	92.81	1.13	9.1	-16.0	-12.9	20.4	31.1	5.87	0.00	BB+	NR	8	1.35	40.47
E—Air Transport 75						********* Consumer Cyclical (15.8%) *********													
ARWS	Air Wisconsin Service	7.75	11.38	68.00	13.53	29.97	1.51	7.2	-3.1	-5.2	20.1	36.5	11.39	0.00	B-	B	12	1.30	42.09
E—Hotel/Gaming 47																			
PDQ-RA	Prime Motor Inns	6.62	36.25	102.25	14.43	106.62	1.14	7.9	-15.4	-12.5	20.6	31.6	6.47	0.24	B+	A-	11	1.30	37.23
E—Recreation 23																			
GNMR	Genmar Industries	7.00	10.88	84.00	8.32	54.62	1.36	7.7	-12.5	-11.4	25.0	41.0	8.33	2.94	B+	NR	11	2.00	43.71
F—Comp. & Peripherals 10						********* Capital Gds-Techn (42.1%) *********													
APCIG	Apollo Computer	7.25	14.00	92.00	18.28	71.28	1.27	7.8	-19.0	-15.9	28.1	43.4	7.88	0.00	B-	NR	11	1.90	56.66
CPQ-RA	Compaq Computer	5.25	46.88	125.00	5.72	213.02	1.17	8.2	-39.1	-29.3	37.3	55.4	4.20	0.00	B+	NR	11	1.55	59.90
CYR-RA	Cray Research	6.12	80.75	107.25	11.56	90.46	1.23	9.2	-18.2	-14.6	23.2	35.3	5.71	0.00	BBB	B+	7	1.35	42.09
PRM-RA	Prime Computer	5.75	18.25	82.25	25.06	84.12	1.12	8.3	-15.7	-12.9	21.6	33.1	6.99	0.00	BB+	B+	10	1.20	45.33
SGATG	Seagate Technology	6.75	16.75	69.00	75.07	51.50	1.04	7.3	-11.7	-10.4	21.1	33.1	9.78	0.00	B+	NR	12	1.40	61.52
F—Computer Software & Services 10																			
AACPR	Anacomp, Inc.	4.12	7.63	50.00	-1.70	87.87	1.79	6.2	-31.6	-27.5	57.1	82.4	8.25	0.00	B3	B-	12	1.60	71.24

SYMBOL	COMPANY NAME	CONV. CPN%	STOCK PRICE	CONV. PRICE	CONVN PREM.	INVEST. PREM.	BLAR ADV.	DUR FLR	LEVERAGE 12Mo.	LEVERAGE 6Mo.	W/INCOME 6Mo.	W/INCOME 12Mo.	CONV. YLD	STOCK YLD	S&P CONV.	S&P STOCK	CCES GR	BETA	STND RISK
F-Electronics	58																		
AFG	AFG Industries	6.50	26.00	108.00	4.53	105.02	1.29	8.0	-20.0	-16.1	26.0	40.3	6.01	0.92	B+	B+	10	1.30	40.47
ZE-RA	Zenith Electronics	6.25	18.00	76.63	33.03	58.24	1.11	8.2	-8.1	-7.7	17.1	27.0	8.15	0.00	BB-	B-	10	1.35	38.85
								******	Capital Goods (5.3%)	********									
G-Machinery	25																		
TMO	Thermo Electron	5.75	14.50	67.88	42.78	52.17	1.09	8.3	-7.5		16.9	26.8	8.47	0.00	BB-	B	10	1.10	42.09
								******	Basic Industries (10.5%)	********									
I-Copper	3																		
PDPRB	Phelps Dodge	3.00	37.00	53.50	12.78	146.10	1.07	9.4	-20.5	-15.9	23.0	34.6	5.60	1.62	BB-	B-	10	1.30	40.47
I—Paper & Forest Products	22																		
POP-RC	Pope & Talbot	6.00	22.25	94.50	10.16	103.84	1.12	8.2	-16.1	-13.1	21.5	32.9	6.34	1.97	BB-	B	10	1.35	37.23
								******	other (5.3%)	********									
M-Mortgage Banking	0																		
CCR-RA	Countrywide Credit	7.00	8.63	85.88	21.90	42.67	1.25	8.7	-10.8	-10.1	22.3	35.1	8.15	2.78	BB+	B+	8	1.50	50.19
PORTFOLIO AVERAGES:					19.94	81.69	1.23	8.15	-15.76	-13.36	24.40	37.71	7.38	0.76		0.73		1.38	46.35

FIGURE 10.2 Calamos Asset Management—Portfolio Analysis Summary   Bond Alternatives   Research Report

SYMBOL	COMPANY NAME		CONV. CPN%	STOCK PRICE	CONV. PRICE	CONVN PREM.	INVEST. PREM.	BLAR ADV.	DUR FLR	LEVERAGE 12Mo.	LEVERAGE 6Mo.	W/INCOME 6Mo.	W/INCOME 12Mo.	CONV. YLD	STOCK YLD	S&P CONV.	S&P STOCK	CCES GR	BETA	STND RISK
********* Credit Cyclicals (4.0%) *********																				
A-Building																				
PHMA	PHM Corp.	69	8.50	8.63	81.00	122.91	24.78	1.00	7.7	-0.0	-2.3	13.3	22.1	10.49	1.39	BBB	B+	10	1.65	50.19
********* Financial (20.0%) *********																				
B-Bank																				
MELPRB	Mellon Bank Corp.	79	1.68	24.63	18.88	134.41	23.10	0.91	13.3	3.6	0.7	8.3	14.4	8.93	5.68	BBB	A-	5	0.95	25.90
BNCHOTC	Branch Corp.		8.75	15.25	104.50	21.63	28.26	1.07	8.2	0.8	-1.3	10.4	17.5	8.37	4.45	A-	A	6	0.55	19.42
B-Financial Services																				
LNF-RA	Lomas & Nettleton	43	7.00	16.13	74.00	71.27	22.87	0.88	8.7	2.0	-0.6	10.7	18.2	9.45	8.67	A-	A	8	1.10	32.38
B-Insurance/Diversified																				
CIPRC	Cigna Corp.	36	4.10	48.00	48.00	36.42	28.78	1.03	10.5	-0.2	-2.1	11.6	19.3	8.54	5.83	A	B	5	1.05	27.52
ABIGOTC	Amer. Bankers Ins. Co.		9.75	9.00	100.00	51.66	28.93	0.98	7.4	0.5	-1.8	12.4	20.7	9.75	5.55	BBB-	B+	9	1.00	32.38
********* Cons Grwth Stapl (12.0%) *********																				
C—Broadcasting/Cable TV																				
TRSPG	Columbia Pictures	62	7.12	6.88	79.00	70.86	19.09	1.17	8.6	-1.5	-3.4	14.6	24.0	9.01	0.00	BBB+	NR	7	2.00	55.05
C-Medical Services																				
AMI-RA	Amer Med International	81	9.50	14.00	92.50	61.08	18.97	1.04	7.0	1.6	-1.2	13.0	21.8	10.27	5.14	BBB	A-	9	1.25	40.47
C-Restaurant																				
WEN-RA	Wendy's International	71	7.25	6.50	75.00	101.23	20.52	0.96	8.6	3.2	0.2	9.8	16.9	9.66	3.69	BBB-	A-	8	1.05	32.38
********* Consumer Cyclical (12.0%) *********																				
E—Air Transport																				
ABF-RA	Airborne Freight	75	7.50	15.88	81.88	42.57	28.12	1.10	8.6	-2.3	-3.9	14.8	24.2	9.16	3.77	BBB-	B	8	1.05	40.47
E-Recreation																				
BBCC-A	Commtron (Bergin Brun)	23	6.87	3.13	63.87	203.63	21.44	0.97	8.0	2.2	-0.6	11.5	19.5	10.76	0.00	BBB-	NR	10	2.00	46.95

SYMBOL	COMPANY NAME	CONV. CPN%	STOCK PRICE	CONV. PRICE	CONVN PREM.	INVEST. PREM.	BLAR ADV.	DUR FLR	LEVERAGE 12Mo.	LEVERAGE 6Mo.	W/INCOME 6Mo.	W/INCOME 12Mo.	CONV. YLD	STOCK YLD	S&P CONV.	S&P STOCK	CCES GR	BETA	STND RISK
E-Retail Stores 67																			
ZY-RB	Zayre Corp.	7.25	19.63	80.50	44.35	23.36	1.13	8.9	-0.3	-2.4	12.8	21.2	9.00	2.03	BBB+	A-	7	1.25	35.62
******** Capital Gds-Techn (16.0%) ********																			
F-Aerospace/Diversified 50																			
GQ-R	Grumman Corp	9.25	19.00	97.50	78.32	25.79	0.95	8.2	1.7	-0.8	10.8	18.2	9.48	5.26	BBB+	B	8	1.10	32.38
F-Comp. & Peripherals 11																			
IBM-RC	IBM	7.87	113.38	104.00	40.94	20.55	1.03	8.9	1.6	-0.5	8.6	14.6	7.57	3.88	AAA	A+	1	1.00	21.04
F-Electronics 58																			
AVT-R	Avnet	8.00	25.63	92.00	86.65	22.96	1.04	9.3	0.6	-1.4	10.8	18.0	8.69	1.95	A+	B-	5	1.35	37.23
SGN-RD	Unitrode (Signal Cos)	8.00	7.50	85.00	353.33	8.83	0.93	9.1	5.8	2.1	7.3	13.1	9.41	2.66	A-	B+	4	1.15	42.09
******** Capital Goods (4.0%) ********																			
G-Machinery 25																			
GULDG	Goulds Pumps	9.87	18.75	103.00	46.94	19.26	1.07	8.0	3.4	0.2	10.0	17.2	9.58	4.05	A-	B	7	0.70	24.28
******** Energy (16.0%) ********																			
H-Coal/Uranium/Geothermal 74																			
MXSPR	Maxus Energy	4.00	7.00	35.50	211.32	9.16	1.04	9.7	8.1	3.4	8.0	14.7	11.26	0.00	BBB-	C	8	1.20	32.38
H-Natural Gas/Diversified 78																			
ENS-RG	Enserch Corp.	10.00	17.88	101.38	59.21	14.19	1.07	7.3	3.7	0.4	10.4	17.9	9.86	4.47	BBB	B	7	0.85	30.76
SWN-RA	Southwestern Energy	8.50	18.00	95.47	71.71	22.89	1.04	8.9	0.7	-1.4	11.1	18.6	8.90	3.11	BBB+	A-	6	1.81	35.62
H-Petroleum/Integrated 70																			
INI-RC	Mobil (Internorth)	10.50	44.88	112.00	-0.17	28.83	1.58	8.0	-5.7	-6.6	23.2	35.5	9.37	4.90	BB+	B+	8	0.95	25.90
******** Basic Industries (4.0%) ********																			
I-Metal Fabricating 19																			
INR-R	Insilco Corp 1/1/2010	9.00	18.75	110.25	21.36	13.13	1.10	1.4	-1.4	-3.2	14.2	23.3	8.16	5.33	BBB-	B+	8	1.00	32.38
******** Transportation (12.0%) ********																			
J-Trucking/Trans Lease 83																			
CAO-RA	Carolina Freight	6.25	18.63	70.00	78.47	17.68	1.03	9.4	1.8	-0.7	10.5	17.7	8.92	2.68	A-	A	6	1.20	37.23
PTRKG	Preston Corp	7.00	11.25	69.00	59.46	14.63	1.02	8.7	4.8	1.1	9.6	16.8	10.14	4.44	BBB-	B	8	0.85	27.52
TRUK	Builders Transport	8.00	14.50	77.00	29.57	9.67	1.34	8.1	2.9	-0.5	13.3	22.6	10.39	0.00	BBB-	NR	8	0.95	35.62
PORTFOLIO AVERAGES:					83.96	20.63	1.06	8.48	1.52	-1.08	11.69	19.56	9.40	3.56		0.49		1.16	34.13

These risk factors indicate the speculative nature of this group. Most of the securities are rated B and BB, indicating the vulnerability of their investment values.

In addition, the underlying common stock beta average of 1.38 and the standard risk of 46.35 percent (average risk would be 33.0 percent) indicate high risk. The risk/reward shows how the risk is reduced. On a total return basis, the aggressive portfolio is estimated to increase 37.71 percent over a 12-month period if the market advances. The downside risk estimate is –15.76 percent, showing a favorable risk/reward advantage.

Investors should be prepared to monitor the portfolio frequently to take advantage of the volatility these stocks demonstrate. The portfolio turnover is generally higher and the liquidity of many of these issues is sometimes very poor. The spread between the bid and ask is often two to three times higher than investment-grade issues. Still, these convertibles may offer investors an excellent way to reduce risk in a very volatile market sector.

CONVERTIBLES AS A BOND ALTERNATIVE

Convertibles are a flexible investment vehicle that can be used to meet various investment objectives. An alternative to the bond market, with some equity participation, would be to select convertibles based on their bond characteristics rather than their equity component. Convertibles can be selected with specific yields to maturity in mind. For example, figure 10.2 presents a portfolio that has good fixed income characteristics.

Screening convertibles for specific features again points to the versatility of the security. Investors seeking high current yield often ignore convertibles because their yields are somewhat lower than nonconvertible securities. However, by accepting a lower current yield, the investor gains the potential of an overall higher total return.

The sample portfolio in figure 10.2 reflects a cross section of convertible securities having current returns nearly the same as nonconvertible debt of similar quality, plus some equity participation. Convertibles trading on the basis of their fixed income attributes and having little equity participation are often referred to as *busted convertibles*. Convertibles in this category are a result of the common stock being well below the conversion price. Conversion premiums are

FIGURE 10.3   Convertible Debt Spread

December 31, 1987	Current Yield	Yield to Maturity
Non-convertible debt	9.60%	11.07%
Convertible portfolio	9.40%	9.60%
Convertible debt spreads	.20%	1.47%

high, sometimes over 100 percent. Since little equity participation is available at this level of stock price, the convertibles trade at or near their investment values. Theoretically, the convertible should always trade above its investment value because the stock may make a dramatic comeback, however remote this possibility may seem at the time. When searching for candidates in this category, the investor reviews the difference between the convertible and non-convertible debt yields of similar quality. This is referred to as the *convertible debt spread.*

The smaller the debt spread, the closer the yield resembles a non-convertible debt instrument. The other important factor is to determine how much equity participation remains in these busted convertibles. The investor judges the trade-off of accepting higher yields for less equity participation, and can then select those convertibles that have both the highest income and the best equity participation for that level of yield. When considering yield measurements, both current yield and yield to maturities should be evaluated.

The portfolio shown in figure 10.2 exhibits both favorable yield characteristics and some equity participation. The yield characteristics of that portfolio are summarized in figure 10.3. Notice that the current yield is 9.4 percent with a yield to maturity of 9.6 percent. The convertible debt spread is 20 basis points (one percent equals 100 basis points) for the current yield and 147 basis points on a yield-to-maturity basis as shown above. The non-convertible debt yields are derived by comparing the average quality rating to that of comparable straight bond yields.

Convertibles can provide an excellent alternative to the bond market. Their main advantage, when used as a bond surrogate, is that they provide an inflation hedge through equity participation. Even minimal equity participation can translate into an increased total return over time.

The extremely favorable convertible debt spread of 147 basis points is a result of the unsettling markets of the fourth quarter of 1987. These spreads have ranged over the years from as little as 125 basis points to as high as 400 basis points. Investors employing this strategy should monitor the spread on a periodic basis. As spreads widen, the portfolio becomes more vulnerable to a market correction.

SUMMARY

The convertible strategy to be employed by an investor depends on the investor's investment objective and risk tolerance. Portfolios can be designed to accommodate both the conservative and the more aggressive investor. The growth of the convertible market in recent years has allowed many different strategies to be employed. Because of this, the overall liquidity of the convertible market continues to improve.

11

Convertible Preferreds for Corporate Investors

Having a large amount of cash on hand may seem like a nice problem for a corporate treasurer to have, but where to place those corporate funds to obtain favorable returns has become an increasingly difficult question in volatile markets. In broad terms, a treasurer has only two alternatives available: the traditional cash management approach using money market instruments, or dividend capture programs, which entail more risk.

When short-term interest rates fell from the double-digit range in the early 1980s to the five percent to seven percent range in 1986–87, the treasurer's cash management problem became much more challenging. When interest rates were higher, the no-risk money market instruments were the obvious choice of many treasurers. The short-term money instruments provided lucrative returns with little risk and not much effort. However, as these rates declined, the after-tax yields in many cases were below an annualized rate of four percent. Variations on the preferred stocks to reduce risk are the adjustable-rate preferreds and the "Dutch-auction" preferreds. Those offer a bidding procedure that sets a new dividend rate every 49 days. The main benefit of these programs is that they provide money market rates and a dividend exclusion to increase the after-tax yield from four percent to 5.5 percent. Treasurers of many corporations are looking for ways to increase their returns without substantially increasing risk.

One such way is to invest in dividend paying stocks. The tax law allows corporations a 70 percent deduction in 1988 for dividends received by another corporation. This substantially increases the after-tax yield on stock portfolios held by the corporation. Since the law requires the stock to be held for a minimum of 45 days, fluctuating stock prices increase the risk. Once the treasurer has decided to increase risk to obtain higher returns, there are several alternatives available to take advantage of the dividend exclusion rule.

The purchase of straight preferred stocks or utility stocks with high dividend yields and relatively stable market prices is an obvious alternative. These choices are vulnerable to changing interest rates and are difficult to hedge.

CONVERTIBLE PREFERRED DIVIDEND CAPTURE PROGRAM

The explosive growth of the convertible securities market provides yet another solution. The main benefit of a convertible preferred portfolio is that it can provide much higher returns and can accommodate hedging strategies to reduce risk. Because convertible preferred portfolios may be used in a number of different ways, the analysis can become complex. However, once understood, the benefit of higher after-tax returns and controlled portfolio risk is well worth the effort.

Convertible preferred programs for corporations have not always been available to the degree that they are now. The convertible preferred market, like the convertible bond market, has expanded greatly over the last few years. Figure 11.1 illustrates the growth of the new issue market.

Convertible preferreds seem like an ideal candidate for the dividend capture strategy because this hybrid security has a hedge already built in. Convertible preferreds pay a fixed dividend, typically quarterly, like straight preferreds. Also, like straight preferreds, they vary in quality, depending on the issuing corporation, and are rated by Standard & Poor's and Moody's. Dividend rates of convertible preferreds are usually less than those of straight preferreds.

For accepting less current income, the convertible holder has the right to convert to the underlying common stock of the issuing corporation. The ability to convert dramatically changes the investment characteristics of this security. The fixed dividend and its status as a senior security give the convertible preferred the safety of a fixed-

FIGURE 11.1   Convertible Preferred Stock New Issues

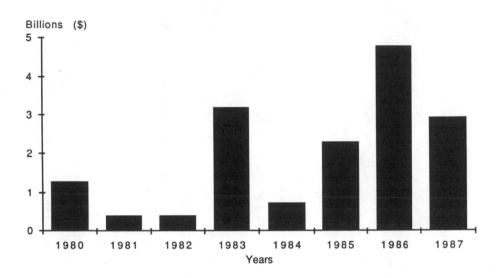

SOURCE: Drexel Burnham Lambert

income vehicle. On the other hand, because conversion to common stock is at the holder's option, any changes in stock price can be reflected in the market price of the convertible preferred, giving the opportunity for potential capital gains. The combination of dividend recapture and capital appreciation is the main reason to utilize a convertible preferred program.

EVALUATING CONVERTIBLE PREFERREDS

The evaluation process for convertible preferreds is the same as that for any convertible security. Chapter 8 reviewed in detail the worksheet analysis of a typical convertible security. Notice that it considers both the fundamentals of the company and the risk/reward analysis of the convertible security. It also includes the interest rate sensitivity and the important ex-dividend dates. The same thorough analysis that was

FIGURE 11.2 Calamos Asset Management Portfolio Analysis Summary Convertible Preferreds

SYMBOL	COMPANY NAME	CONV. CPN%	STOCK PRICE	CONV. PRICE	INVEST PREM.	CONV. PREM.	BLAR ADV	DUR FLR	LEVERAGE 12Mo.	LEVERAGE 6Mo.	W/INCOME 6Mo.	W/INCOME 12Mo.	CONV. YLD	STOCK YLD	S&P CONV.	S&P STOCK	CCES GR	BETA	STND RISK
B-Financial	43								*********	Financial (13.6%)	*********								
HIPRD	Household Intl.	6.25	42.38	94.00	15.34	60.92	0.98	9.90	-7.90	-7.50	14.00	22.50	6.64	4.71	A-	B+	6	1.05	28.14
B-Insurance (Property Casuality)	16																		
FGPRA	USF & G Corp.	4.10	32.50	46.75	32.33	22.00	0.99	10.80	-0.30	-2.40	11.50	19.50	8.77	7.63	A-	B	6	1.05	29.80
B-Insurance/ Diversified	36																		
CIPRC	Cigna Corp.	4.10	51.50	49.75	31.79	26.19	1.10	11.00	-0.60	-2.30	12.30	20.00	8.24	5.43	A	B	5	1.05	28.14
					*********	Consumer Staples (4.5%)	*********												
D-Food Processing	48																		
STAPR	Staley Cont.	3.50	19.38	41.00	48.04	34.71	1.03	10.60	-2.80	-4.00	13.30	21.70	8.53	4.12	BBB-	B-	8	1.10	36.42
E-Auto Parts -OEM	80				*********	Consumer Cyclical (13.6%)	*********												
SMCPRC	Smith AO 2.125	2.12	15.38	21.50	17.37	16.35	1.39	12.10	-2.60	-4.90	18.40	30.50	9.88	5.20	BB+	B-	8	1.25	41.39
E-Recreation	23																		
WCIPRA	Warner Communication	3.62	26.00	54.75	26.32	66.13	1.14	10.90	-12.10	-10.20	19.00	29.20	6.62	1.53	BBB	B-	7	1.10	41.39
E-Tire and Rubber	4																		
GRPRD	Goodrich B.F.	3.50	33.63	42.00	37.39	38.00	1.04	10.60	-2.00	-3.30	12.80	20.80	8.33	4.63	BB+	B-	8	1.05	29.80
F-Comp. & Peripherals	10				*********	Capital Gds-Techn (4.5%)	*********												
UISPRA	Burroughs Pref. (UNI)	3.75	32.88	59.75	8.75	75.26	1.11	10.80	-10.50	-9.20	16.20	25.50	6.27	2.79	BBB	B+	7	1.10	28.14
G-Machinery	25				*********	Capital Goods (9.1%)	*********												
CBHPRB	CBI Industries Pref.	3.50	20.13	39.75	34.27	21.52	1.15	11.20	0.00	-2.20	11.80	19.90	8.80	2.98	BBB+	B	6	0.80	31.45
CUMPR	Cummins Engine	3.50	48.13	42.75	36.86	40.46	1.07	10.60	-2.30	-3.30	13.50	21.60	8.18	4.57	BBB-	B-	8	0.95	29.80
					*********	Energy (13.6%)	*********												

SYMBOL	COMPANY NAME	CONV. CPN%	STOCK PRICE	CONV. PRICE	CONV. PREM.	INVEST PREM.	BLAR ADV	DUR FLR	LEVERAGE 12Mo.	LEVERAGE 6Mo.	W/INCOME 6Mo.	W/INCOME 12Mo.	CONV. YLD	STOCK YLD	S&P CONV. STOCK	S&P STOCK	CCES GR	BETA	STND RISK
H—Natural Gas (Utility)		89																	
ALGPRA	Arkla Pref. A	3.00	17.00	38.88	30.91	38.67	0.99	11.60	-4.80	-5.40	14.00	22.60	7.71	6.35	A-	A	6	0.95	34.76
H-Oilfield Services/Equipment		41																	
BHIPR	Baker Hughes	3.50	14.25	41.25	47.69	26.10	1.12	11.20	-2.60	-4.00	13.70	22.50	8.48	3.22	BBB+	NR	6	1.25	41.39
H-Petroleum Producing		54																	
GREB	Gulf Resources & Ch	1.30	10.88	17.00	25.00	79.15	1.09	12.00	-10.70	-9.30	17.70	27.60	7.64	0.00	B	B-	11	0.65	38.07
I-Chemical/Diversified		35																	
******** Basic Industries (22.7%) ********																			
IGLPRA	Int'l Minerals & Chem	3.75	34.00	52.00	25.56	59.46	1.02	10.40	-6.50	-6.40	13.80	22.00	7.21	2.94	BBB-	B	8	0.85	29.80
I-Copper		3																	
PDPRB	Phelps Dodge	3.00	39.00	54.63	9.26	133.08	1.24	10.10	-21.10	-16.40	25.50	38.20	5.49	0.00	BB-	B-	10	1.30	41.39
I-Metals & Mining-General		8																	
FTXPR	Freeport-McMoran	1.87	20.88	23.50	25.05	50.40	1.10	12.10	-8.10	-7.90	16.80	26.90	7.97	2.87	BB-	B	9	1.10	38.07
I-Paper & Forest Products		22																	
BCCC	Boise Cascade	3.50	61.25	51.75	23.34	62.64	1.35	10.90	-5.50	-4.70	18.90	27.80	6.76	3.10	BBB	B	7	1.20	29.80
PCHPRB	Potlatch Corp.	3.75	26.38	57.00	14.56	67.20	1.09	10.80	-9.90	-8.70	16.50	26.00	6.57	3.48	BBB	B	7	1.15	31.45
J-Trucking/Trans Lease		83																	
******** Transportation (4.5%) ********																			
XTRPRB	Stra Corp. Pref. B	1.93	23.50	21.00	23.59	24.67	1.27	12.40	-2.80	-4.50	15.80	26.00	9.22	2.72	BBB-	B-	8	1.05	38.07
L-Multiform		68																	
******** Conglomerates (4.5%) ********																			
ITTO	ITT Corp, Ser O	5.00	49.00	81.75	15.29	70.04	1.30	10.50	-12.80	-10.40	21.90	33.00	6.11	2.04	A	B	5	1.05	38.07
M-Cement		42																	
******** Other (9.1%) ********																			
MMRPRA	Moore McCormick Re	3.68	19.25	44.75	39.45	55.31	1.06	9.60	-5.70	-5.80	15.40	24.30	8.24	2.70	BB-	B	10	0.90	34.76
M-Maritime		53																	
SCRPRD	Sea Containers	4.12	17.00	40.50	47.51	34.50	1.15	8.80	-2.10	-3.90	15.20	24.90	10.18	0.29	B	B-	11	1.10	39.73
PORTFOLIO AVERAGES:					27.98	50.13	1.13	10.89	-6.11	-6.26	15.87	25.18	7.81	3.33		0.91		1.05	34.54

discussed earlier is applied to convertible preferreds. The worksheet again becomes the main tool in the decision-making process.

Convertible preferreds provide the corporate treasurer with the flexibility to choose among several variations of a convertible strategy. Which program the treasurer wishes to implement depends on the time horizon and the desired risk tolerance level. The longer the time horizon, the higher the probability that the strategy will achieve its investment objective. It should be emphasized from the onset that a convertible, or for that matter any straight preferred or common stock program, should not be viewed as a checking account. There are costs involved in setting up any program that need to be amoritized over time. There are also commission costs for executing trades and the important bid-ask spread of a marketable security. Even treasurers using adjustable rates have found that bid-ask spreads can be very significant and negate months of dividend income. Over short periods of time, day-to-day market fluctuations add an unknown additional cost factor. The longer the time period, the greater the likelihood that overall cost factors will be minimized.

Although a convertible preferred program has similar liquidity to other securities in the public financial markets, the treasurer should determine a minimum time horizon for these funds. If funds are needed for other corporate purposes in less than six months, then a preferred or stock program is not recommended. Assuming that the time horizon is sufficient for using convertible preferreds (a minimum of six months to a year is a good rule of thumb), then the risk/reward parameters of the strategy should be the next consideration. The risk/reward analysis, which considers the volatility of returns, is the tool most useful to the treasurer in selecting the proper program for the corporation.

BASIC CONVERTIBLE PREFERRED PROGRAM

The most straightforward investment strategy would be to establish a portfolio of convertible preferreds. This basic program offers the corporation a combination of tax advantage yield and capital gains. The dividend yield of convertible preferreds is typically less than that of straight preferreds. In the market environment of December 1987, the yield for straight preferreds was 9.02 percent, while the average yield for convertible preferreds was 7.8 percent. This difference of 122 basis points, or 1.22 percent, is less than it has been in many years. By accepting the lower current yield of a convertible preferred, the holder

---

**FIGURE 11.3   Lipper Convertible Preferred Index vs Money Market
Instruments**

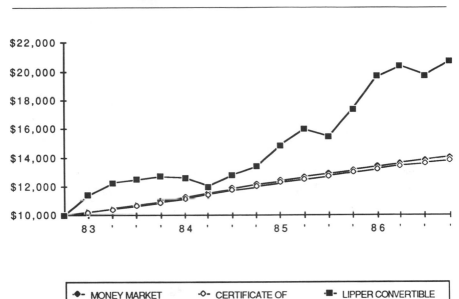

•- MONEY MARKET	-○- CERTIFICATE OF DEPOSIT	-■- LIPPER CONVERTIBLE PREFERRED INDEX

SOURCE: Lipper Convertible Analysis Report published by Lipper Analytical Services, Inc.

receives the opportunity for capital gains. This important aspect of a convertible preferred program can significantly increase the total return of the program.

Convertible preferreds have outperformed money market instruments and certificates of deposit by a wide margin. Figure 11.3 indicates the performance of the convertible preferred market on a total return basis. The Lipper Convertible Preferred Index, introduced in 1983, has been trading over a period of generally rising stock prices. This favorable stock market environment has created capital gains opportunities, which is an important aspect of the convertible preferred program. Some analysts associate rising stock prices with inflation. The same forces that make common stocks an inflation hedge over time also work to make convertible securities an inflation hedge.

The Lipper Convertible Preferred Index indicates how convertible preferreds performed, in general, without regard to any selection pro-

---

FIGURE 11.4   Convertible Preferreds and Taxes

For Calendar Year 1986
Lipper Convertible Index

Dividend Yield	8.0	
Capital Gains	11.0	
Total Return	+ 19.0	

	Column A* 1986	Column B** Under New Laws
Between Tax Return	19.00	19.00
Dividend	8.00	8.00
Tax	.55	.54
After Tax Yield	7.45	7.46
Capital Gains	11.00	11.00
Tax	3.54	3.74
After Tax Gain	7.46	7.26
After Tax Return	14.91	14.72

*Based on 46% corporate tax rate and 50% of capital gains long-term.

**Based on 34% corporate tax rate effective January 1, 1988.

---

cess. Using the techniques discussed in previous chapters, one would choose convertible preferreds that had superior risk/reward characteristics, which should improve performance and decrease volatility.

TAX IMPLICATIONS OF CONVERTIBLE PREFERRED PROGRAM

The Tax Simplification Act of 1986 changed the rules for corporate taxes. The 85 percent dividend exclusion is now 70 percent, and there is no longer a deduction for long-term capital gains. However, the highest marginal corporate tax rate has been reduced from 46 percent to 34 percent for 1988. Figure 11.4 indicates how a 19 percent total return will be affected by the tax law changes. Column B computes the total return of 19 percent using the rates under the new tax law. The changes have lessened the potential after-tax return slightly, but the advantages are still attractive to corporate investors.

FIGURE 11.5   Relative Market Performance
             March 31, 1987 through April 15, 1987

Lipper Convertible Preferreds	−1.1%
S&P 40 Utilities Index	−7.9%
S&P 500 Stock Index	−4.1%

Figure 11.4 indicates the after-tax return using 1986 as an example. The assumption is that the corporation is in the highest marginal tax bracket. The before-tax total return of 19 percent is made up of two components and is indicated in Column A. First, the dividend component of eight percent enjoys the 85 percent dividend exclusion. The after-tax return on income is 7.45 percent. During 1986, the corporation had the benefit of excluding 60 percent of long-term capital gains; therefore, the after-tax return on capital gains was 8.98 percent, a net after-tax return of 16.38 percent. Returns such as these are not unusual and are attainable with the proper use of convertible preferreds. The main point here is that the changes in the tax law have not affected the attractiveness of convertible preferreds.

Discussions of returns are not complete unless they address the issue of risk. The treasurer's most difficult task is to assess the corporation's tolerance for risk. Figure 11.3 compared convertible preferreds to the minimum-risk investments of money markets and certificates of deposit. The expected return increases with convertible preferreds, but so does the degree of risk. Figure 11.3 indicates the number of negative returns per quarter over this period of time. Quarters such as the third quarter of 1986, which saw the S&P 500 Stock Index drop nearly seven percent for the quarter, caused negative returns for convertible preferreds for the quarter.

In March and April of 1987, short-term interest rates rose and stock prices fell due to the U.S.-Japan trade restriction and the falling value of the dollar. Figure 11.5 indicates how these events affected the various asset classes during that period. Note that convertible preferreds sustained only minor losses compared to straight preferreds, utility company stocks or blue-chip stocks. This indicates that convertible preferreds in advancing stock markets are not as directly affected by rising interest rates.

A company's tolerance for risk should be based on the treasurer's assessment of interest rate risk, inflation risk and stock market risk. Once interest rate risk and inflation are considered, a convertible preferred program may well be less risky than a straight preferred program. The importance of the time horizon becomes apparent when reviewing the charts in this chapter. The longer the time horizon, the higher the probability that the return objective can be met without having to close out the program in unfavorable market conditions. In addition, the volatility of returns can be controlled by hedging techniques. These techniques may allow the treasurer to further reduce the inherent portfolio risk of fluctuating market prices.

HEDGING CONVERTIBLE PREFERREDS

The flexibility of convertible preferreds is that they can be used with two hedging techniques: a covered call writing program and/or the purchase of index put options. These techniques do not eliminate risk, but they can substantially reduce risk. With any risk reduction technique, there is a trade-off. With convertible preferreds, returns are reduced during the up quarters, but protection is increased in the down quarters. The net effect should be an overall reduction in the quarter-to-quarter fluctuations. That means less volatility and hence less risk.

COVERED CALL WRITING WITH CONVERTIBLE PREFERREDS

Hedging convertible preferreds is similar to hedging convertible bonds, which will be discussed in chapter 12. The main difference is that care must be exercised not to jeopardize the tax advantage of the preferred dividend. The tax law has made this distinction to assure that a position is at risk and is not merely a maneuver to capture dividends at no risk. The same tax law also states that the use of the convertible stock hedge (shorting stock against a convertible preferred) eliminates the tax deduction status, thereby effectively preventing the use of the technique. When options are sold against the convertible preferred, they are either qualified or unqualified. A qualified option is one that does not jeopardize the tax deductibility of the preferred dividend, while an unqualified option is one that does. A thorough knowledge of the tax rules is helpful in managing a convertible preferred program. Following is a brief discussion of those rules.

TAX HOLDING PERIOD REQUIREMENTS

1. The convertible preferred stock must be held for at least 46 days.
2. If the preferred stock is cumulative, with an arrearage of more than a year in dividends, the stock must be held for at least 91 days.
3. The deduction is not allowable if a short sale of common stock (substantially identical security) is made against a convertible preferred.
4. The holding period is reduced for any period during which the taxpayer's risk of loss with respect to the stock is diminished because the taxpayer has:

    A. An option to sell, is under an obligation to sell, or has made (and not closed) a short sale of substantially identical stock or securities;

    B. granted an option to purchase substantially identical stock or securities; or

    C. reduced the risk by virtue of holding one or more other positions with respect to substantially similar or related property.[1]

The writing of *qualified covered call options* against convertible preferreds does not reduce the holding period and is not considered substantially identical securities.

A covered call option is qualified if:

- The option is a listed option trading on national exchanges.
- The option has more than 30 days until expiration.
- The option is not deep-in-the-money.
- The option is not granted by an options dealer in connection with his activity of dealing in options.
- Gain or loss with respect to the option is not ordinary income or loss.

The thrust of the rules is to prevent a no-risk hedge position being established to capture the tax-favored dividends. That is why short sales and deep-in-the-money options are prohibited. The tax rules define a deep-in-the-money option as an option with a strike price that is lower than the lowest qualified benchmark.

---

[1]Commerce Clearing House, Inc., *Federal Tax Guide Reports,* 1987, pp. 1165–3.

The *Commerce Clearing House Tax Guide* explains qualified benchmark in the following manner:

> Generally, the lowest qualified benchmark is the highest available strike (exercise) price that is less than the "applicable stock price" (the closing price of the optioned stock on the most recent day on which it was traded before the option was granted or, if more than 110 percent greater than the most-recent-day price, the opening price on the date of grant). However, there are exceptions to the general definition of the lowest qualified benchmark. (The lower the strike price is in relation to the market value of the underlying stock, the more likely it is that the market value of the call will parallel that of the stock.)
>
> (1) If an option is granted more than 90 days before it expires and if the strike price is more than $50, the lowest qualified benchmark is the second highest strike price that is less than the applicable stock price.
>
> (2) If the applicable stock price is $25 or less and if, but for this exception, the lowest qualified benchmark would be less than 85 percent of the applicable stock price, the lowest qualified benchmark is equal to 85 percent of the applicable stock price.
>
> (3) If the applicable stock price is $150 or less and if, but for this exception, the lowest qualified benchmark would be less than the applicable stock price reduced by $10, the lowest qualified benchmark is equal to the applicable stock price reduced by $10.

For purposes of the loss deferral rule, a covered call option is not treated as qualified if gain from the disposition of stock to be purchased under the option is included in gross income in a taxable year after the taxable year in which the option is closed and if the stock is not held for more than 30 days following the date on which the option is closed. The covered call exception also does not apply in the case of stock that is disposed of at a loss in one year, but the gain on the option is not includible in gross income until the following year and the option is not held for at least 30 days after the related stock is disposed of at a loss (.25). In determining whether this holding period requirement is satisfied, rules similar to those applicable in determining whether a taxpayer is eligible for the dividend received deduction under Code Sec. 246(c)(3) and (4) will apply (without regard to the exception to those rules for a qualified covered call option).

Effective for positions established after June 30, 1984, in taxable years ending after that date, any loss realized from a qualified covered call option granted by the taxpayer, which has a strike price that is less than the applicable stock price, will be treated as a long-term capital loss if gain from the sale of the stock when the loss is realized would be long-term capital gain. Also, the holding period for stock subject to the option will not include any period during which the taxpayer is the grantor of the option.[2]

As a general guide, in-the-money options of more than 12 percent should be avoided because of the possibility of losing the deduction.

The use of margin (debt financing) reduces the amount of the deduction received for dividends to the extent of the interest paid to purchase the stock.

Tax rules change frequently and are interpreted differently by professionals. When utilizing a convertible preferred program, it is advisable to seek tax counsel to assure that the deductions are secure and meet all requirements.

HEDGING CONVERTIBLE PREFERRED PORTFOLIOS

A convertible preferred portfolio can be hedged in two ways. The first is to hedge an individual position. Typically, this is accomplished by selling a covered call on a listed option against the long convertible preferred. Because of variables such as option premium levels, conversion premium on the convertible and market conditions, not every position in the portfolio should be hedged. Hedged positions would be entered into only when the risk/reward relationships are favorable. The technique is discussed in detail in chapter 12.

HEDGING WITH INDEX PUT OPTIONS

The second aspect of convertible hedging is the use of index put options. This allows for the control of market risk.

Since not all attractive convertible preferreds have options or are attractive option-writing candidates, investors can use index put op-

---

[2]Ibid., p. 2101.

FIGURE 11.6   Convertible Preferred Index—Unhedged vs. Hedged

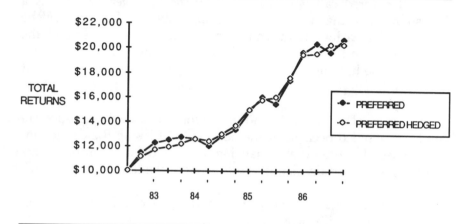

SOURCE: Lipper Analytical Services, Inc.: Convertible Preferred Market Index and research by Calamos Asset Management, Inc.

tions to further reduce portfolio risk. Index options are becoming increasingly popular as a means to provide portfolio insurance against
declining markets. Index puts are options that are tied to broad-based
indexes like the S&P 500 or Value Line and to narrow-based indexes
that are tied to specific industry groups. Again, the specific hedging
strategy is covered in detail in chapter 13.

The principle behind using index puts for insurance purposes is
that as the index declines in value, the put gains in value. Like all options, there are specified strike prices and time periods. Index puts are
purchased at premiums that can vary in response to market sentiment.
This can make it difficult to estimate the cost of this insurance. The
valuation of premium levels is an important consideration for the convertible strategist utilizing index puts. The advantage to using index
options rather than index futures is that the cost is fixed and upside potential is not limited for other than the premium cost. With options,
once the index rises above the strike price, the option may become
worthless. With futures, as the index increases, the future contract that
was sold increases in value and becomes an extremely costly item.

The use of index puts is a cost-effective means to protect portfolio
value and is most useful when there is a high correlation between the
index and the portfolio. Figure 11.6 illustrates how index put strategies

---

FIGURE 11.7   Convertible Preferred Quarterly Returns

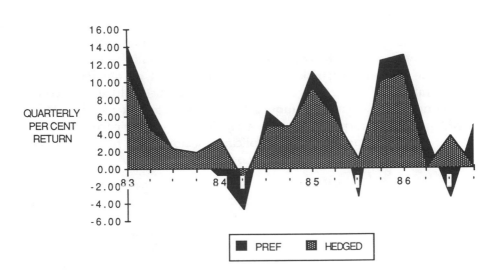

SOURCE: Lipper Analytical Services, Inc.: Convertible Preferred Market Index and research by Calamos Asset Management, Inc.

---

can reduce volatility. During the up phases the puts expired worthless, reducing the return by the cost of the put premium. During down phases the puts gained in value, offsetting the decline in the portfolio asset value. Figure 11.7 illustrates how this strategy affects quarter-to-quarter fluctuations. Notice the negative quarters of the unhedged index and how the hedging has reduced the return in the up quarters, increasing the returns in the down quarters. During this period all but one of the negative quarters would have been eliminated by the hedging technique.

Although the returns from a combination of writing call options and buying index puts have not been illustrated, this combination gives the treasurer the maximum flexibility in controlling risk. The strategy is complicated to execute and should be managed by either a specialist in convertible hedging or a treasurer well versed in the intricacies of that market. Convertible hedging can affect the holding period and the dividend exclusion rule, so tax consequences of each position need to be thoroughly reviewed.

SUMMARY

The flexibility of convertible preferreds in a corporate cash management program gives the corporate treasurer the ability to increase returns while adjusting risk to the tolerance level of the individual corporation. Whether convertible preferreds are used alone or in conjunction with hedging techniques to increase after-tax returns, their contribution to corporate cash as a profit center of the corporation is assured. This important but complicated sector of the financial markets will continue to attract more corporate treasurers.

12
Convertible Hedging

The purpose of hedging is to reduce and control risk. A perfect hedge is one which has eliminated any future profit or loss. In convertible hedging the objective is not to achieve perfection, but to control risk while retaining acceptable profit opportunities. In a sense, convertible securities without hedging provide a hedge against the volatility of the underlying common stock. As it has been demonstrated, convertible securities can be evaluated to ascertain their particular risk/reward parameters. Convertible hedging combines the use of other instruments and adjusts the risk/reward relationship to a different profit profile. That profit profile can be predetermined and designed by the investor. Therefore, convertible hedging allows investors additional flexibility to control risk.

There are a number of hedging techniques to be applied with convertibles. Each technique has its exclusive advantages and disadvantages. In this chapter we will cover the convertible stock hedge and convertible option hedging.

CONVERTIBLE STOCK HEDGE

The convertible stock hedge is a well-known technique applied largely by convertible arbitragers, convertible market makers and convertible hedge funds. Due to its complexity, it is used to a lesser degree by individual investors. The convertible stock hedge is accomplished by selling the underlying stock short against the convertible security. To determine how investors may be able to use this technique, we will consider each of its ingredients.

The Long Position: Convertible Security

The convertible security for this hedge can be any convertible security, convertible bond, convertible preferred stock or warrant. Not all convertibles can be used favorably with this technique. The most likely candidates have the following attributes:

- *Low conversion premium.* The amount of convertible conversion premium is an important consideration. As the underlying common stock increases in value, the conversion premium is gradually reduced. In a convertible stock hedge, the convertible bond is increasing in value as the stock increases, but the short sale of stock is offsetting these gains. Therefore, the best candidates are convertibles with low conversion premiums.

- *Positive yield advantage.* The convertible should enjoy a yield advantage over its underlying common stock. The short sale of stock requires that the seller is responsible for paying the dividend.

- *Low premium over investment value.* The convertible should be trading close to its investment value for the convertible price to be cushioned when the stock declines in value.

- *Avoid overvalued convertibles.* Since they tend to trade on a fair value price track, convertibles should be avoided if they are overvalued as determined by the convertible pricing model. Overvalued convertibles may decrease to their normal valuation without any change in the underlying stock price.

The above attributes are similar to the ones that should be used in the selection process for convertibles, as described in early chapters. The convertibles that are most suitable for hedging are often the same as those that possess the most favorable unhedged characteristics.

Short Position: Underlying Common Stock

Each convertible converts into a specific number of shares of common stock. The convertible stock hedge is set up by selling the underlying stock short against the convertible security. The Securities and Exchange Commission's rule on short sale states that they can be executed only in a rising market. Therefore, the following conditions need to be met to execute a short sale on stock exchanges.

- *Uptick or plus tick rule.* The last sale of the stock must be at a higher price than the preceding sale.

- *Zero plus tick rule.* The last sale is unchanged, but higher than the preceding different sale.

- *Short exempt.* Short sales can be made without meeting the above rules if the short sale is made with the anticipation of covering the sale by the conversion of the convertible within a short period of time. This is used frequently when closing out a convertible position by selling the stock first and then converting the bond. This allows the investor to be assured of a stock price without falling victim to administrative delays in the conversion process of the convertible.

Before a short sale of stock can be transacted, the broker must borrow the shares from another investor in order to deliver and complete the sale of securities. The administration is handled in brokerage firms by the stock loan department, whose function is to find the stock, usually from other margin customers or from institutions, to accommodate the trading activity. Even large firms have active stock loan operations to facilitate short sale trading activity. Once the stock has been borrowed it can remain outstanding indefinitely. However, the institution that has loaned the stock can recall it at any time. Occasionally, this may result in a *buy-in* to cover the short sale. The broker pays the institutions, based on a percentage of market value, for the stocks they have loaned.

The short sale can only be done in a margin account; therefore, to use the convertible stock hedge technique, a margin account must be employed. Margin accounts are governed by Regulation T of the Federal Reserve Board. Under those rules, a short sale of a convertible against a convertible bond does not require any additional margin. The short sale is considered a *covered short sale*.

A confusing concept to many investors is *mark-to-market*. When the short sale is made, the proceeds of the sale must be segregated by the broker into a subaccount: the short account. That subaccount must always contain the exact amount of funds necessary to buy back the short sale. As the stock changes in price, funds are transferred within the margin account, from one subaccount to another, to maintain the proper balance. If the stock has increased in value, money is transferred from the general account to the short account to bring the account in balance. If the stock has moved down in price, funds are transferred from the short account to the general account. These transfers are made for stock price moves of as little as an eighth of a point. The short account credit balance is a frozen credit that the investor cannot use even to offset debits in other subaccounts. As with all credit balances in the account, the broker does receive the use of the funds. From the investor's point of view, the net effect of this movement of funds back and forth between subaccounts is zero, but it must be done to conform to margin rules.

Convertible Stock Hedge Profit Profiles

Thus far we have discussed the mechanics of a convertible stock hedge. We will now cover in more detail how it can be applied under various conditions. Figure 12.1 is an abbreviated version of the now familiar convertible worksheet analysis. The convertible stock hedge adjusts the risk/reward of the convertible, so the beginning point is to *determine* the risk/reward and the price track of the convertible security. Other factors discussed at length in previous chapters and detailed in the convertible evaluation worksheet should be considered. For illustrative purposes here, we will ignore those fundamental segments and concentrate on the hedge profile. We will also assume, for the example, that the most probable price range is an arbitrary plus or minus 50-percent move. When applying this to actual examples the most accurate price distribution should be used, as discussed in previous chapters.

The convertible in figure 12.1 has a favorable risk/reward relationship to the underlying common stock. On a total return basis, assuming a one-year holding period, the convertible enjoys 70 percent of the upside potential of the common stock for only 27 percent of its downside loss. Each convertible can be exchanged for 16.44 shares of common stock. Three profit profiles will be reviewed to show the flexibility of this technique.

Bullish Hedge

An initial position of 100 convertible bonds are purchased at 112 for an investment of $112,000, with the simultaneous short sale of 300

FIGURE 12.1 Convertible Stock Hedge Example

XYZ Company 7.75 – 03/01/1996

Common Stock Market Price	=	$59.25
Convertible Market Price	=	112.00%
Conversion Ratio	=	16.44 shares

Investment:

Long Position: 100 bonds at $1,120.00 = $112,000
(remains same for each hedge)

Short Position:

BULLISH HEDGE	300 shares at	$59.25 = $17,750
NEUTRAL HEDGE	900 shares at	$59.25 = $53,325
BEARISH HEDGE	1,500 shares at	$59.25 = $88,875

	–50%	*–25%*	*0*	*+25%*	*+50%*
Assumed Stock Price	29.63	44.44	59.25	74.06	88.88
Estimated Convertible Price	90.43	99.65	112.00	127.48	146.08
BULLISH HEDGE:					
Profit/Loss on Conv.	(21571)	(12350)	0	15477	34082
Profit/Loss on Stock	8886	4443	0	(4443)	(8886)
Bond Interest	7750	7750	7750	7750	7750
Stock Dividends Paid	0	0	0	0	0
Total Profit or Loss	(4935)	(157)	7750	18784	32946
Return on Investment %	(4)	0	+7	+17	+29
NEUTRAL HEDGE:					
Profit/Loss on Conv.	(21571)	(12350)	0	15477	34082
Profit/Loss on Stock	26663	13331	0	(13331)	(26663)
Bond Interest	7750	7750	7750	7750	7750
Stock Dividends Paid	0	0	0	0	0
Total Profit or Loss	12842	8731	7750	9896	15169
Return on Investment %	+11	+8	+7	+9	+14
BEARISH HEDGE:					
Profit/Loss on Conv.	(21571)	(12350)	0	15477	34082
Profit/Loss on Stock	44438	22219	0	(22219)	(44438)
Bond Interest	7750	7750	7750	7750	7750
Stock Dividends Paid	0	0	0	0	0
Total Profit or Loss	30617	17619	7750	1008	(2606)
Return on Investment %	+27	+16	+7	+0	(2)

shares of common stock at a price of $59.25 per share. Figure 12.1 indicates the profit and loss of the position. Notice that if the stock were to advance dramatically over a 12-month period, the convertible would increase in value for a gain of $34,082. That is determined by the then stock price of $88 7/8. Since a short sale was made at $59 1/4, a loss of

FIGURE 12.2   Convertible Stock Hedge Profiles

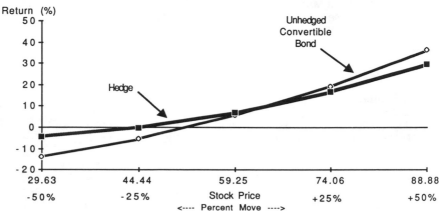

Bullish Stock Hedge Return Profile

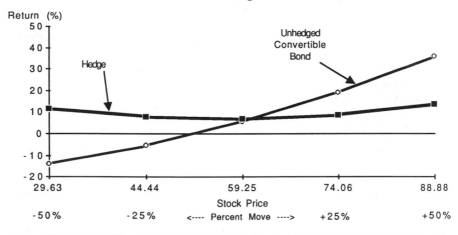

Neutral Stock Hedge Return Profile

$8,886 has also been registered. In addition, interest has been earned on the convertible, and any stock dividends must be paid for to arrive at the total profit of $32,946 on the hedge position. It is estimated that a 29 percent return on investment would be realized in this situation.

A bullish hedge is set up to prevent losses if the stock were to decline in value instead of increasing as the investor had hoped. With the

---

FIGURE 12.2   Convertible Stock Hedge Profiles (Continued)

Bearish Stock Hedge Return Profile

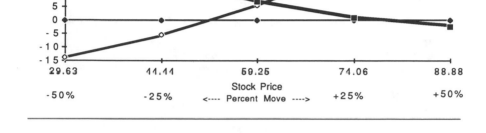

---

stock showing a sizable loss of 50 percent, the benefit of stock hedging becomes evident. The convertible decreases in value as the stock declines, but at a much lesser rate. As shown in the profit and loss estimate, the convertible realizes a $21,571 loss because of the decline in the value of the stock. The short sale of stock now realizes a profit of $8,886, offsetting a large portion of the convertible's loss. The interest on the convertible provides the balance, for a total loss of only $4,935. A negligible loss, considering the dramatic decline of the stock.

A bullish hedge trades the upside potential of the stock for increased downside safety. Figure 12.2 graphically illustrates the profit profile of the convertible stock hedge. Notice how the hedge alters the convertible bond profit profile, providing less upside potential for greater downside safety. The profit profile can be further modified by simply varying the number of shares sold short.

Neutral Hedge

Figure 12.2 also presents the profit profile for a neutral hedge. The amount of stock sold short has been increased to 900 shares. This provides a suitable return over a wide range of stock prices and is not dependent on the stock either increasing or decreasing. The neutral hedge

---

FIGURE 12.3   Convertible Stock Hedge: Leverage

XYZ 7.75–03/01/1996

Investment
  Long Position:
  Cash Investment $112,000
  50% Margin   56,000
  Initial Investment $ 56,000

  Short Position:
  Short Sale   300 shares at $59.25 = $17,750 credit
  Margin Requirement   -0-

Percent Change	–50%	–25%	0	+25%	+50%
Assumed Stock Price	29.63	44.44	59.25	74.06	88.88
Est. Conv. Price	90.43	99.65	112.00	127.48	146.08
Total Return	–11.5%	–3.3%	6.9%	21.6%	38.2%

BULLISH HEDGE:

Risk/Reward Analysis					
Profit/Loss on Conv.	(21571)	(12350)	0	15477	34082
Profit/Loss on Stock	8886	4443	0	(4443)	(8886)
Bond Interest	7750	7750	7750	7750	7750
Stock Dividends Paid	0	0	0	0	0
Margin Interest	(2950)	(3490)	(3920)	(4460)	(5400)
Total Profit or Loss	(7885)	(3647)	3830	14324	277546
Return on Investment	–14%	–7%	7%	26%	49%

---

is most effective when the interest yield on the convertible is attractive and protection is sought against fluctuating stock prices.

Bearish Hedge

For an investor who is bearish, the convertible stock hedge with a bearish bias can be a low-risk means to participate in declining stock prices. By increasing the short sale to nearly the full amount of 1,500 shares, a bearish position is accomplished, as shown in figure 12.1. If the investor is correct and the stock declines by 50 percent, a 30 percent profit should be realized. The profit results from the short sale of stock more than offsetting the loss on the convertible. A small upside loss would occur if the investor were incorrect and the stock rose dramatically instead of falling in price. The profile is shown graphically in figure 12.2

FIGURE 12.4   Convertible Stock Hedge: Leverage Profit Profile

---

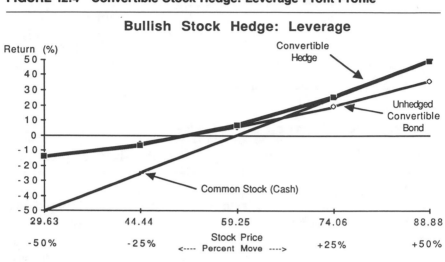

Convertible Stock Hedge: Leveraged

Like any investment technique, how convertible hedging is used is more important than broad generalizations about its risks and rewards. Even the use of leverage can be relatively safe if done intelligently. Figure 12.3 shows the same position used earlier, but with 50 percent leverage. The initial margin requirement for convertibles usually follows that of stocks, and here it is assumed to be 50 percent. The initial investment becomes $56,000, with the remainder borrowed from the broker, upon which interest is charged. The interest charge will vary depending on the debit balance in the account. The debit balance is affected by the mark-to-market requirement on the short position, as discussed earlier. Notice how interest costs vary due to the mark-to-market requirement. The debit balance is automatically reduced in a declining market while it increases in a rising market. The worksheet takes this into account to arrive at the proper estimate of profit and loss of the hedge position.

Even with a leveraged position, downside risk is effectively controlled by varying the short position. It's interesting that a leveraged position using the convertible stock hedge technique, on a risk/reward basis, has assumed less risk than owning the stock outright on a cash basis. The cash basis investor would receive a 50 percent increase for a

50 percent move in the stock, whereas the convertible hedger would receive 49 percent. If the stock decreases 50 percent, the cash basis investor would obviously lose 50 percent. On the other hand, the convertible position would show a loss of only 14 percent. This is shown graphically in Figure 12.4. Notice how the profit profile of the leveraged position overlaid on the cash basis stock position shows nearly the same upside potential and less downside risk.

Pitfalls of the Convertible Stock Hedge

The convertible stock hedge offers flexibility in designing a profit profile to match the investor's particular objective. We have concentrated thus far on the rewards of convertible hedging. Unfortunately, there are also pitfalls. The convertible stock hedge profit profile is based on a number of assumptions that must be evaluated. Some of the same assumptions about convertibles that were discussed previously, namely changing interest rates, changing fundamentals of the company and other factors, all affect the price estimate of the convertible price track. In some respects, they need to be considered even more carefully with convertible hedging.

For example, if a convertible stock hedge were set up with the convertible having a reasonable conversion premium of 15 percent, and a takeover attempt on the stock ensued, the convertible hedge could show an immediate loss of the conversion premium (15 percent). This can occur because often the only way the convertible holder can participate in the takeover is to convert to the underlying common stock. The worst case for the holder of an unhedged convertible would probably be an *opportunity* loss, whereas the convertible hedge holder could have two *real* losses on both sides of the hedge.

Because of its conservative nature, leverage can be applied to the convertible stock hedge to allow the investor to become more speculative. In fact, some hedge funds apply 90 percent leverage using this technique.[1] The problem with this much leverage is that a slight miscalculation can result in significant losses. Hedge funds using very high margins with this technique saw their equity reduced substantially as volatility increased and bid and ask spreads widened as a consequence of the stock market crash of 1987.

---

[1]Regulation T, NASD Rules of Fair Practice Section 30, Appendix A, Section 4(8)(b)

Other risks include the forced buy-in of a short position and clos-ing out the convertible hedge at a time dictated by the buy-in rather than when the investor desires. There are also costs to set up and close the hedge. The costs involve not only commissions for executing the trades, but the spread between the bid and ask prices. The spreads be-tween securities vary greatly from issue to issue and are one of the un-certainties with which the investor must cope. When using leverage, these costs are amortized over a small initial investment and become an even larger factor.

Convertibles may seem very liquid at one price level and extremely illiquid at lower prices. This is especially true of below investment-grade issues of small companies. If the decreasing stock price is due to changing fundamentals of the company, the estimate of the convertible price track probably will not hold, causing a greater loss on the con-vertible than anticipated. Although the convertible will not decrease at a greater rate than the common stock, it is disconcerting to find the convertible stock hedge with a bearish profile to be trading dollars on the downside.

Investors must view the convertible stock hedge as an intermediate to long-term investment. It would be very unusual to realize large losses in a convertible stock hedge portfolio, even if actual portfolios varied from the estimates. Time is needed to amortize the costs of set-ting up the position and the spread of the securities. An important as-pect of the total return is the convertible's yield component and, obviously, time needs to pass to earn that interest. Although complex, a convertible stock hedge is an effective technique to achieve above-average returns while controlling risk.

CONVERTIBLE STOCK OPTION HEDGING

Not every convertible security can be set up as a convertible stock hedge, so the convertible hedger seeks additional ways in which to control risk. Where the underlying common stock has listed stock op-tions available, additional hedging techniques are available. It is as-sumed that the reader is familiar with the basic principles and the risks and rewards of stock options.[2] The goal is not to detail option hedging,

---

[2]For a basic understanding of listed stock options, consult the risk disclosure booklet titled *Characteristics and Risks of Standardized Options.* It is available from Options Clearing Cor-poration, the options exchanges or any broker dealing in listed stock options. An excellent

but to show how stock options, combined with convertibles, can give an investor another means to control risk.

A call option gives the holder the right to buy the underlying stock at a specified price, called the *exercise price*, for a specified period of time, the *expiration date*. Each contract is standardized at one hundred shares of stock, and the cost of the contract is called the *option premium*.

Call options may be sold or *written* against stocks called *covered* call writing. The option writer receives the option premium and is obligated, if and when assigned an exercise to deliver stock according to the terms of the contract. Only the option buyer can exercise an option.

Convertible Call Option Hedge

Many of the companies that issue convertibles have stock options listed on the option exchanges. Unfortunately, not every convertible can be used effectively with options. How they are used is largely determined by a worksheet analysis that shows both the potential profit and the potential loss of the position. There are not any simple rules of thumb to make this process less time consuming.

The Mechanics

Each convertible bond converts to a specified number of shares of the underlying common stock. As long as the number of call options sold, or written, against the underlying stock represented by the convertible is no greater than the amount of shares into which the convertible can be converted, the options are considered covered. A covered option against a convertible requires no margin and can be accomplished in the cash account of the investor's brokerage account. The option premium is immediately available to the investor and can be used to reduce the initial cost of a convertible option position.

If the option is exercised, the convertible holder can either convert the convertible to stock and deliver against the exercise, or buy the stock on the exercise day to cover the sale. The decision is based on which choice offers the best economic advantage. Most often the investor would buy the stock and sell the convertible security to cover the exercise. The convertible may have accrued interest, as well as

source for detailed information on advanced option strategies is *Option Pricing and Strategies in Investing* by Richard M. Bookstaber.

FIGURE 12.5   Convertible Call Option Hedge

XYZ – 7.75% of 03/01/1996

Common Stock Market Price	=	$59.25
Convertible Market Price	=	112.00%
Call Option Premium	=	$5.25
Conversion Ratio	=	16.44 shares
Expiration Date	=	7.20 months

Covered Hedge:

100 at	$1,120.00	=	$112,000
16 calls sold at	$500.25	=	8,400
Initial Investment		=	$103,600

Specified Hedge:

100 at	$1,120.00	=	$112,000
10 calls sold at	$525.00	=	5,250
Initial Investment		=	$106,750

	-50%	-25%	0	Exercise Price	+25%	+50%
Assumed Stock Price	29.63	44.44	59.25	65.00	74.06	88.88
Estimated Conv. Price	90.43	99.65	112.00	117.00	127.48	146.08
COVERED HEDGE:						
Profit/Loss on Conv.	(21570)	(12350)	0	5636	15477	34082
Profit/Loss on Call	8400	8400	8400	8400	(6100)	(29800)
Bond Interest	4650	4650	4650	4650	4650	4650
Total Profit or Loss	(8520)	(700)	13050	18686	14027	8932
Return on Investment %	(8)	(1)	13	18	14	9
Annual ROI (.60 years) %	(14)	(1)	21	30	23	14
SPECIFIED HEDGE:						
Profit/Loss on Conv.	(21571)	(12350)	0	5636	15477	34082
Profit/Loss on Call	5250	5250	5250	5250	(3813)	(18625)
Bond Interest	4650	4650	4650	4650	4650	4650
Total Profit or Loss	(11671)	(2450)	9900	15536	16314	20107
Return on Investment %	(11)	(2)	9	15	15	19
Annual ROI (.60 years) %	(18)	(4)	15	24	25	31

---

some conversion premium. Both factors should be considered before converting to deliver for an exercise.

Convertible Option Hedge: Risk/Reward

To determine whether a convertible option hedge has a suitable profit potential, use the convertible option worksheet. Figure 12.5 shows an abbreviated worksheet similar to that shown with convertible stock hedging. Again, the more detailed analysis of the basic convertible is not discussed here but should not be ignored. For illustrative purposes we will cover only the hedging position and assume that the detailed analysis of the convertible has already been accomplished.

The initial investment for the now infamous XYZ convertible bond is $103,600. This represents the purchase of the bonds for $112,000 and the option premium received of $8,400. The 100 bonds represent 1,640 shares of common stock, so 16 call option contracts (each contract equals 100 shares) were sold on a covered basis.

The price range of the common stock must be estimated to determine the profit/loss on the position. Also, the exercise price of the option and the price of the options at various levels are important factors. Figure 12.5 illustrates how the option price would change at different stock prices. The profit/loss estimate of the position is calculated on the expiration date of the option. At that time, the option contract must be closed, so that becomes an important time period in which to calculate the profit/loss estimates. The option price is a straightforward calculation. The option will be at its intrinsic value on expiration date. If the stock price is *below* the exercise price, the option will be worthless. If the stock price is *above* the exercise price, then the option will be worth the stock price minus the exercise price. With this and previously discussed convertible factors in mind, the profit/loss estimates are completed. The return on investment (ROI) is calculated to the exercise date and then annualized. Both the ROI and the annualized ROI are important to determine if this is a suitable hedge position.

Annualized ROI for option positions allows comparison between various option positions. Since options expire at different times throughout the year, the annualized ROI will give an indication as to which position provides the better opportunity. On the other hand, the annualized number assumes that option premium levels remain the same and that the investor will be able to sell the option at the same premium level again and again. This is frequently not the case. Therefore, both ROIs become important in assessing the profit opportunity.

Notice the profit potential of the position over the wide range of stock prices. If the stock remains near its current level, the profit potential is excellent. The returns shown in this example are not unusual. Also notice how the profit is reduced if the stock increases dramatically to 88⅞. This happens because the conversion premium of the convertible decreases as the stock increases. Any conversion premium must erode as the stock increases in value. This factor is important in

---

FIGURE 12.6   Convertible Option Hedge Profit Profiles

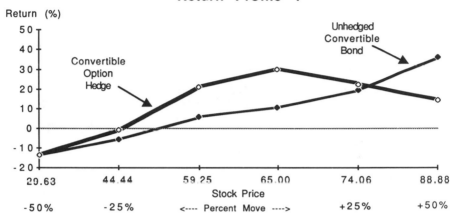

Convertible Covered Call Write
Return Profile 1

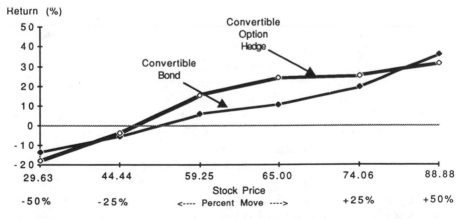

Convertible Partial Call Write
Return Profile 2

---

determining the number of calls to sell against a convertible security. If the convertible security has a high conversion premium, selling covered calls could result in an upside loss. This is another reason the convertible option worksheet is a necessity.

FIGURE 12.7   Common Stock Covered Call Option Hedge

XYZ – Common Stock
COVERED HEDGE: 1600 @ 1120 = $94,800
   16 calls sold @ 500.25 = $ 8,400

	–50%	–25%	0	Exercise Price	+ 25%	+ 50%
Assumed Stock Price	29.63	44.44	59.25	65.00	74.06	88.88
Profit/Loss on Stock	(47400)	(23700)	0	9200	23700	47400
Profit/Loss on Call	8400	8400	8400	8400	(6100)	(29800)
Dividend Income.	0	0	0	0	0	0
Total Profit or Loss	(39000)	(15300)	8400	17600	17600	17600
Return on Investment	(45.1)	(17.7)	9.7	20.4	20.4	20.4
Annual ROI (60 years)%	(75.1)	(29.5)	16.2	34.0	34.0	34.0

NOTE: Initial Investment: $94,800 less $8,400 = $86,400

In the example shown, the return is stabilized at a stock price of
88⅞. The option hedge would show similar returns no matter how
much the stock increased above 88⅞. This is also shown in the profit
profile graph in figure 12.6. Notice how the profit is the maximum at
the exercise price then gradually decreases as the stock varies from that
point. The option premium income, the interest earned on the convertible and the fact that the convertible declines at a lesser rate than that
of the common stock provide a good measure of downside safety. For a
dramatic decline in the common stock of 50 percent, the convertible
option hedge covered basis shows an annualized loss of only 15 percent. For a more likely stock decline of 25 percent, the convertible option hedge has provided a break-even situation.

Figure 12.7 shows a worksheet using covered call writing against
common stock. When comparing this situation to that of the convertible option hedge, it is evident that the convertible option hedge provides a superior risk/reward opportunity. Figure 12.8 illustrates the
relationship. The upside potential is greater when using the common
stock instead of the convertible bond, but there is little reduction in
risk. The convertible option hedge provides a better balance of reward
on the upside to additional downside safety. In addition, by varying
the amount of calls written (partial covered option hedge) the profit
profile can be altered to provide greater upside potential.

FIGURE 12.8 Convertible Option Hedge Profit Profiles

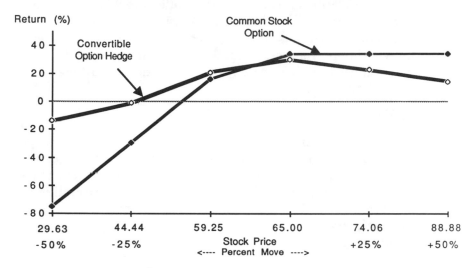

Common Stock Covered Options Writing vs. Convertible Covered Option Hedge

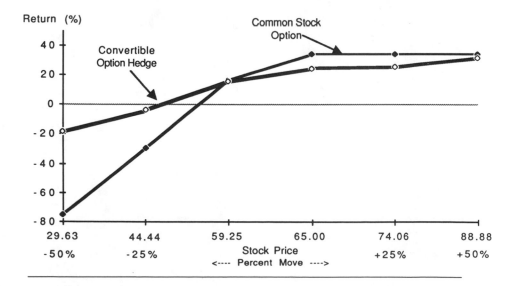

Common Stock Covered Call Compared to Convertible Partial Covered Option Hedge

OTHER CONVERTIBLE STOCK OPTION STRATEGIES

In addition to stock options on calls, there are also stock put options. Put options increase in value as the stock decreases from its exercise price because puts give the investor the right to sell the stock for a specific price over a specified time period. Put options could be purchased with convertibles to provide additional downside protection. Or some combination of covered calls and put purchases could provide interesting risk/reward opportunities. There are many variations of the convertible option hedging theme, each with its particular advantages.

SUMMARY

Convertible hedging with stock options provides some interesting opportunities. On the other hand, monitoring and selecting the correct investment situation is very time consuming. Stock options are often illiquid and have wide spreads that can cause additional frustration in executing transactions. Nevertheless, more stock options have been added and the convertible option hedge, once discovered, can result in excellent profit opportunities.

13

Convertible Hedging with Put Options

In addition to call options on stock, there are also stock put options. Put options can be purchased with convertibles to provide additional downside protection, and some combination of covered calls and put purchases can provide interesting risk/reward opportunities. There are many variations on the convertible option hedging theme, each with its particular advantages.

Most investors accept the notion of call options, but put options at first glance seem confusing.

> A put option gives the holder the right to *sell* the underlying stock at a specified price, called the *exercise price*, for a specified period of time, the *expiration date*. Each contract represents 100 shares of stock, and the cost of the contract is called the option *premium*.

An investor may purchase a put option in hopes of profiting if the stock declines in value. Because a put option gives the investor the right to sell the stock for a specific price over a specified time period, the put gains in value as the stock trades below the option's exercise price. If the investor misjudged and the stock increased in value, the put option would become worthless at the time of expiration. The loss is limited to the cost of the put. A popular strategy in bull markets is to sell put options and thereby gain the option premium as the stock increases in value. This is a high-risk strategy because as stocks decline, the put options' gain in value can create substantial losses. Our discussion will focus on the use of put options as a conservative defensive strategy to provide insurance against investment losses.

Put options can be thought of as insurance because they provide benefits if stocks decline, and the insurance premium is paid for a specified period of time. The amount of protection desired by the investor is then related to how much that protection will cost. Since many convertibles already have a level of protection because of their fixed income attributes, the main benefit of using put options with convertibles is that the cost of put protection can be reduced.

The use of put options with convertibles can give the investor additional flexibility to alter the profit profile of the overall investment. The purchase of put options becomes a cost factor that increases the initial investment. The cost of a put option is affected by many of the same factors that influence the convertible's price. The main difference is that the option market is much more sensitive to near-term volatility than the convertible market. Because of that, the put option can seem expensive when the stock experiences increasing near-term volatility. Therefore, its use needs to be carefully considered.

The purchase of a convertible bond and of a put on the underlying common stock illustrates how these options can be used effectively with convertibles. Again, the worksheet analysis is the best means to evaluate the risks and rewards of the strategy. Figure 13.1 under Profile A outlines the profit and loss on the purchase of 100 convertible bonds and 16 put options. The hedge ratio is equal to one because the 100 bonds represent 1,600 shares of stock and 16 puts also represent 1,600 shares of stock. This is the same convertible bond that was illustrated in previous chapters. Notice how the cost of the put seriously deteriorates the current yield on the convertible bond. Without the puts, the convertible's annual current yield would be 6.9 percent. If the stock remains at current levels, the current yield on the bond is reduced to an annualized rate of three percent. However, this yield does offset the cost of the puts.

Ironically, with this hedge, the investor is most vulnerable to loss if the stock declines slightly and remains at the exercise price of the put option. At that level, the put expires worthless and the convertible declines from 112 to 108.5. Because the interest income did not overcome the price decline of the convertible and the cost of the puts, the position shows its maximum loss at an annual rate of a negative 2.8 per-

---

FIGURE 13.1   Convertible/Put Option: Hedge Ratio 1.0

XYZ Convertible Bond 7.75% – 03/01/1996
Put Option Expires 219 days
Exercise Price of $55.00 and market price of $162.50 per contract

HEDGE POSITION: 100 @ $1,120.00 per bond =	$112,000
16 puts bought @ $162.50 per option =	2,600
Initial Investment =	$114,600

Profile A: Hedge Ratio: 1.0

Stock Price Range	–50%	–25%	Exercise	0	+25%	+50%
Assumed Stock Price	29.63	44.44	55.00	59.25	74.06	88.88
Est. Conv. Price	90.43	99.65	108.05	112.00	127.48	146.08
Profit/Loss on Conv.	(21570)	(12350)	(3950)	0	15480	34080
Profit/Loss on Put	38000	14300	(2600)	(2600)	(2600)	(2600)
Bond Interest	4650	4650	4650	4650	4650	4650
Total Profit or Loss	21080	6600	(1900)	2050	17530	36130
Return on Investment %	18.4	5.8	(1.7)	1.8	15.3	31.5
Annual ROI (.60 yrs) %	30.7	9.6	(2.8)	3.0	25.5	52.5

---

cent. With the cost of the puts, the upside potential of this position is still attractive. If the stock were to increase 50 percent over the life of the option, this position would increase 31.5 percent. The value of the put is evident if the stock were to decline significantly over that same period of time. This position would gain 18.4 percent for a 50 percent decline in the common stock price. Figure 13.2 graphs the profit profile of this position. Notice that losses are shown if the stock declines slightly, but profits can be realized if the stock moves dramatically up or down.

This technique works well with convertibles because it provides an additional level of safety. With convertibles, the costs can be controlled. The cost to provide this amount of safety using common stock and puts would be prohibitive. Figure 13.3 sets up a common stock position with the purchase of put options. Common stock is used instead of the convertible, but all other factors remain the same. Notice how expensive the program becomes. At the exercise price of 55, the annualized return on investment using common stock is a negative 16.1 percent, compared to a negative 1.7 percent for the convertible hedge.

FIGURE 13.2   Convertible/Put Option: Profit Profile A

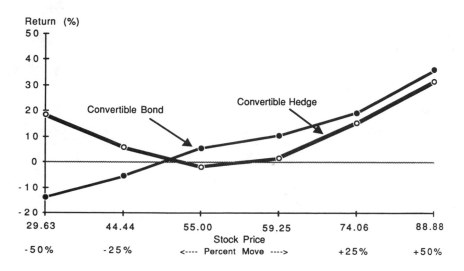

NOTE: Returns based on options period of time to expiration.

FIGURE 13.3   Common Stock/Put Option Hedge

XYZ Common Stock   Dividend Yield   0%
Put Option Expires 219 days
Exercise Price of $55.00 and market price of $162.50 per contract

HEDGE POSITION: 1,600 shares @ $59.25 per share = $94,800
16 puts bought @ $162.50 per option =   2,600
Initial Investment = $97,400

Profile A:

Stock Price Range	−50%	−25%	Exercise	0	+25%	+50%
Assumed Stock Price	29.63	44.44	55.00	59.25	74.06	88.88
Profit/Loss on Stock	(47,400)	(23,700)	(6800)	0	23,700	47,400
Profit/Loss on Put	38000	14300	(2600)	(2600)	(2600)	(2600)
Dividend Income	0	0	0	0	0	0
Total Profit or Loss	(19400)	(19400)	(9400)	(2600)	21100	44800
Return on Investment %	(9.7)	(9.7)	(9.7)	(2.7)	21.7	46.0
Annual ROI (.60 yrs) %	(16.1)	(16.1)	(16.1)	(4.5)	36.1	76.7

FIGURE 13.4 Put Hedging Common Stock vs. Convertible

Stock Price Range	–50%	–25%	Exercise	0	+25%	+50%
Assumed Stock Price	29.63	44.44	55.00	59.25	74.06	88.88
AROI % STOCK	(16.1)	(16.1)	(16.1)	(4.5)	36.1	76.7
AROI % CONVERTIBLE	30.7	9.6	(2.8)	3.0	25.5	52.5

FIGURE 13.5 Profit Profile Put Option Hedges Common Stock vs. Convertible

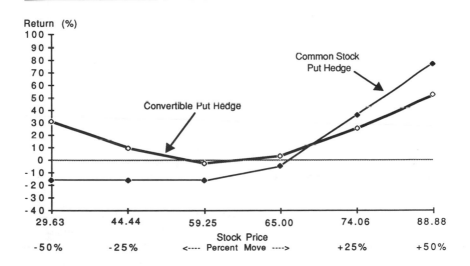

Figure 13.4 lists the AROI and compares the strategies. The common stock strategy provides greater upside potential but does not provide sufficient downside safety. The convertible provides a balanced return over the complete spectrum of stock prices. Figure 13.5 illustrates the advantage of using a convertible put option hedge over the common stock put option position. The graph depicts the extra advan-

---

FIGURE 13.6   Convertible/Put Option Hedge

XYZ Convertible Bond 7.75% – 03/01/1996
Put Option Expires 219 days
Exercise Price of $55.00 and market price of $162.50 per contract

HEDGE POSITION: 100 @ $1,120.00 per bond = $112,000
10 puts bought @ $162.50 per option =   1,625
Initial Investment = $113,625

Profile B: Hedge Ratio .63

Stock Price Range	–50%	–25%	Exercise	0	+25%	+50%
Assumed Stock Price	29.63	44.44	55.00	59.25	74.06	88.88
Est. Conv. Price	90.43	99.65	108.05	112.00	127.48	146.08
Profit/Loss on Conv.	(21570)	(12350)	(3950)	0	15480	34080
Profit/Loss on Put	23750	8938	(1625)	(1625)	(1625)	(1625)
Bond Interest	4650	4650	4650	4650	4650	4650
Total Profit or Loss	6830	1238	(925)	3025	18505	37105
Return on Investment %	6.0	1.1	(0.8)	2.7	16.3	32.7
Annual ROI (60 years) %	10.0	1.8	(1.4)	4.4	27.1	54.4

---

tage the convertible provides on the downside. Because the convertible declines less than the common stock, it provides a handsome profit, while the stock position shows a serious loss.

The versatility of the convertible put option hedge is shown by the investor's flexibility to vary the hedge ratio. For example, instead of using a hedge ratio of 1.0, the position could be given a bullish tilt by using fewer put options. Figure 13.6 illustrates the convertible put option hedge with a hedge ratio of .63.[1] Ten put options are purchased to protect the convertible bond investment. This reduces costs in a sideways market while still retaining adequate downside protection. Should the stock decrease 25 percent, this position shows a break-even

---

[1]Hedge Ratio = 1, is where the number of stocks represented by the convertible is equal to the number of options. In this case: 1,000 shares/1,600 shares = .63.

FIGURE 13.7   Profit Profile B Convertible/Put Option Hedge Graph

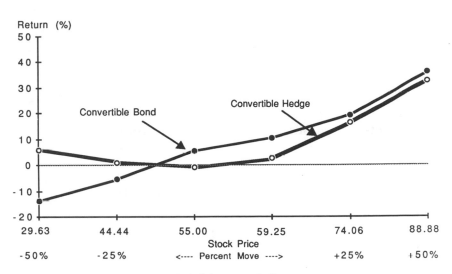

NOTE: Returns based on option's period of time to expiration.

while providing significant upside gains. Figure 13.7 depicts the profit profile of the position. The convertible investor can design the hedge for his or her desired profit profile.

The convertible put option hedge can be an extremely useful technique. It can protect a profit in a convertible that had been previously purchased. The protection can be added or taken off independently of the convertible position. The drawback of the strategy is that option premium levels vary from issue to issue. Premium levels also vary due to general market volatility and at times can be extremely expensive. Hedging with slightly out-of-the-money options, as illustrated in the preceding examples, can reduce the costs, but close attention to premium levels is required to execute the strategy successfully. In addition, many stock options are often illiquid, with wide spreads between the bid and ask prices. This has been particularly true since the introduction of index options.

MANAGING PORTFOLIO RISK WITH INDEX PUT OPTIONS

Index options provide an additional hedging tool for the convertible investor. In March of 1983, the S&P 100 Index was launched under its original name, the CBOE 100, and many other indexes have been introduced over the years. Index options have the standardized features of listed stock options, except that when an index option is exercised, the holder receives the cash value instead of any securities. Index options can be either calls or puts.[2] Our discussion will center on the use of index puts as a means to hedge convertible portfolios.

An index put option is a contract to sell the index value at a specified price (the exercise price) for a specified period of time (the expiration date). Each contract is for 100 shares of the index. Therefore, if the index is at 200, each contract represents $20,000 in stock value. The index put option gains in value as the index falls below its exercise price. The market value of the index put at any specific time is called its premium.

There are a number of features about index puts that make them effective vehicles for controlling market risk in convertible portfolios:

- Index options are not affected by takeovers, tender offers and other events peculiar to individual companies.

- Convertible swaps within the portfolio can be made without interfering with the desired hedge ratio.

- The index's volatility can be estimated much more accurately than that of individual stock positions. Fair value prices can be easily determined for index options.

- Because of the cash settlement of index options and the liquidity of the index option market, transaction costs are lower.

- Index options expire monthly, rather than the three-month cycle for many individual stock options, giving additional flexibility to hedge the portfolio.

---

[2]For a basic understanding of listed stock options, consult *Characteristics and Risks of Standardized Options*, available from The Options Clearing Corporation, options exchanges or any broker dealing in listed options.

• Many index options have been introduced, allowing investors to select the appropriate index for their particular needs.

Combining index put options with convertibles is an effective means to hedge the entire portfolio. The most difficult risk factor for investors to hedge against is systematic risk. Index put options give investors a means to control systematic risk of convertible portfolios. As with all hedging techniques, there are trade-offs that must be measured to determine how much a reduction in risk has cost in potential returns. Blindly buying puts without the detailed analysis needed to evaluate the accompanying costs will not produce favorable returns. Returns will most likely be based on chance rather than a systematic evaluation process. The evaluation process cannot be ignored because the associated costs with hedging portfolios can be substantial.

Convertible Portfolio Index Option Hedge

Hedging is an attempt to avoid or lessen loss by making counterbalancing investments. The objective of the convertible portfolio index option hedge is to achieve higher risk-adjusted rates of return than may be expected if the portfolio remained unhedged. In this chapter we will develop the methodology to evaluate hedged convertible portfolios. Conceptually, put options should increase in value to offset any decrease in value of the convertibles. A properly hedged position should provide good protection in the declining phase, while not significantly jeopardizing the profit potential in advancing markets. Proper analysis shows that overestimating the hedge ratio can result in a stagnated portfolio with the effect of trading dollars, whether the market advances or declines. The consequence of such a strategy is overall poor performance.

Figure 13.8 assumes a three-month holding period over which the investor chooses to hedge a common stock portfolio. The index put option provided good downside protection, but at the expense of the dividend yield in a sideways market and some upside potential. Figure 13.8 illustrates the advantage of using index puts and the necessary steps that must be taken to determine the amount of hedging to be accomplished.

FIGURE 13.8   Common Stock Portfolio

Portfolio A: Common Stock

	Stock Market Change		
	−10%	0	+10%
Index Option Value	180	200	220
Portfolio Change	−7%	0	+7%
Portfolio Dividends	+1%	+1%	+1%
Unhedged Portfolio Returns	−6%	+1%	+8%

Portfolio B: Hedged with Index Put Options

	Stock Market Change		
	−10%	0	+10%
Index Option Value	180	200	220
Portfolio Change	−7%	0	+7%
Portfolio Dividends	+1%	+1%	+1%
Cost of Index Puts	−2%	−2%	−2%
Value of Puts	+10%	0	0
Hedged Portfolio Returns	+2%	−1%	+6%

Portfolio Characteristics:
    Assumes three-month holding period.
    Dividend yield = 4% annually.
    Portfolio beta = .70.
    Index put option cost based on 2% per quarter.

Figure 13.9 indicates the theory of hedging with index puts by constructing the return profile of a typical fully hedged convertible portfolio. With the index currently at 264, the unhedged performs better than the hedged portfolio at the current level and above. The difference in performance is the cost of the put protection. Should the index decrease in value, the hedged portfolio maintains its value except for the cost of the put premium. In practice, many steps are needed to execute the hedged strategy.

Determining the Risk/Reward of the Convertible Portfolio

The first step is to determine the risk/reward of the convertible portfolio. The convertible portfolio summary discussed in chapter 9 provides

---

FIGURE 13.9 Convertible Securities Index Option Hedge Return Profile

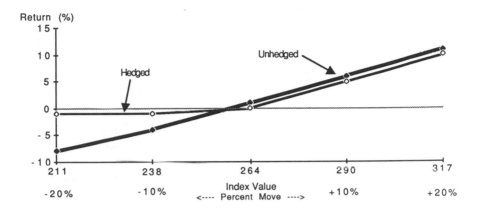

---

needed data and conveniently measures the upside potential and downside risk of the portfolio. As discussed in previous chapters, both a dollar-weighted upside beta and dollar-weighted downside beta are estimated for the portfolio.

Projecting a portfolio's sensitivity to changes in a market index can be accomplished by calculating a weighted portfolio beta. These values can be useful in determining the effect and costs of index hedging. Figure 13.9 assumes that the upside beta of the convertible portfolio is .70 and the downside beta is .30. Therefore, the range of the portfolio value as compared to the market index can be easily determined. The second step is to determine the number of puts to purchase to protect the convertible portfolio.

Since the downside beta is .30, one has to buy only 30 percent of the puts needed for a common stock portfolio with a beta of 1.0 to offset the decline of the convertible portfolio. In this case, a hedge ratio of .30 is used to provide a near break-even should the market index decline by ten percent over the three-month period under consideration.

FIGURE 13.10   Convertible Portfolio

Portfolio A: Unhedged

	Stock Market Change		
	−10%	0	+10%
Index Option Value	180	200	220
Portfolio Change (Total Return)	−3.0%	1.8%	+7.0%
Return On Investment	−3.0%	1.8%	+7.0%

Portfolio B: Hedged With Index Put Options

	Stock Market Change		
	−10%	0	+10%
Index Option Value	180	200	220
Portfolio Change (Total Return)	−3.0%	1.8%	+7.0%
Cost of Index Puts	−0.6%	−0.6%	−0.6%
Value of Puts	+3.0%	0	0
Hedged Portfolio Returns	−0.6%	+1.2%	+6.4%

Portfolio Characteristics:
   Assumes three-month holding period.
   Convertible upside beta is .70, downside beta is .30.
   Index put option cost based on 2% per quarter.
   Cost adjusted to provide near break-even on downside.

In the example illustrated in Figure 13.10, there are a number of assumptions that must be reviewed to realistically determine the value of hedging convertible portfolios with index puts.

- The accuracy of the weighted betas depends on how the convertible price track is estimated.

- Interest rates are assumed to be stable over the three-month period, and the convertible portfolio is assumed to be well diversified to minimize unsystematic risk.

- Perhaps the most material of assumptions is the level of the put premiums. Premium levels can be measured by the implied volatility of the market.

Put premiums can vary significantly from period to period as market conditions change, making it difficult to estimate the cost of hedging portfolios. Figure 13.11 indicates the changes in option premium

---

FIGURE 13.11   S & P 100 (OEX) Implied Volatility 1987

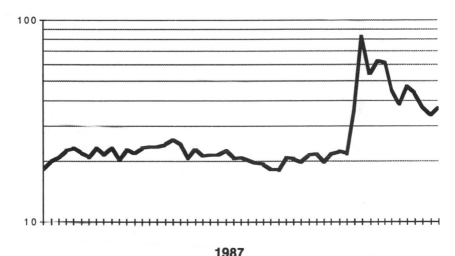

Annual
Standard
Deviation
(%)

1987

NOTE: Data January 1, 1987 through December 31, 1987.

---

levels for various indexes during 1987. Notice the extreme levels attained by these indexes over this relatively short period of time.

Historical Perspective for Convertible Hedging with Index Puts

There has not been a great deal of evidence on the performance of convertible hedging with index puts because they have only been in existence since early 1983. However, by backtracking we can estimate how a hedged convertible portfolio may have performed over various market cycles. Figure 13.12 indicates the performance of convertibles going back to the beginning of 1978. The quarterly performance on a total return basis is listed along with the Value Line Composite Index. The cost of hedging (the put premium) is estimated using the Black-Scholes option model. Notice how these costs vary from quarter to quarter, with the lowest cost being 1.34 percent in third quarter of 1981 to 5.10 percent for the fourth quarter 1986.

The data used in figure 13.12 to estimate the put premium (cost of hedging) was prepared under the assumption that put options are purchased at the beginning of each quarter. At the end of the quarter they have either expired worthless or have been sold for their intrinsic value. Also, the put options when purchased are exactly at their strike price.

The convertible investor employing hedging strategies should understand that option premium levels may vary minute by minute. For example, in figure 13.12 the fourth quarter of 1987 hedging cost of 2.8 percent seemed inexpensive, considering the stock market action of October 19th, but when the panic atmosphere pushed the put option premium to an exorbitant 20 percent, the costs made hedging prohibitive.

Figure 13.13 graphs these results against the Value Line Index and the unhedged portfolio. Observe how the hedged portfolio has smoothed the returns over time. Figure 13.14 shows the returns on a quarter-by-quarter basis. The unhedged convertible portfolio reduces the peaks and troughs from the market index. The hedged convertible portfolio further reduces and eliminates many of the negative quarters.

In panel 1 of figure 13.14, notice the high correlation between the Value Line Index (XVL) and the Convertibles (CAM). Panels 2 and 3 indicate the favorable comparison of the hedged convertible portfolio (HDG 1) to both the XVL and the S&P 500.

Figure 13.15 graphs the risk-adjusted returns of the alternative investments. This illustrates the trade-off between upside potential and downside risk. The security market line is shown by the T-bill return and the S&P 500 Stock Index. Considering risk as the volatility of quarterly returns, the convertibles show higher returns at less risk than the stock market. The hedged convertible portfolio also reveals that the use of put options reduces risk further. It's clear that index puts allow convertible investors to fine-tune the risk/reward of a portfolio, to control risk and to attain their investment objectives.

In the last two chapters we have discussed the use of stock options and index options. Each has its own peculiar characteristics and can be used to control risk within the convertible portfolio. Premium levels

FIGURE 13.12   Convertible Hedging with Index Puts
(quarterly percent changes)

YEAR/ QUARTER	CONVERTIBLES (CAM)	VALUE LINE INDEX (XVL)	PUT PREMIUM (%)	HEDGE RETURN (HDG 1)
1979–4	4.36	–1.00	2.41	2.59
1980–1	–10.08	–12.90	2.14	0.36
1980–2	17.50	16.50	1.74	15.50
1980–3	13.10	14.20	2.77	9.91
1980–4	1.40	2.10	2.62	–1.61
1981–1	4.40	6.90	1.90	2.22
1981–2	5.00	0.60	1.66	3.09
1981–3	–7.00	–16.30	1.34	7.76
1981–4	8.50	6.20	1.51	6.76
1982–1	–3.10	–9.10	1.93	3.78
1982–2	2.10	–3.80	1.70	3.95
1982–3	10.90	9.40	2.10	8.49
1982–4	12.80	20.50	2.86	9.51
1983–1	12.20	12.80	2.83	8.95
1983–2	7.40	14.20	2.56	4.46
1983–3	–2.60	–2.70	2.38	–2.64
1983–4	0.20	–2.40	2.10	0.19
1984–1	–0.50	–6.30	1.83	3.70
1984–2	–2.70	–5.20	1.83	0.40
1984–3	6.50	5.60	1.74	4.50
1984–4	3.50	–2.40	1.83	3.80
1985–1	7.90	9.30	1.78	5.85
1985–2	7.10	1.50	1.91	4.90
1985–3	–3.00	–6.00	1.66	1.09
1985–4	9.87	7.60	2.27	7.26
1986–1	14.50	12.34	2.21	11.96
1986–2	3.40	2.08	3.54	1.41
1986–3	–1.18	–9.50	2.47	5.48
1986–4	2.71	3.93	5.10	–3.16
1987–1	13.08	22.06	3.50	9.06
1987–2	1.16	5.99	3.90	–3.33
1987–3	3.30	5.53	3.20	–0.38
1987–4	–12.80	–24.48	2.80	8.46
AVERAGE QTR RETURN %	3.94	2.34		4.37
STANDARD DEVIATION	7.12	10.46		4.50
COEFFICIENT VARIATION %	180.76	446.91		102.90

Notes:
1) Convertible performance based on selected convertible portfolios.
2) Value Line Index (XVL) has been used in this study; other indexes would show similar results.
3) Put option premium is based on the implied volatility using the Black-Scholes option model.

FIGURE 13.13   Index Option Portfolio Hedge Cumulative Return

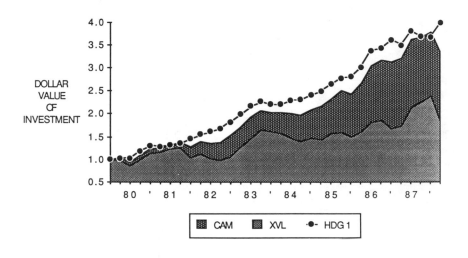

NOTE: Data September 31, 1979 through December 31, 1987.

and liquidity play an important part in whether the investor can effectively use these hedging techniques. Figure 13.16 shows the market share of both stock options and index options for all U.S. exchanges for the period 1984 through 1987. Notice how the activity in stock options increased over that of index options during 1987. At times writing options against convertibles may not be attractive, while at other times it's extremely attractive. Market conditions play an important role in the availability of hedging opportunities, and the investor must be alert to these changing conditions.

FIGURE 13.14   Quarterly Returns

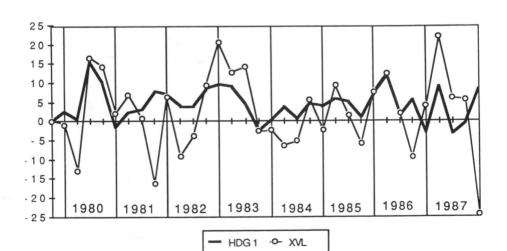

September 30, 1979 through December 31, 1987

FIGURE 13.14   Quarterly Returns (Continued)

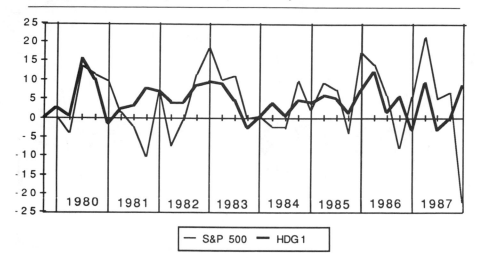

FIGURE 13.15   Capital Market Line
September 30, 1979–December 31, 1987

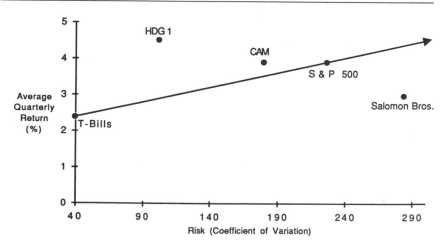

NOTES:
   CAM - Calamos Asset Management, Inc.
   HDG 1 - Calamos Asset Management with full hedge.
   S&P 500 - Stock market proxy.
   Salomon Bros. - Bond market proxy.

**FIGURE 13.16 Market Shares of Equity and Index Options
All U.S. Option Exchanges, 1984–1987**

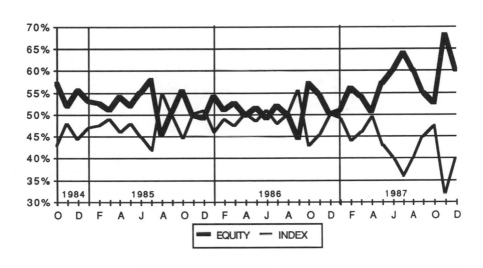

SOURCE: The Options Clearing Corporation

14

Convertible Performance

When investors are introduced to convertibles, they often feel that they are "too good to be true." Convertibles provide the best of both worlds: fixed income with stock market participation. There is no doubt, as has been demonstrated in previous chapters that a convertible provides a low-risk alternative to the underlying common stock. In particular situations, there is little question as to the value of a convertible over its stock counterpart. Does what seems obvious in an individual security translate to the convertible market as a whole? It is helpful for the investor to know how convertible securities have performed over different market conditions. Can convertible indexes provide such a view?

In the 1980s, the convertible market grew dramatically and the investment community responded by introducing a number of convertible indexes to track that market. The firms introducing these indexes attempted to gain recognition as the Dow Jones Average of the convertible market. Investment consultants favor indexes as a means to compare the performance of convertible money managers. However, the problem with convertible indexes is that they often provide a misleading and erroneous view of the convertible market. Convertibles should be selected on the basis of one's investment objectives. As has been discussed, convertibles can be purchased as an alternative to the bond market or the stock market. Still, it is useful for investors to examine the convertible market in detail, and the indexes are helpful to that end.

There are a number of problems with all indexes, despite their popularity.

It is well known that the Dow Jones Industrial Average is not broadly representative, since it is made up of only 30 stocks and is weighted by price, rather than shares outstanding. The S&P 500 has been used as a model for index funds and is a popular measure of performance for pension funds. It represents a cross section of corporate America and is weighted by shares outstanding. It is often considered an unmanaged proxy for the market, but in truth it's an index managed by five employees of the Standard & Poor's Corporation. They meet weekly to decide on changes. In 1987 alone, there were 21 changes to the index, and in some months as many as five additions or deletions. The index has been criticized for reflecting the investment fads of the time while sacrificing diversification.[1]

The Value Line Composite Index of 1,700 stocks includes some over-the-counter stocks. It provides a wide representation of stock in many different industries. It is equal-dollar weighted, meaning that any time the price of one of the stock changes, the number of shares are adjusted to bring all the stocks in balance. Very few investors would attempt a comparable investment program with its prohibitive transaction costs.

There are many indexes besides the ones mentioned here, each looking at the market from a different perspective. Investors need to understand the biases of each index before using them to draw inferences about performance.

Therefore, with the problems associated with indexes in general, a convertible investor should be aware of how a convertible index has been designed. Creating a convertible index is not an easy task. Indexes can be flawed simply by the way their calculations are accomplished. For example, a convertible index that weights the performance of convertibles by the amount of the issue outstanding is ignoring more than 50 percent of the convertible market. Also, does it make any sense to include a convertible that is trading at a price of 250, 150 percent above par, in a convertible index? Both Western Union, presently in reorganization, and Cincinnati Financial, trading at 333 percent

---

[1]Marshall E. Blume and Jack P. Friedman, *Encyclopedia of Investments* (New York: Warren, Gorham & Lamont, 1982), p. 321.

above par, are included in some indexes. Neither of these issues has any of the attributes usually associated with convertible investing.

The indexes discussed here have been created by convertible research departments or advisory services.

FIRST BOSTON CONVERTIBLE SECURITIES INDEXES

First Boston introduced three convertible indexes: a general convertible index, called The First Boston Convertible Securities Index, and two subindexes, the Convertible Bond Index and Convertible Preferred Index. The groundwork for these indexes was originally laid by the Harris Trust and Savings Bank of Chicago, so little back-testing was required.

Features

- The indexes begin in January 1982 and start with an initial price of 1,000.

- To be included in the index, domestic convertible bonds and convertible preferred stocks must have a Standard & Poor's rating of B- or better and an issue size of $50 million or more. Preferreds must have a minimum of 500,000 shares outstanding.

- The index includes dollar-denominated Euroconvertibles issued by domestic companies. Those issues also must have a Standard & Poor's rating of B- or better and a minimum size of $100 million.

- The index includes 278 issues with a market value of $44.5 billion as of July 1987.

- At the beginning of each calendar year, a new list of issues is determined that satisfy the eligibility criteria.

- All changes in the index are done at month end, except for those whose call date occurs in the first ten days of the month. In that case, they are deleted in the prior month. This may be unrealistic because calls have the near-term effect of depressing stock prices, and causing an immediate loss of accrued interest. The prior month's closing price may not be an accurate measure for those few issues where the market has not anticipated the call.

- The indexes are capital weighted. Each issue's price is multiplied times the amount of shares outstanding.

Overall, the First Boston Convertible indexes are well thought out and reflect the opportunities for institutional size portfolios. Since large issues dwarf most of the issues included in the index, this may not represent how the large institutional money manager would construct a convertible portfolio. Still, it has value in observing how the convertible market in general is reacting to different market conditions.

GOLDMAN SACHS CONVERTIBLE 100

In January of 1986, Goldman Sachs created an index aimed at the institutional investor. The index is tilted toward the larger issues. The inclusion criterion for convertible debentures is at least $100 million in principal amount; convertible preferreds must have at least $100 million in market value. Initially 100 issues met those guidelines, representing $20 billion in market value.

Features

- The index began with a value of 100 as of December 31, 1984, and is updated monthly based on a total return.
- It is dollar-weighted and well diversified across many industry groups. This index is not capital weighted.
- Reflects the high capitalization sector of the financial market.
- Securities within the index are replaced when called or redeemed.
- A change to the index was made in April of 1987 to take into account convertibles that, due to price moves, no longer have any typical convertible attributes. Therefore, convertibles with a conversion premium of 100 percent or more and a yield of five percent or less are replaced in this index.

Although the Goldman Sachs 100 does seem to reflect its initial objective of providing an indication of the high cap sector of the market for institutional investors it is not necessarily reflective of high quality. There are some serious drawbacks to using this index as a measure of performance. Like any index that is dollar weighted and has a widely diversified portfolio, it seems unlikely that any investor would make portfolio changes of that nature on a monthly basis. The index contains issues of which 49 percent are investment grade, plus some fallen angels, such as LTV and Global Marine. These two issues were rated CCC, which would seem to be unlikely holdings for an institutional portfolio. Very few money managers would continue to buy a defaulted bond monthly as it decreased in price. Any recovery in these issues would have equal weighting to the other issues. The change in April of 1987 was an attempt to correct this shortcoming.

KIDDER PEABODY & COMPANY
CONVERTIBLE BOND INDEX

Introduced in August of 1985 with data being backtracked to December 31, 1974, the index consists of 30 issues, all convertible bonds that were felt to have sufficient price history to construct the index.

Features

* Based on 30 issues selected by the research department without any set criteria given.
* The index is a total return and dollar weighted index. It is not capital weighted.
* The index includes data over a relatively long period of time.

In our opinion this index is too narrow to be representative of the convertible market. The conclusion from the index was that convertibles are equity alternatives—not surprising with the issues selected. It would be difficult to use this index as a proxy for the convertible market because its selection criteria are not clear. This subgroup of convertibles has over the years moved in line with the stock market except for 1987.

LIPPER CONVERTIBLE INDEXES

Lipper Analytical has a convertible securities index calculated on a total return basis and four subindexes. The total return index was introduced in March of 1984 with a value of 100 as of December 27, 1982. The indexes are calculated and adjusted weekly for new issues, calls and reduction of existing issues. Lipper covers both convertible bonds and convertible preferreds with a price only index.

Features

* Distinguishes between price and total return for both convertible bonds and convertible preferreds.

- The indexes are published weekly in *Barrons.*
- Adjustments are made weekly reducing distortions from calls and other factors.
- Indexes are dollar weighted and therefore skewed toward the lower quality sector of the market.
- Includes 382 bonds with market value of $25.7 billion and 203 convertible preferreds with market value of $16.4 billion as of December 31, 1987. Does not include many of the Eurobond convertible issues.

LIPPER CONVERTIBLE MUTUAL FUND INDEX

In addition to the convertible securities indexes, Lipper also provides the Lipper Convertible Securities Fund Index, an index of the convertible mutual funds. This index includes all types of convertible funds including dual purpose funds. Starting with seven funds in 1976, it has grown to include 29 funds in 1987. Only since 1985 has there been a meaningful number of convertible funds with which to create an index. Results of the years prior to 1984 may not be representative because of the small number of funds and the inclusion of a non-convertible fund in the index. Figure 14.1 shows the performance of convertible mutual funds as compared to the stock and bond markets.

In any case, the convertible mutual fund index is a reflection of the many different fund management styles. Many of the convertible funds use market timing and are not fully invested in convertibles. Another fund which for years invested totally in non-convertible fixed income, actually changed its name to include the word convertible because of the recent convertible popularity. Although it was not a convertible fund until mid 1987, this fund is included in the index from 1976, the inception of the index. It is further distorted by including funds with small initial investments on the same basis as fully invested larger funds.

However, Lipper does provide many categories in which to compare convertible mutual fund performance. The categories based on size and investment objective provides a means to compare relative performance.

VALUE LINE CONVERTIBLE INDEX

The Value Line Convertible indexes were introduced in March of 1982. One index shows only price appreciation, while the other indicates performance on a total return basis. Value Line has a long history of convertible research and its index represents how convertibles perform in general.

Features

- The indexes are based on 585 convertibles followed in the Value Line Service, representing a market value of $53 billion (most of them domestic convertible issues).

- The indexes are dollar weighted on a weekly basis. The index values are not calculated at the end of each month, making comparisons difficult with other market indexes. Investors could not possibly manage their portfolio on the same basis as this index is constructed, since it would need to be adjusted weekly to reflect the equal dollar weighting.

- The Eurodollar convertibles are not included, but there are indications that they may be in the future.

- Small issues have the same weighting as large issues. The indexes are not capital weighted.

The Value Line Convertible Indexes are a good indication of how the average convertible is performing. It is not a suitable gauge for the performance of a convertible portfolio.

SUMMARY: CONVERTIBLE INDEXES

In general, convertible indexes provide a broad view of how the convertible market as a whole is reacting to various market conditions. Each index describes a particular aspect of the convertible market according to how the index was prepared. Figure 14.2 compares the construction parameters and their influence on market sectors between high and low cap companies, credit quality, and whether there is an equity or income bias.

The question remains whether any general convertible index, even a well-designed one like the First Boston Convertible Securities Index, should be used as a measure of performance for a convertible portfolio.

Convertibles can be managed to achieve a particular investment objective. A random selection of convertibles does not indicate whether the investor was successful in achieving the investment goal.

FIGURE 14.1 Convertible Indexes

	FirstBoston Convertible Securities	Goldman Sach's Convertible 100	Kidder Peabody Convertible Index	Liper Convertible Index	Value Line Convertible Index
Beginning Date of Index	Jan-82	Dec-84	Jan-74	Dec-82	Jun-82
Current Market Value	44.5 billion	20 billion	6.9 billion	25.7 billion	53 billion
Number of issues	278	100	30	382	585
Frequency of calculation	monthly	monthly	monthly	weekly	weekly
Weighting	capital	dollar	dollar	dollar	dollar
Euroconvertibles	yes	no	no	no	no
Convertible Preferreds	yes	none	none	none*	yes
Subjective changes	no	yes	yes	no	no
Capitalization bias	High cap companies	High cap companies	none	Low cap companies	Low cap companies
Credit quality bias	none	none	none	lower quality	lower quality
Equity/Income bias	none	none	equity	none	none
Data as of	Dec-87	Dec-87	Mar-88	Dec-87	Dec-87

Note: All indexes based on total return
*publishes separate convertible preferred index

FIGURE 14.2   Convertible Funds vs. Bond and Stock Markets

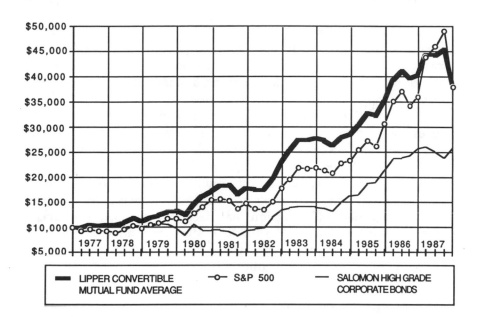

For example, an investor seeking low-risk equity through the convertible market may feel the objective had not been achieved when compared to a general convertible index. If interest rates and equity prices declined, the indexes would show an increase in convertible prices as their bond value responded to the lower interest rates. In all likelihood, the convertible selected for lower-risk equity participation would increase very little and lag behind the general convertible indexes. Didn't the convertible investor achieve his or her objective?

On the other hand, the investor who constructs a convertible bond portfolio based on yield characteristics and is willing to forego much of the upside equity participation may lag behind the indexes in a *strong* stock market. Therefore, it is more important to gear the performance to the attainment of a particular investment objective rather than a general index.

ARE CONVERTIBLES A SEPARATE ASSET CLASS?

With the growth of convertibles in the 1980s, pension fund consultants and managers are debating whether convertibles constitute a separate asset class. Pension fund managers spend a great deal of time deciding on asset allocation among alternative investments. The status of the convertible market has advanced to a point where it deserves to be considered a separate asset class, but this was not always the case. Because of its small size, sprinkled among a small number of industry groups, convertible investing could not be taken seriously by the large pension funds. Not knowing whether to put convertibles in the equity category of fixed income, many consultants placed them in the famous "other" category. Those conditions have changed dramatically, so convertibles now deserve their own separate asset class.

For this to be done, convertibles must be evaluated on their own merits. From an asset allocation point of view, convertibles can provide the much-needed protection that fixed-income portfolios lacked in the inflationary times of the 1970s. A significant allocation to convertibles would have provided a higher total return at less risk than comparable fixed-income portfolios.

CONVERTIBLES COMPARED TO MARKET INDEXES

Convertible indexes tell part of the story of how convertibles have done over time. It is interesting to compare the convertible market to the universe of underlying common stocks that have issued convertibles. This clearly reflects in broader terms how convertibles have performed over different market conditions. Figure 14.3 does just that. For example, during the stock market crash of 1987, it was generally perceived that convertibles did not do as well as should have been expected. However, upon close examination, we see that convertible issues declined 17.7 percent, while their underlying common stocks declined 31.7 percent. The convertibles decreased nearly half as much as their common stocks. In fact, if the decline were over a longer period of time, allowing the yield advantage to exert itself, the difference would have been even greater. The convertible held up under the most severe market conditions in history. This in light of the fact that according to the same research conducted by Smith Barney, convertibles actually outperformed their underlying common stocks in the bull phase of

FIGURE 14.3 Performance of Convertibles Compared to Underlying Stocks

| Security | 9/30/1987 to 11/16/1987 | | 12/31/1986 to 11/16/1987 | | 1986 | | 1985 | | 12/31/1984 to 11/16/1987 |
	Price	Total Return	Price	Total Return	Price	Total Return	Price	Total Return	Average Annual Total Return
Convertibles	−18.70%	−17.70%	−7.00%	−0.60%	+4.00	+12.30%	+16.80%	+26.50%	+13.30%
Underlying Common Stock	−31.70%	−31.50%	−3.70%	−2.60%	+9.00	+11.10%	+23.70%	+25.90%	+12.00%

SOURCE: *Smith Barney Convertibles* Vol. 1, No. 10, December 3, 1987, Pg. 4

1985 and 1986 as well as for the period from December 31, 1984, through November 16, 1987.

Convertible Performance: Another View

Clearly, convertible indexes give investors a frame of reference with which to view the convertible market. The question of relative performance remains open. We have emphasized throughout this book that one should purchase convertibles that are undervalued and contain favorable leverage. There are not any satisfactory indexes providing a measure of performance based on that decision process. However, we feel the Calamos Convertible Composite of Managed Accounts does provide a fair representation of the process over time. It should be noted that the evaluation process for convertibles discussed in this book has not been in use throughout the entire period covered. The convertible evaluation techniques have evolved over the years and what has been presented also includes the latest innovations to convertible money management. For that reason, the relative performance of convertibles should improve in the future.

In figure 14.4 the Calamos Convertible Composite[2] is compared to the performance of the S&P 500 Stock Index and the Salomon Brothers Long-term Bond Index. Interest and dividends are reinvested in both indexes and the composite to provide a total return comparison.

Notice how convertibles preserved capital in the early 1980s, while the bond market was in near chaos. Interest rates in 1980 alone were as high as 21 percent and as low as eight percent. The effect of interest rate volatility on the non-convertible bond market verified the benefits of convertible investing in those times. The bull market beginning in August of 1982 pulled convertibles and most other financial instruments to new highs simply because all investment strategies seem to work well in bull markets. Observe the corrections of the stock market during this period and how the composite retraced less, preserved capital and stood ready to resume an upward trend from the previous plateau.

This is an important aspect of convertible investing. Convertibles actually take advantage of the market volatility and, over time, will outperform the more volatile stock market, assuming that the investor

---

[2] Appendix to this chapter presents a detailed explanation of the Calamos Convertible Composite.

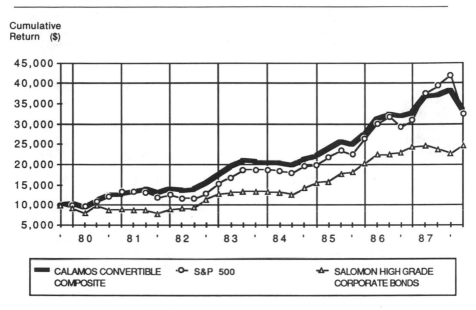

FIGURE 14.4 Calamos Convertible Composite Comparative Performance Tax-Exempt Accounts (September 30, 1979–December 31, 1987)

maintains a favorable risk/reward relationship in the portfolio. This means that as convertibles increase in price during a bull market phase, they are sold and replaced with other convertibles possessing a favorable risk/reward relationship. The convertible portfolio is continually monitored so that the risk/reward remains at the desired level.

The risk of any investment is measured by the variations in returns on a periodic basis. Figures 14.4 and 14.5 measure the relative risk of the composite to that of various indexes and to the no-risk investment of three-month Treasury bills. The composite exhibited less volatility and higher total returns than the bond market or the stock market.

Some view this as an aberration. In theory, the security market line is linear, bonds are not supposed to fluctuate more than stocks, and convertibles are not supposed to be the best performing asset class. There are sound reasons why this occurred and why it should continue into the future. Convertibles as an asset class have a positive performance bias in inflationary and volatile markets. If inflation is no

---

FIGURE 14.5   Risk Analysis—Calamos Convertible Composite (September 30, 1979 through March 31, 1988)

	T-BILLS	STOCKS(1)	BONDS(2)	BONDS(3)	CALAMOS CONVERTIBLE COMPOSITE
Cumulative Return	119.5%	244.3%	154.1%	151.5%	253.7%
Quarterly Geometric Mean	2.34%	3.70%	2.78%	2.75%	3.79%
Standard Deviation	.92	9.05	8.62	5.42	7.01
Coefficient of Variation	39.2	244.0	310.0	197.0	185.0
Annualized Return	9.7%	15.7%	11.6%	11.5%	16.0%

RISK MEASUREMENT: Based on 34 quarters. The Coefficient of Variation is the standard deviation as a percentage of the mean. This produces a *percentage dispersion* figure used to compare the volatility of different sets of data.

(1) Based on the Standard & Poor's 500 Stock Index
(2) Based on the Salomon Brothers High Grade Long-term Corporate Bond Index
(3) Based on the Shearson Lehman Hutton Government/Corporate Bond Index

---

longer a problem and market volatility subsides, then convertibles will not outperform stocks over time. But that does not seem to be occurring in our times: Financial markets continually exhibit alarming levels of volatility, and few investors and analysts are convinced that inflation is no longer a problem.

The Calamos Convertible Composite has provided an annualized return on investment of 16.0 percent since its inception in 1979. It covers the bull market from the summer of 1982 to the summer of 1987 and the double-digit inflation environment from 1979 to 1982. Convertible investing has been tested under severe market conditions involving both inflation and deflation.

FIGURE 14.6   Relative Risk Analysis Convertible Strategy vs. Stocks/Bonds (September 30, 1979–March 31, 1988)

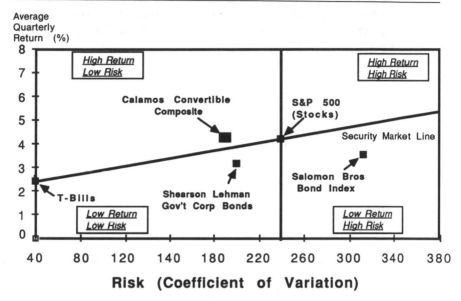

NOTE: This graph shows that convertibles have provided higher total returns and risk adjusted returns than either the stock or bond markets.

CONCLUSION

In the past 14 chapters we have journeyed from the basics of convertible securities, to the mechanics of evaluation, and through analysis in a highly technical theoretical framework. It is hopeful that the investor has gained knowledge to implement this information into successful investment practices. The subject is complicated and reflects the complex financial markets of our time. It has often been said that "the financial market is not a playing field, but a battlefield." To avoid becoming a casualty takes an enormous amount of time, effort, knowledge and discipline. In this book, specific "buy now, sell now" guidelines have been avoided intentionally. Simplistic market rules, often viewed as discipline, have caused investors to substitute a rule for critical analysis. We have elaborated on the risks and rewards of convertible investing. For some investors, convertibles can be a complete investment strategy to gain above-average returns at a lower risk. To others they can be used as an integral part of the asset allocation problem. Successful investing is much like the evolution of any science: It requires continual questioning. The more we understand the better we are able to cope with changing market conditions. To interpret the shadows on the wall of Wall Street what is needed is wisdom, and as Socrates said, Wisdom is knowing what I don't know.

APPENDIX A: Calamos Convertible Composite

 A MEMBER OF ARTHUR YOUNG INTERNATIONAL

Arthur Young

One IBM Plaza
Chicago, Illinois 60611
Telephone: (312) 645-3000
Telex: 190182

The Board of Directors
Calamos Asset Management, Inc.

We have examined the Calamos Composite Returns included in the accompanying Schedule of Calamos Composite Returns on Managed Accounts of Tax-Exempt Investors for each of the calendar quarters in the period October 1, 1979 to December 31, 1987. Our examination was made in accordance with generally accepted auditing standards and, accordingly, included such tests of the accounting records and such other auditing procedures as we considered necessary in the circumstances.

In our opinion, the schedule referred to above presents fairly the composite returns (as defined) of the accounts of tax-exempt investors managed by John P. Calamos for each of the calendar quarters in the period October 1, 1979 to December 31, 1987, on the basis described in the notes to the accompanying schedule.

Arthur Young & Company

April 6, 1988

Schedule of Calamos Composite Returns
on Managed Accounts of Tax-Exempt Investors

Quarter Ended	Calamos Composite Returns	Rates of Return Salomon Brothers High Grade Long-Term Corporate Bond Index (unaudited)	S & P 500 Stock Index
12/31/79	4.4%	−8.0%	0.1%
3/31/80	−10.1	−13.5	−4.1
6/30/80	17.5	25.2	13.5
9/30/80	13.1	−11.1	11.2
12/31/80	1.4	1.3	9.5
3/31/81	4.4	−1.1	1.4
6/30/81	5.0	−2.2	−2.3
9/30/81	−7.0	−9.3	−10.3
12/31/81	8.5	12.9	6.9
3/31/82	−3.1	3.6	−7.3
6/30/82	2.1	2.5	−0.6
9/30/82	10.9	21.4	11.5
12/31/82	12.9	11.5	18.2
3/31/83	12.2	3.7	10.0
6/30/83	7.4	1.3	11.1
9/30/83	−2.3	−0.3	−0.2
12/31/83	0.3	−0.1	0.4
3/31/84	−0.5	−1.4	−2.4
6/30/84	−2.5	−4.6	−2.6
9/30/84	7.1	13.4	9.7
12/31/84	4.1	9.1	1.9
3/31/85	7.7	2.0	9.2
6/30/85	7.3	12.5	7.3
9/30/85	−3.2	1.7	−4.1
12/31/85	10.6	12.1	17.2
3/31/86	14.3	10.8	14.1
6/30/86	3.6	0.7	5.9
9/30/86	−1.8	1.9	−6.9
12/31/86	2.9	5.5	5.6
3/31/87	12.2	1.9	21.2
6/30/87	.8	−4.0	5.0
9/30/87	3.3	−4.7	6.6
12/31/87	−12.7	8.6	−22.5
Cumulative Return	233.8	146.7	225.1
Average Compound Annual Return	15.7		

See accompanying notes.

Notes to Schedule of Calamos Composite Returns on Managed Accounts of Tax-Exempt Investors

1. General

    The Calamos Composite Returns calculations include all investment advisory accounts of tax-exempt investors managed by John P. Calamos on a fully discretionary basis during the period October 1, 1979 to December 31, 1987. All such accounts had similar investment objectives (maximum total return consistent with preservation of capital) and were invested principally in convertible securities. Mr. Calamos was the portfolio manager of these accounts and a principal in the firm of Noddings-Calamos Asset Management, Inc., an investment adviser. Mr. Calamos formed Calamos Asset Management, Inc. on April 7, 1987.

    The composite returns have been calculated without consideration of the effect of any income taxes thereon. The results for individual accounts and for different periods may vary. Other performance calculation methods might produce different results. Past performance may not be a reliable indicator of future performance.

2. Calculation of Composite Returns

    The composite returns have been determined in accordance with standards established by the Investment Counsel Association of America, Inc. for each period by (a) adding (i) the quarter ending value of managed accounts plus (minus) (ii) cash withdrawals (additions) less (iii) the quarter beginning value of managed accounts and dividing the result by (b) the sum of (i) the beginning value of managed accounts plus (minus) (ii) one-half of additional account contributions (withdrawals) unless such addition or withdrawal was ten percent or more of the value at the beginning of the quarter, in which event such contributions or withdrawals are reflected on the actual receipt or disbursement date.

    Dividends and interest have been reinvested. Management fees were excluded from the calculation. Account contributions (capital inflows) or withdrawals (capital outflows) were halved in the denominator to present the average amount invested.

The value of managed accounts includes cash, interest and dividends receivable and receivables for securities sold less payables for securities purchased. Convertible securities were valued by using (a) market quotations, or independent pricing services which use prices provided by market makers or estimates of value obtained from yield data relating to instruments with similar characteristics or (b) the value of the conversion feature, whichever is greater. Securities traded on a national exchange and securities listed on the NASDAQ National Market are valued at the last sale price on the exchange or market where primarily traded or listed or, if there is no recent sale, at the last current bid quotation. Securities not so traded or listed are valued at the last current bid quotation if market quotations are available.

Average compound annual return represents the level annual rate which, if earned for each annual period in a multiple year period, would produce the actual cumulative return over that period.

3. Salomon Brothers and S&P 500 Rates of Return

Rates of return for the Salomon Brothers High Grade Long-term Corporate Bond Index and the Standard & Poor's 500 Stock Index (both unaudited) were determined by Computer Directions Advisors, Incorporated (CDA Investment Services). The S&P 500 Stock Index is a capitalization weighted index. The Salomon Brothers Index is a high-grade long-term corporate bond index of industrial and utility bonds rated AA or better with an average maturity of 23 years. Both indices are on a total return basis with income and dividends reinvested.

Calamos Convertible Composite

Construction Parameters

A. Includes all investment advisory accounts that are:
1. Managed exclusively by John P. Calamos
2. Tax-Exempt and ERISA
3. Managed on a fully discretionary basis
4. Similar in investment objectives

B. The Composite is based on ending quarterly equity values of the various accounts. The rate of return of each account is adjusted for cash flow. Portfolio cash flow is defined as contributions minus withdrawals. The net cash flow for each quarter is time weighted.

C. The accounts comprising the Composite are dollar weighted in calculating quarterly returns.

D. Time-Weighted Rate of Return: Quarterly returns are linked to determine the ending cumulative return of one dollar invested at the beginning of the investment period.

E. Total Return: Returns for the Composite and all other indexes in this report assume reinvestment of the prior quarter's net increase.

F. Returns are net of execution costs. Management fees vary depending on account size and have not been included in the returns.

G. This analysis covers an 8$^1/_2$ year period commencing September 30, 1979, to March 31, 1988. While this was a period of generally rising common stock prices, it included interim periods of substantial market declines. The results shown should not be considered a prediction of future performance.

H. The Calamos Convertible Composite has been audited by Arthur Young through December 31, 1987. Figures for 1988 have not been audited. The Calamos Convertible Composite increased 6.2 percent for the first quarter of 1988.

BIBLIOGRAPHY

Alexander, Gordon J., and Roger D. Stover, "Pricing in the New Issue Convertible Debt Market." *Financial Management*, no. 6 (Fall 1977): 35-39.

Alexander, Gordon J., and Roger D. Stover, "The Effects of Forced Conversion on Common Stock Prices." *Financial Management*, no. 9 (Spring 1980): 39-45.

Altman, Edward, Robert G. Haldeman and P. Narayanan, "Zeta Analysis: A New Model to Identify Bankruptcy Risk of Corporations." *Journal of Banking and Finance*, no. 1 (1977): 29-54.

Blume, Marshall E., and Jack P. Friedman, *Encyclopedia of Investments*. Boston: Warren, Gorham and Lamont, 1982.

Bookstaber, Richard M., *Option Pricing Strategies in Investing*. Addison-Wesley Publishing Company, 1981.

Brigham, Eugene F., "An Analysis of Convertible Debentures: Theory and Some Empirical Evidence." *Journal of Finance*, no. 21 (March 1966): 35-54.

Clasing, Henry K., *The Dow Jones-Irwin Guide to Put and Call Options*. Illinois: Dow-Jones Irwin, Inc., 1975.

Cox, John C., and Mark Rubinstein, *Options Market*. New Jersey: Prentice-Hall, Inc, 1985.

Downes, John, and Jordan Elliot Goodman, *Dictionary of Finance and Investment Terms*. 2d ed. Barron's, 1985.

Francis, Jack C., *Investment Analysis and Management*. New York: McGraw-Hill Book Company, 1980.

Gastineau, Gary L., *The Stock Options Manual*. New York: McGraw-Hill Book Company, 1975.

Graham. Benjamin, D.L. Dodd and S. Cottle, *Security Analysis: Principles and Techniques* 4th ed. New York: McGraw-Hill Book Company, 1962.

Ibbotson, Roger I., and Rex. A. Sinquefield, "Stocks, Bonds, Bills and Inflation: Year by Year Historical Returns (1926-1974)." *Journal of Business* 49, no. 1 (January 1976): 11-47.

Ingersoll, Jonathan E., "A Contingent Claims Valuation of Convertible Securities." *Journal of Financial Economics*, (May 1977): 289-321.

Ingersoll, Jonathan E., "An Examination of Corporate Call Policies on Convertible Securities." *The Journal of Finance*, no. 2 (May 1977): 463-78.

Jarrow, Robert A., and Andrew Rudd, *Option Pricing*. Illinois: Richard D. Irwin, Inc., 1983.

Jennings, E.H., "An Estimate of Convertible Bond Premiums." *Journal of Financial and Quantitative Analysis*, no. 9: 33-56.

King, Benjamin F., "Market and Industry Factors in Stock Price Behavior." *The Journal of Business* 39, no. 1 (January 1966): 139-90.

King, Raymond, "Convertible Bond Valuation: An Empirical Test." *The Journal of Financial Research*, no. 9 (Spring 1986): 53-69.

Merton, R.C., "On the Pricing of Corporate Debt: The Risk Structure of Interest Rates." *The Journal of Finance*, no. 29 (May 1974): 449-70.

Mikkelson, Wayne H., "Convertible Calls and Security Returns." *Journal of Financial Economics*, no. 9 (September 1981): 237-64.

Reilly, Frank K., *Investment Analysis and Portfolio Management*. 2d ed. New York: The Dryden Press, 1985.

Schwartz, E.S., and M.J. Brennan, "Analyzing Convertible Bonds." *Journal of Financial and Quantitative Analysis*, no. 15 (November 1980): 907-29.

Schwartz, E.S., and M.J. Brennan, "Convertible Bonds: Valuation and Optimal Strategies for Call and Conversion." *The Journal of Finance*, no. 5 (December 1977): 1699-715.

Thorp, Edward O., and Sheen T. Kassouf, *Beat the Market*. New York: Random House, Inc., 1967.

Weinstein, Mark I., "The Effect of a Rating Change Announcement on Bond Price." *Journal of Financial Economics*, no. 5 (December 1977).

Glossary of Terms

Accrued Interest—Bond interest accrues daily based on a 360-day year. The accrued portion is that which has been earned since the last interest payment date.

Adjustable Rate—Interest rate or dividend which is adjusted periodically, usually based on a standard market rate such as that prevailing on Treasury bonds or notes. Typically, such issues have a set floor or ceiling that limits the adjustment.

Antidilution Clause—Protection allowed to convertible security holders whereby the conversion ratio may be raised or lowered under certain conditions. Stock dividends or stock splits are the most common occurrences that result in an adjustment to the conversion ratio via the antidilution clause.

Arbitrage—The simultaneous purchase and sale of securities to take advantage of pricing differentials created by market conditions.

Beta—A measure of a stock's relative volatility in relation to the market. A beta of 1.0 would indicate average market volatility. A beta of 2.0 would reflect twice the market volatility.

Bond Value—Also known as investment value. The price at which a bond would have to sell as a straight debt instrument relative to yields of other bonds of like maturity, size and quality.

Breakeven Time—Bond yields typically are greater than dividend returns on the underlying common. The breakeven measures the time it would take for the added return on the bonds to equal the conversion premium. This is also known as the payback period. Possible redemption of the bonds could invalidate the calculation.

"Busted Convert"—A convertible selling essentially as a straight bond. Assuming the issuer is "money good"—that is, can continue to meet interest obligations—such issues have very little equity participation.

Buy-in—If stock can no longer be borrowed to maintain a short position, the broker will be required to buy-in to close the short position.

Call Feature—A right to redeem debentures prior to maturity at a stated price, which usually begins at a premium to par (100 percent) and declines annually. Of late, new convertible issues are non-callable for at least two years, except under very limited circumstances.

Call Terms and Provisions—Call terms and provisions are outlined in the securities indenture and are determined at or prior to issuance. The call terms typically indicate under what circumstances the security can be called, the date and the price. Convertible securities often have provisions that are subject to the underlying stock's price. For example, the convertible security cannot be called for three years from issuance unless the stock price exceeds 150 percent of the conversion price for 30 consecutive days.

Capitalization—A measure of the firm's equity market value. Multiply the total common shares outstanding by the market price of the common stock.

Cash-Plus Convertible—Convertible security which requires payment of cash upon exercise.

CCES grade—The grading system used by Calamos Research to classify convertible risk. A grade of 1 is the highest quality while the lowest grades are assigned a 20. This allows for a wider classification of grades than obtained through the rating services.

Conditional Call—Circumstances under which a company can effect an earlier call. Usually stated as a percentage of a stock's trading price during a particular period, such as 140 percent of the exercise price during a 40-day trading span.

Conversion Parity—The value of a bond or convertible preferred based solely on the market value of the underlying equity. Also known as conversion value.

Conversion Premium—The amount by which the market price of a convertible bond or convertible preferred exceeds conversion value, expressed as a percentage. It is a gauge of equity participation.

Conversion Price—Stated at the time of issue, the price at which conversion can be exercised. Usually expressed as a dollar value.

Conversion Ratio—The conversion ratio determines the number of shares of common stock for which a convertible can be exchanged. The conversion ratio is determined upon issuance of the security and is typically protected against dilution. To determine conversion ratio, divide $1,000 par value by the conversion price.

Conversion Value (Stock Value)—The equity portion of the convertible bond. It is based on the conversion price set by the company at the time the bond is issued. This price in turn determines the number of shares of stock into which each bond can be converted. This can be determined by multiplying the common stock price by the conversion ratio. Conversion value represents the intrinsic value or equity value of the bond in stock.

Convertible Debenture—A general debt obligation of a corporation which, also under conditions set forth in the indenture, can be converted into common stock.

Convertible Debt Spread—The difference between the convertible and the non-convertible debt yields of similar quality securities.

Convertible Instrument—A bond or preferred stock that can be exchanged—hence converted—into the common stock of the issuing corporation.

Convertible Preferred—A preferred stock that is also convertible into common stock. It is similar to a convertible bond, except that it represents equity in the corporation. Unlike interest payments, dividend income is not a pretax income item for the issuing corporations. Corporations holding convertible preferreds are entitled to a 70 percent exclusion of dividends.

Convertible Risk Level—This is an indication of the broad overall risk level of the convertible, including both equity and bond risk measures. It is a means to distinguish between the various opportunities available on the basis of relative risk. Three levels of risk are recommended: low, medium and aggressive.

Covered Short Sale—A short sale against a convertible security is considered covered because the convertible may be converted to cover the short sale at any time. No additional margin is required for a covered short sale.

Current Yield—Stated interest or dividend rate, expressed as a percentage of the market price of the convertible security.

Debt/Equity Ratio—Indication of a firm's leverage.

Dollar Premium—The difference between the market price and the conversion value, expressed in number of dollars or points.

Duration—Weighted average time to full recovery of principal and interest payments for fixed-income security.

Effective Exercise Price—The exercise price is adjusted for a bond usable in lieu of cash upon exercise.

EROI (Expected Return on Investment)—This is a statistical measure of the convertible security's expected return.

Exchangeable Convertible Preferred Stock—A convertible preferred stock that can be exchanged for a convertible bond with the same terms at the option of the issuer.

Exchangeable Investment—Similar to a convertible bond or convertible preferred stock, but exchangeable into the common stock of a different public corporation. Also can refer to an instrument exchangeable under certain circumstances into another security of the issuing company.

Exercise Price—Price at which the underlying stock is either purchased or sold. Exercise prices are stated in option contracts, convertible securities, scores and warrants.

Expected Return—Expected value or mean of all the likely returns of investments contained in a portfolio. The mean value of the probability distribution of possible returns.

Expiration Date—Last date on which an option, warrant or right of convertibility can be exercised.

Fair Value Price—The price at which neither the buyer nor the seller has an advantage.

Financial Considerations—Conservativeness of a company's accounting practices, financial goals and policies.

Forced Conversion—To call a debenture. Companies usually will force conversion when the underlying stock is selling well above the conversion price. In this way, they assure that the bonds will be retired without requiring any cash payment.

Hedge Ratio—The number of underlying common shares sold or represented by an option divided by the number of shares into which the bonds are convertible.

Hedging—Trading techniques involving the sale of one security or option against a purchase of another related security. The object is to minimize risk in one position while attempting to profit from inefficiencies in the market's valuation of the various securities.

Index Options—Calls and puts on indexes of stock.

Investment Grade Convertibles—Those rated as investment grade quality, BBB or better, by Standard & Poor's or Baa or better, according to Moody's.

Investment Premium—The amount that the market price of the convertible is above its investment value, expressed as a percent of the investment value.

Investment Value (Bond Value)—The fixed-income component of the convertible. This is determined by calculating an equivalent bond value based on the assumption that the bond is not a convertible. The coupon and maturity date are used to decide this value, and over the short term it represents the investment floor.

Investment Value Yield—Estimated yield to maturity utilized to calculate the straight bond portion of the convertible. This can be determined by evaluating any straight debt the company may have outstanding or yield to maturity of similar quality debt in the marketplace.

Issue Size—Indicates the size of the convertible issue in millions of dollars for bonds and millions of shares for preferreds. Issue size can be helpful in determining the liquidity of an issue.

Junk Bond—Low-quality bonds issued by smaller companies. Convertibles in this category are generally rated B or below by Standard & Poor's.

Mark-to-Market—The accounting adjustment used to maintain the short account in line with current market prices.

Next Call Price—Determined at or prior to issuance, this is the price at which the issuer may redeem the bond or preferred stock. The call price is usually above the par value of the security in order to compensate the holder for the loss of income prior to maturity. The earliest call price is most significant in evaluating a bond.

Option Premium—Dollar value of an option.

Overvalued Convertibles—Since convertibles tend to trade on a fair value price track, convertibles that are overvalued as determined by the convertible pricing model should be avoided. Overvalued convertibles may decrease to their normal valuation without any change in the underlying stock price.

Par Value—The face value of the security. Bonds are typically issued at $1,000 par value, and interest on bonds is stated as a percentage of par value. Preferred stocks have par values, and their dividends are expressed as a percentage of par value.

Parity—See *Conversion Value.*

Positive Yield Advantage—The convertible should enjoy a yield advantage over its underlying common stock. The short sale of stock requires that the seller is responsible for paying the dividend. The difference between the convertible's yield and the yield of the underlying stock.

Short Exempt—Short sales can be made without meeting the uptick rules if the short sale is made with the anticipation of covering the sale by the conversion of the convertible within a short period of time. This is used frequently when closing out a convertible position by selling the stock first and then converting the bond.

Standard & Poor's Stock Rank—Indicates the company's consistency of dividend payments and stability in earnings.

Standard Risk—See *Volatility*.

Stock Dividend Yield—The annual dividend rate divided by the current stock price.

Stripped Yield—Return on the debt portion of a bond/warrant unit after subtracting the value of the issued warrant segment.

Swap—To sell one security to purchase another. The aim is usually to enhance yield while maintaining equity position in a security.

Synthetic Convertibles—Combining a non-convertible debt instrument with a warrant, score or option to create the characteristics of a convertible issue.

Systematic Risk—The portion of a stock risk due to general movement of stock prices.

Total Risk—See *Volatility*.

Trading Flat—Bonds trading flat are bought and sold without the payment of accrued interest. Income bonds and bonds in default trade flat.

Trust Indenture—The legal document spelling out the specific terms of a bond issuer as well as the rights and responsibilities of both issuer of the security and the holder.

Underwriter—The lead underwriter for the security. This is useful because the lead underwriter often makes market in the security and can provide information on the security and company.

Unsystematic Risk—Risk of a stock specific to the company's financial condition or industry group.

Upside Beta and Downside Beta—This measure indicates the convertible's price sensitivity to changes in the overall stock market (not including the income portion of the convertible).

Uptick or Plus-Tick Rule—The last sale of the stock must be at a higher price than the preceding sale.

Usable Bond—Bond issues as part of a unit (bond plus warrant) can be used in lieu of cash to exercise the warrant.

Variance—See *Volatility*.

Volatility—The standard deviation of the stock's return over a specified period of time. The measure of total risk. (Also called variance and standard risk.)

Warrant—Option to buy a stock at a stated price, extending up to ten years. Warrants themselves bear no dividend and no voting rights.

Warrant Premium—The difference between the market value of the warrant and its exercise price expressed as a percentage.

Yield Advantage—Convertible's yield minus the common stock dividend yield.

Yield to Maturity—The rate of return on a bond, which takes into account the market price, interest payments and time until date of maturity.

Zero Plus-Tick Rule—The last sale is unchanged, but higher than the preceding different sale.

Index

Computer Software for Convertible Investors

Computer software will be available (late 1988) for easy access to the computations and worksheets illustrated in this book.

The programs are written for the IBM PC and Apple Macintosh computers.

For further information and availability, send your name and address to:

Calamos Convertible Evaluation Service
2001 Spring Road, Suite 750
Oak Brook, Illinois 60521